SOCIALISM
AND THE
INTELLIGENTSIA
1880–1914

History Workshop Series

General Editor

Raphael Samuel, *Ruskin College, Oxford*

Already published

SOCIALISM AND THE INTELLIGENTSIA 1880–1914

Edited by
CARL LEVY

Routledge & Kegan Paul
London and New York

First published in 1987 by
Routledge & Kegan Paul Ltd
11 New Fetter Lane, London EC4P 4EE

Published in the USA by
Routledge & Kegan Paul Inc.
in association with Methuen Inc.
29 West 35th Street, New York, NY 10001

Set in Garamond
by Input Typesetting Ltd
and printed in Great Britain
by T.J. Press Ltd, Padstow, Cornwall

Library of Congress Cataloging in Publication Data

Socialism and the intelligentsia 1880–1914.

(History workshop series)
Includes bibliographies and index.
Contents: Introduction: historical and theoretical
themes/Carl Levy —— Sydney and Beatrice Webb/
Royden Harrison —— Max Weber and German social democracy/
Wolfgang J. Mommsen —— [etc.]
  1. Socialism——Europe——History. 2. Middle classes——
Europe——History. 3. Education——Social aspects——
Europe——History. 4. Class consciousness——Europe——
History. I. Levy, Carl, 1951– . II. Series.
HX238.S6 1987   335.0094   86–31449

ISBN 0–7102–0722–0
ISBN 0–7102–1257–7 (pbk.)

British Library CIP Data also available

In memory of
Frances Levy

Book education and not skill is now the road to status and, with diminishing exceptions, even skill has moved into the world of diplomas. And, of course, the road into that world has been broadened. There was a time when miners might want their sons out of the pit at all costs, but engineers were content to offer their sons a presumably improving version of their own prospects. How many of the sons of toolmakers today are content to become toolmakers? ...

... When the last men who have driven and cared for steam locomotives retire – it will not be long now – and when engine-drivers will be little different from tram-drivers, and sometimes quite superfluous, what will happen? What will our society be like without that large body of men who, in one way or another, had a sense of the dignity and self-respect of difficult, good, and socially useful manual work, which is also a sense of a society not governed by market-pricing and money: a society other than ours and potentially better? What will a country be like without the road to self-respect which skill with hand, eye and brain provide for men – and, one might add, women – who happen not to be good at passing examinations?

E. J. Hobsbawm, *Worlds of Labour*, London, Weidenfeld & Nicolson, 1984, pp. 271–2

In our own time the division between high-born and base-born has become a fiction, transparent to every eye. But the distinction between the lowly manual world and the lofty intellectual one continues – no longer as lord and serf, but as officer and subaltern, party cadre and party member, expert and everyone else. Even after the rights of property have been unmasked, those of intellectual labour remain.

R. L. Heilbroner, *New York Review of Books*, 5 November 1981, p. 52

Class antagonism within the ranks of revolutionary cadres remains the great unwritten history of nineteenth-century radical politics.

R. Sennett, *The Fall of Public Man*, Cambridge University Press, 1977, p. 253

Contents

Contributors

David Beetham is Professor of Politics at Leeds University and an expert on modern European social and political theory. His most recent books are *Marxists in Face of Fascism* (1984) *Max Weber and the Theory of Modern Politics* (2nd edn, 1985) and *Bureaucracy* (1987).

Royden Harrison MA, D.Phil., FR (History) S. Formerly Senior Tutor in Industrial Studies and then Reader in Political Theory at the University of Sheffield. Professor of Social History, University of Warwick, 1969–82. In addition to being the co-founder and co-editor of the *Bulletin of the Society for the Study of Labour History*, 1960–1982, Harrison has authored, edited and compiled five books in English apart from substantial works in Italian and Japanese. He contributed to both the first and second volumes of *Essays in Labour History* as well as contributing dozens of articles to academic and literary journals.

Carl Levy is a Research Fellow at Eliot College, the University of Kent at Canterbury. He has published articles and essays on Max Weber, Antonio Gramsci and Italian social history.

Wolfgang J. Mommsen. Studied history, philosophy, history of art and political science at Marburg, Cologne and Leeds universities. Habilitation 1967 at Cologne University. Since 1968 Professor of Modern History at Dusseldorf University. Visiting professorships at Cornell University, Ithaca, NY, St Antony's College, Oxford, School of Advanced International Studies, Johns Hopkins University, Washington, DC, and the University of Western

Ontario, London, Ontario. Visiting Member of the Institute of Advanced Study in Princeton, 1968. From August 1977 to June 1985 Director of German Historical Institute, London. Publications include *Max Weber und die Deutsche Politik* (2nd edn, 1974; English trans. 1985), *Das Zeitalter des Imperialismus* (1967), *The Age of Bureaucracy* (1974) and *Imperialismustheorien* (1987). Co-editor of *Geschichte und Gesellschaft. Zeitschrift für Historische Sozialwissenschaft.*

Jonathan Rée teaches Philosophy at Middlesex Polytechnic in London. His book *Proletarian Philosophers* was published by Oxford University Press in 1984. His latest work, a study of philosophy and literature entitled *Philosophical Tales*, has recently been published by Methuen.

Stephen Yeo teaches History at the University of Sussex. He writes about the history of religion (*Religion and Voluntary Organisations in Crisis*, 1976), as well as about the history of working-class associations such as co-ops, friendly societies and clubs. He published an article on 'A New Life: The Religion of Socialism in Britain 1883–1896' in *History Workshop Journal*, no. 4. He was active in the Federation of Worker Writers and Community Publishers, particularly the Brighton community publishing group called QueenSpark. He is particularly interested at the moment in the question 'whose story?' – in other words, not just the history of the working class but history as perceived by the working class; and he recently published an essay on this subject in the *Journal of Contemporary History.*

Acknowledgments

One of this volume's origins was an Open University seminar held in London in November 1982. I should like to thank Adam Westoby and John Raynor for their support during my stay at the Open University. I would also like to thank all those friends and colleagues who lent help and criticism, particularly Chris Rootes, Jonathan Zeitlin, Stephen Yeo, James Joll, Jonathan Rée, David Beetham, David Sugarman, Pat Thane, John Breuilly, David Howell, Dylan Morris, James Young, Ron Eyerman, Elias Berg, Tobias Abse and Katrin Andersson. An extra warm thanks goes to Raphael Samuel, who encouraged the publication of these essays.

Val Oswald, Joanna Snow and Linda Williams helped type sections of this book. Their assistance was invaluable.

Royden Harrison's contribution to this volume was first published in *Nihon Rōdō Kyōkai Zassi* (the monthly journal of the Japan Institute of Labour), Nos. 298 and 299, February and March 1985, Tokyo. I should like to thank its editors for their kind permission to republish it here.

Although this book is a collective enterprise, I, needless to say, take full responsibility as its editor.

Carl Levy

I
Introduction: Historical and Theoretical Themes

Carl Levy

The expansion of the European middle classes of the late nineteenth and early twentieth centuries, together with their political significance, have recently been increasingly studied by social historians. Much of this, however, has been concerned with the propertied middle classes.[1] At the same time students of contemporary social structures have devoted increasing attention to the role of the highly educated but unpropertied strata, East and West.[2] Within the literature and its debate the relations between the educated middle classes and the origins and development of modern socialist organisations during the era of the Second International (*circa* 1880–1914) have been frequently commented upon, and occasionally examined in more detail in particular periods and contexts. There has never been a study examining the role of the educated middle classes generally during this formative period for major modern socialist organisations and movements. While socialist intellectuals of the period have been widely studied, this has largely been in biographical treatments or as the principals in doctrinal disputes and institutional histories. A study of the appeals of socialism for the educated middle and lower middle classes has been lacking.

The essays in this volume address this theme. They originate from a seminar held at the Open University's London centre in November 1982, but in their final version they have been greatly revised and supplemented by entirely new contributions.

In this introductory essay I shall set the problem in its historical context. This will be followed by a discussion of the theoretical questions the contributors raise. In my conclusion I will discuss the particular problems raised by the Russian case.

A NEW PROJECT

The history of an idea seems an appropriate place to commence. Using points raised in Wolfgang Mommsen's and Royden Harrison's contributions to this volume, we might start by a comparison of the Webbs and Weber.

Both shared strikingly similar intellectual preoccupations, firstly in their elitest sociologies, and secondly in their hankering after social imperialist solutions to the 'social' question. Increasingly they considered state intervention in the economy and social life as a way to regulate industrial disputes and eradicate urban or rural pauperism. Stephen Yeo, in his contribution, quite rightly quotes Stefan Collini's contention that in Britain, amongst the highly educated public before 1914, the ideological fault-line was individualism vs collectivism as socialism rather than capitalism vs socialism.[3] However, I would argue that particular idioms influenced different national educated middle classes, and each nation's civil society set limits to, or opened opportunities for collectivist or reformist liberal intellectuals' participation in popular socialist or labour movements, in contrast to their reformers from above.

It is certainly the case that the Webbs always felt less distant from the British labour movement than Weber did from the German Social Democratic Party (SPD). The Fabians shared marginalist economics and an explicit quest to justify economically the higher salaries of the educated with the *Verein für Sozialpolitik*. But because of local conditions the Fabians succeeded in affecting both Independent Labour Party (ILP) political propaganda and the political education of trade-union officials, whilst the *Verein* were more or less excluded from SPD politics, although they evinced sympathy for reforms not very different from those which the SPD proposed.[4]

The remainder of this essay will place Collini's field of force within a broader European context. In the first half I shall highlight the various differences within states which heightened or lessened the importance of educated middle-class socialists. Throughout this introduction I shall also raise the distinct problems of the self-made party bureaucrat and lower middle-class white-collar worker within party structures. However, first I turn to the external pressures which shaped socialist parties' relationships to the broader middle-class electorate.

Suffrage

One of the most important yardsticks for measuring educated middle-class participation in socialist movements was the constraints of suffrage.[5] Almost from their debut on the national scene socialist parties were pitching their propaganda at middle-class voters. Until about 1910–1914 the effects of plural voting, rigging and literacy requirements restricted suffrage significantly. In Britain and France residential requirements disenfranchised many workers. In Germany the three-class Prussian voting system weakened Bismarckian male suffrage, and in any case the Reichstag's power was limited by the Junker bureaucracy, the military and the Kaiser himself. In most cases women were excluded from electoral participation on the national level. Because none of these parties, with the exception of the SPD, acquired a mass membership for a considerable period before 1914, the Italian, French and British, to cite important examples, sought votes from non-party members. Such constituencies might include smallholders, independent artisans, white-collar public sector workers and the professionals.

Following upon the inherent logic of these tactics, socialist 'election machines' frequently instituted formal or informal alliances with radical liberal groups or parties which possessed collectivist programmes and were usually populated by the educated middle classes. These alliances sought, rather optimistically on the whole, to fuse elements of what were seen as 'modernising productive bourgeoisies' with mass constituencies of industrial and rural proletariats through variations upon the theme of 'gas-and-water socialism'. These programmes promised the renovation of urban infrastructures and housing as well as the expansion and partial democratisation of educational opportunities. We certainly need to know a great deal more about these phenomena. A typology of European municipal socialism, a form of socialism when it was put

3

into practice which affected the daily lives of ordinary people to a greater extent than parliamentary politics, remains to be devised.

My own admittedly preliminary survey suggests that both municipal and national approaches encountered enormous difficulties, and its intentions must, I believe, be weighed against actual implementation. In France, for example, the non-socialist Radicals were on the whole deeply suspicious of social programmes and far more comfortable with shared Radical/Socialist anti-clerical legislation. In Britain, the Liberals were divided, but even those collectivists were not above stealing Labour's thunder, and increasing tensions between the labourist and the socialist currents within its erstwhile partner's constituent organisations. On the whole, the SDP is a quite different matter. Except for southern alliances, national and Prussian attempts were unsuccessful. The National Liberals, and even the more radical anti-Junker *Hansa-bund*, were firmly attached to the anti-socialist coalition. Attempts at creating electoral pacts with the Progressives in 1912, for example, merely drove their supporters into the arms of this bloc. Only in Sweden and Denmark do effective socialist-liberal intelligentsia alliances appear *before* the World War. And it is interesting to note that in Norway, where suffrage had been granted by 1905, a polarisation of the working class and liberal intelligentsia was so much more evident.[6]

To sum up, voting restrictions causing the uneven profile of the manual-worker socialist vote, and a low degree of party organisation in most of Europe, heightened the potential importance of the educated as electoral allies, but the outcomes are far from clear-cut and we need more cross-national studies of political behaviour to determine their influence.

INTELLECTUALS AND SOCIAL MOVEMENTS

If the external, electoral influence of the educated middle class was a complex, negotiated relationship, what of the undoubted importance of their representatives within party organisations and leadership? It seems to me that Stedman Jones's recent sketches for a possible history of the Labour Party might be incorporated into the project outlined in this book. Perhaps we should imagine party structures as contested terrains where various knowledges validate the power and status of members, but where no single discourse (even the much studied 'scientific socialism') is capable of direct translation into power. To paraphrase Stedman Jones, agendas arise from a 'vacant centre' where various 'groups possessing different and sometimes incompatible political languages of widely varying provenance' establish 'a changing balance of forces' which is informed by 'their discursive self-definition primarily from without'.[7]

These observations affect the way we examine the nature of socialist parties, particularly their class composition, an essential prerequisite in assessing the weight of the educated middle classes within them. Elsewhere I have written at length on the social class composition of socialism during the Second International. Here I will summarise my findings in order to introduce a broader discussion of how the educated middle classes influenced party organisation and ideology.

In my previous work I demonstrated that not only was the intervention of the educated white-collar or entrepreneurial middle classes determined by specific national factors (a point which I will expand on), but that socialism appealed to a wide variety of workers and peasants who were as affected by the peculiarities of local conditions as their middle-class comrades. Certainly all socialist parties' mass base derived from the manual working class. But this in itself says little. The variety was as interesting as the qualifying adjective manual. There was no essential link between the socialism of these parties and the factory proletariat.

First, there were skilled textile workers, printers, locksmiths and other artisans; including a smattering of pre-industrial political shoemakers. They were the respectable self-educated workers who carried with them an older craft-based radicalism. But they shaded into a new wave of machine operatives (turners, precision tool makers, engineers and engine drivers) who were attracted to the scientistic and technocratic socialisms synthesised by various educated scientific socialisms. (And I say socialisms advisably because revolutionary and anarcho-syndicalists in Italy or Spain were as attracted to the idiom as socialist engineers in Germany.)

But socialism could also appeal to certain working-class or rural communities where communitarian feelings outlived the collapse of older paternalist hierarchies. When industrial organisation or the cruel logic of the world capitalist marketplace disintegrated their older world, these peasants and workers could become rapidly radicalised. Thus, and this example is particularly significant for the numbers supplied to pre-war socialism, the landless labourers of the Po Valley; the peasants of the Var; or the proto-proletarians of the Urals, the worker-peasants, entered socialist politics. In all of these cases communitarian socialism rather than technocratic or scientific socialism was an important ideological ingredient.

On the other hand, 'well-suited' candidates for socialist or even labourist conversion from older loyalties were not always so forthcoming. In the Ruhr's mines and steel mills paternalism reigned until the arrival of immigrants around 1910; Lib-Lab miners federations represented Northumberland colliers until the courts threatened their very existence; and in France the 'yellow unions' had more members than the vastly overestimated syndicalists, and only the World War and the Popular Front government of the 1930s stimulated a shift away from this powerful and little studied paternalism.

To sum up our argument so far: working and lower-class attraction to socialism was varied, inconsistent and unpredictable. Equally, when we turn to the educated middle classes, socialism was embraced for a variety of reasons. Romantic and communitarian impulses are discernible amongst artists and literati. However, scientific or technocratic arguments increasingly gained more attention in the late nineteenth century. This can be demonstrated by focussing on the 1880s, a crucial decade in which the ideology of the Second International is first formulated. Indeed, this ideology precedes the actual formal organisation of many modern socialist parties.

Older types of popular radicalism are criticised and overturned by self-defined 'scientific socialists'. This is not merely a shift associated with 'Marxism after Marx', rather Marxism is the most elegant and intellectually engaging version of a wider discursive practice. Thus Marxist vulgarisations by Engels or Kautsky, the Fabian anti-Marxist *Essays*, and works by various French and Italian positivist professors all proclaim the birth of scientific socialism. These works all praise modernity, particularly the modernity of science, the scientist, the professional, but also that other symbol of the new era: the industrial proletariat of the first gigantic modern factories. In all of these texts 'the people' is replaced by the proletariat. For scientific socialists the urban, prop-ertyless, factory operator, especially skilled male engineers, possessed the skill, muscle and discipline to transform the capitalist system into a smokestack utopia. The scientific socialists admired the successful bourgeois professional who had declared for socialism. Unlike the Russian populists (the *narodniki*) or their Western admirers, scientific socialists did not believe that the educated need feel guilt due to comfortable lives based upon creden-tials or 'cultural capital' so long as they performed a useful service to humanity. One of these services might just be to disseminate scientific socialism itself.

But these are only images and idioms found within texts. They say little about who actually appropriated or appreciated them. Nor does it follow that the first generation of 'scientific socialists' were triumphant politically, psychologically or culturally within socialist or broader social movements. Even the educated them-selves possessed a dissident anti-industrial and romantic tradition, even William Morris was perhaps more romantic than scientist. Furthermore, as my review of class composition of socialist parties has just demonstrated, most socialist workers, scientific socialist imagery notwithstanding, were not 'disciplined' factory operatives or skilled engineers but artisans and labourers in smaller shops. Pre-socialist plebeian radicalism may have been losing its vigour but certainly was not moribund. The oral transmission of radical thought associated with centuries of heretical movements may have lost some of its importance to trade-union and party presses but still flourished in southern Europe and even, I would argue, in 'modern' England and Germany. The little traditions ignored and at times contested the scientific socialists's 'great traditions'.

In short, the ways in which party priorities were set owed a great deal to ideas and customs which educated or self-educated socialists imported from non-socialist sources. Some of the beliefs and utopias within socialism reflected those little explored elective affinities and class-blind cleavages of broader civil society, such as the British Victorian principles of work and respectability, the peculiarly German separation of all manual workers from the white-collar world, the pronounced productivism of trade-union officials, set against the 'moral economies' of ex-peasant or peasant socialists (particularly evident in France and Italy), or the continent-wide bifurcation of modern science and classical humanism, reflected if not perfectly aligned within socialism as one between the romantic or bucolic and the technocratic.[8]

The circulation of socialist ideologies in any given national setting owed a great deal to the combined and uneven development of the state and civil society. Similarly, to understand how socialism was appropriated by those sanctioned as brain-workers, and to what extent the 'certified' were given opportunities to participate in internal party politics, one would have to examine the nature of different Western European experiences of industrialisation, different legal traditions, different religious histories and differences in popular associational culture and its relationship to the informal or accredited 'systems' of knowledge.

I will approach my check-list through the social history of the widely employed nouns 'intellectual' and 'intelligentsia'. There are slippages between definitions of the highly educated as intellectuals, as professionals or as university graduates. But these different definitions reflect varying national labour markets, university systems and state formations.

Starting in the 1880s and 1890s, for example, the German socialists preferred the term 'university graduate' (*Akademiker*) to 'intellectual'.[9] For British counterparts the term 'professional' men or women, or even 'men of letters', was more meaningful than 'intellectual'. Their definition differed from the sociological one the Germans adopted. For the British the 'professional', and especially the 'man of letters', carried with his title a normative resonance either as a 'cleric' or sage or as a more democratic *narodnik*-like Russian populist, who abandoned, or at least attempted to abandon, a comfortable middle-class life-style.[10] In Italy the analogous term might carry both meanings, where the first generation of anarchists, following Russian practice, fled academia for manual trades, and a second positivist generation of pioneering physicians, sociologists and criminologists saw no contradiction between successful bourgeois careers and their socialist beliefs. Indeed, one reinforced the other. Certainly the Italian case must be set apart from other Western European examples due to the sheer numbers of university graduates and literati who joined or sympathised with the Partito Socialista Italiano in the 1890s.[11]

The French, more than any other nationality, popularised the conception of the successful writer, university professor or scientist committed to leftist or socialist politics. The *Manifesto of the Intel-*

lectuals, published during the Dreyfus affair, demonstrates how the noun *intellectuel* presupposed social beings different from the Russians or Italians of the 1860s and 1870s. The *Manifesto* was deeply immersed in French cultural and political history, reinforcing a tradition which is traced back to the Revolution, but underlined by the important intervention of artists, poets and writers in the revolutions of 1830, 1848 and, to a certain extent, 1871.[12] There was a distinctive Parisian connection between certain *Grandes Écoles* (the *École Normale* above all), the middle and upper layers of the republican and anti-clerical bureaucracy and literary politicos. Even the Sorelian syndicalist and right-wing counterattack against the 'Dreyfusard revolution' a few years later arose from the same Parisian hothouse.

The contrast with Britain could not be greater, as it lacked the centralising bureaucracies, the large university enrolments or the formality which characterised intellectual life in France and other industrial second-comers. As Eric Hobsbawm wrote in a classic survey of Fabianism:

> The bureaucrats, the technologically and scientifically trained manager or businessman, even the office worker, or for that matter a national system of primary, secondary and higher education were common-place in Germany and France from the early nineteenth century, but not in Britain.[13]

This, of course, did not prevent a series of professional middle-class groups from influencing the radicals, Chartists, Model Trade Unionists and pioneering socialists of the 1880s.[14] However, the terms of engagement, I would suggest, were different. These individuals found a ready audience amongst trade unionists and artisans raised in similar traditions of debate and earnest self-improvement. When the British did in fact adopt the noun 'intellectual' in the 1890s, it was meant to negate this specific tradition of political activism. The largely literary British intelligentsia assumed an ascetic, detached and largely apolitical conservative vocation.[15]

In young nation-states intellectuals or professionals were at first placed in a quite different position. In Italy and Germany, for instance, the humanist middle class and university intelligentsia retained their dominance until the late nineteenth century by assuming the role of guardians of the national language and indeed, at least before unification, as nation-builders. In nations where, at least initially, dialect rather than standard national languages was the rule, where region, religion or caste fractured civil society, the educated classes were bound to play a role far outside their actual numbers.[16] In Germany the Bismarckian 'civil-service' state easily enticed or intimidated the intelligentsia. Italy is, as I have noted, quite different. Here the state remained weaker and inefficient, industrialisation more uneven, and the anti-papal political elite discredited by the apparent failures of the *Risorgimento* as well as isolated from the large Catholic landowners, who might have played an analogous role to the Junkers within the state apparatus. The educated middle classes, while perhaps not suffering from unemployment as badly as is usually implied, did resent the failure of reform after national liberation, which undoubtedly radicalised some of them.

Finally, in the subject nations of Eastern Europe, intellectuals were more likely than not attracted to national populist movements albeit for the important exceptions of the marginalised Jewish intelligentsia and student or intellectual exile circles based in Switzerland. This was certainly the case in the Balkans and is also evident in Poland where intellectuals divided within socialism between nationalists and internationalists. And even in highly industrialised Bohemia, intellectuals such as Masaryk were more inspired by the Czech national movement than social democracy. Foreign intellectuals could also play prominant roles in a host's socialist parties. It is worth recalling that many leading intellectuals within the SPD (Kautsky, Luxemburg or Parvus, to name three) were foreigners whose socialisation outside the German tradition of *Bildung* perhaps allowed them greater opportunity to transcend rigid mental boundaries. And in Italy Russian middle-class women, such as Kuliscioff or Balabanov, exercised greater influence on the PSI elite before 1914 than their Italian sisters.[17]

Associations

The extent and nature of associational life, that is to say, the ability of the self-educated to establish their own trade unions, co-operatives and clubs, delineated those social spaces where the 'certified' and the popular merged.

Associational life was firstly affected by law. The laws which might repress trade unions and strikers might not affect the involvement of the educated middle classes in socialist parties. Industrial legislation in practice may have been equally repressive in Italy, France or Germany, but civil rights for the educated were more readily granted in France, Italy or Great Britain than in Wilhelmine Germany.[18] In this respect the German university graduate who declared openly for the SPD experienced a uniquely uncomfortable life in comparison to his/her socialist graduate comrades in other Western European states. Robert Michels, who had been active in both the Italian and German socialist movements before 1914, readily and rather bitterly described the differences.[19] Many graduates' careers were abruptly terminated because civil-service posts (including academic jobs) were prohibited to socialists, forcing them to become journalists or lawyer/journalists. And this could be contrasted with Austria where professors were free to join the Socialist Party and helped stimulate a famous circle of Austro-Marxist intellectuals (Karl Renner, Otto Bauer, Max Adler, Gustav Eckstein and Rudolf Hilferding).[20]

Religion was another crucial variable of associational life. Both Weber and Gramsci understood this, citing the intimate relationship between the clergy and the faithful in sectarian Protestant Britain and North America as stimulating rich voluntary organisational and anti-statist traditions. And these, in the writings of each, are contrasted with Russia, where a convergence of state and church stifled the growth of voluntary associations.

Jews always played a disproportionate role in German and other European socialist movements. In Germany and central Europe incomplete assimilation was caused by the *numerus clausus* in universities and the closure of more conservative professions. And just because of these informal and formal restrictions, the Jewish intelligentsia were more likely to be socialised within the oppositional or critical cultures of the newer or less prestigious professions and thereby be more available and receptive to socialist movements. Anti-clericalism, as an associational phenomenon, partially derived from reactions to the threat of clerical organisation, and it inspired much of the language and substance of socialist politics in Belgium, France, Italy and Spain. Albeit in the last case the rationalist generation of new intellectuals at the turn of the century (the generation of 1898) were anticlerical radicals rather than socialists or anarchists. But even if the anarchists or socialists did not attract large numbers of intellectuals before 1914, the Barcelona libertarians did recruit some important artists, poets and educationalists.[21] But religious life generated other outcomes as well. Anti-clericalism, as an associational phenomenon, partially derived from reactions to the threat of clerical organisation, and it inspired much of the language and substance of socialist politics in France, Italy and Spain.

In France the Paris Commune's bloody aftermath destroyed a generation of self-educated socialist artisans; university graduates after 1871 played important roles in the states' socialist and libertarian movements. In four of the five parties which defined the splintered movement before the creation of a unified socialist party (SFIO) in 1905, classically trained journalists and free professionals – masters of anti-clerical rhetoric – held sway. Even in 'workerist' anarchism and syndicalism the 'enlightened' journalist/lawyer, attracted to notions of rationalist libertarian education and culture, dominated national and, at times, local organisations.[22] The Independent Socialist parliamentary group, led by Jaures and other *normaliens*, is perhaps the most extraordinary example of the dominance of high intellectuals in the French socialist movement.[23] Here, too, the language of rationalism and anti-clericalism popularised their appeal.

The German case should be placed between the anti-clerical and Anglo-American examples. Most early recruits to the SPD were male skilled Protestant workers from areas where popular involvement in the church and its influence on local social life had already weakened. Both the Roman Catholic Church and the Protestant state churches were more conservative than British churches. And as in Catholic dominated countries, socialist associationalism stimulated an important Christian largely Catholic labour movement, with strongholds in the Ruhr and the Rhine industrial areas. Unlike their British counterparts the Protestant churches were much closer to the state, and the Kaiser, as their temporal leader, made sure that radical or reformists clergy were kept in line. Germany also lacked a vigorous free or dissenting church movement, that was so important in stimulating British Christian Socialism, which in turn provided leaders and cadre to the SDF and the ILP; and British socialists with their political languages, political apprenticeships and vital ties to Liberal dissenting and Anglican educated middle-class sympathisers.

The failure of a middle-class based Christian Socialism in

Germany highlights an important difference with the British case. However, in Scandinavia the dissenting tradition seems to have played a role analogous with Britain's. In Sweden, for instance, the Lutheran Church allowed greater leeway within its walls than German Protestant churches but dissenters from Småland and Norrbotten were important socialist pioneers. Throughout Scandinavia the linkage between the powerful temperance movements and socialism opened another important avenue of influence with dissenting Protestantism.

Patterns of capitalist industrialisation also affected that key form of associationalism – trade-union organisation. Only in Germany, Britain, Belgium and Scandinavia were rates of unionisation sufficiently high for socialist or labourist representatives to be generated from the working class itself.[24] In this regard comparisons of neighbouring Belgium and the Netherlands are quite revealing. Whereas the highly unionised working-class Belgian party contained important rationalist intellectuals such as Vandervelde, Huysmans, Destré or De Brockère, only a small percentage of the entire intelligentsia joined the party. In the Netherlands, however, where trade unionism generally and worker representation in the party were far weaker, the weight and numbers of intellectuals within the party as well as their influence on the intelligentsia outside its boundaries was that much greater. The characterisation of the Dutch party as being the party of Protestant pastors, lawyers and students may be exaggerated but not that far from the truth.

Linkages between socialist movements and trade unions were affected by developments within elite and popular politics, and as John Breuilly has shown, liberalism preserved its dominance in Britain for example longer than in Germany because of a series of unique cultural and political factors.[25] Nevertheless, by the early 1900s there are many similarities between British and German working-class parliamentary representation.[26] Twenty-three out of twenty-six of the Labour Representation Committee's successful candidates in 1906 were trade-union officials, and in the much larger SPD *Reichstagfraktion* of 1903 fifty-three out of eighty-one deputies were similarly employed.[27]

It is certainly true that while in Britain the rather small ILP gained its influence from locally negotiated agreements with Lib–Lab trade unions whose membership was counted in hundreds of thousands, the German SPD and the Free Trade Unions adopted a more openly socialist approach, in reaction to the authoritarian state which repressed a liberal alternative. However, it is with low rates of unionisation in France and Italy, where combined socialist and syndicalist membership never exceeded 8 per cent, that one finds a radically different social composition of parliamentary representatives.[28]

If we compare the Germans and the Italians the differences are extremely revealing. While nearly 88 per cent of the *Gruppo Parlamentare Socialista* (GPS) in 1903 were university graduates, only 16 per cent of the German deputies were. Of the twenty-four graduates in the GPS, nine were professors – three times the grand total for the entire Reichstag in that year![29]

But one should not overlook the differences between the German and British labour movements. For at least half a century before its neighbours, Britain possessed a massive labour movement of trade unionists. The ability of the British labour movement to create an impressive network of co-operatives and trade societies by the middle of the nineteenth century, capable of producing a leadership largely independent of middle-class intellectuals, inspired foreign observers. Royden Harrison quite rightly underlines the deep interest which the British trade-union movement inspired in the European intelligentsia who lived in, passed through or were interested in Britain before 1914. Bernstein, Lenin and Sorel all studied it, and the Webbs' theoretical industrial sociology is based very closely upon its history.[30]

Social spaces

We also need to know a great deal more about how socialist ideology was understood by the self-educated.[31] It is probably true that socialist ideologies were reinterpreted by trade unionists to serve pragmatic needs. For example, even if the Berlin party school of the SPD was run by such radical intellectuals as Mehring and Luxemburg, students assimilated their methods of study rather than their ideological passions.[32] And what we know of the books read by the working-class rank and file and trade-union officials in the SPD seems to show that they were largely unaffected by the Marxist texts produced by party intellectuals. Surveys of worker libraries and of memoirs of leading trade unionists demonstrate that the books that made them politically aware were few in number;

perhaps Bebel's vulgarisation of positivist Marxism, *Women under Socialism*, Edward Bellamy's technocratic utopian projections and Lassalle's pamphlets were the limit of their political reading. But these were overtaken by a steady diet of 'penny dreadfuls' and occupational manuals, although Kautsky's and other intellectuals' prolific production may have been more seriously considered by what William Guttsman terms the SPD's 'functionaries' democracy' – the thousands of white-collar officials and enthusiasts whom the party needed by 1910.[33] It should also be noted that the depth or range of reading by other nations' socialist publics did not vary greatly from that of Germany, even if pamphlets by Lassalle or Bebel were replaced by those of Morris or Ferri; Bellamy, who needs greater investigation, was a universal favourite.[34]

We lack studies which reveal how cultural and intellectual networks of the 'certified' and the popular encountered each other. What are required, I would argue, are synthetic monographs which join together evidence from working-class clubs and schools with works, like the suggestive contributions of Regis Debray and Raymond Williams, which focus upon the middle-class literary café, the university, the dinner-table or friendship circle.[35]

One might distinguish the Latin 'coffee-house' culture of French, Italian or Austro-Hungarian intelligentsias from the Anglo-Saxon 'dissenting club' or earnest confab of dinner-table journalists and university collectivists, as crucially important and little studied nationally specific sites where various traditions, and formal or informal knowledges, were circulated and cross-fertilised. Both popular and 'certified' networks served as party 'universities', labour exchanges for intellectuals or apprentice brainworkers and informal 'policy-making units'.

The lower middle class

Finally, a cross-national comparison would have to trace the ways in which the lower middle class of white-collar teachers and state functionaries, as well as clerks and commercial travellers, intervened within pre-1914 socialism. Here, too, influence was largely determined by specific national historical and cultural legacies, although the flexibility of party tactics become an important variable as they established their own organisational momentum about 1914.

In Germany the white-collar middle class – the *Angestellten* and

Beamten – were separated from manual workers to a much greater degree than British clerks and certainly French public *employés* were. As Jürgen Kocka has shown, the very words employed to describe German white-collar workers belonged to the pre-capitalist corporate mentality which they largely adopted.[36] But, as David Blackbourn notes, the long-standing argument that the SPD became embourgeoisified through growing artisan and petty-entrepreneurial middle-class support can be turned around to mean that some elements of the middle class were not as resolutely anti-socialist as is commonly believed.[37] In Italy and France local socialist parties' organisations were more likely than not populated by small-time lawyers, journalists, primary or secondary-school teachers, state functionaries and pharmacists. Furthermore, as I mention in my contribution, teachers, commercial travellers and clerks were particularly visible in the ILP.[38]

How these groups related to both party intellectuals and professionals, on the one hand, and manual working-class socialists, on the other, is still largely unexplored territory. But we might look more closely at older radical ideas – the myth of the 'free-born Englishman' or the French conception of the eternal battle of people against *le gros* – and how socialists appropriate the slogans of the 'middling class' to the needs of a newer white-collared constituency.[39]

THEORETICAL DISCUSSION

The new class

Although these essays deal mainly with European socialism and the educated middle classes between 1870 and 1914, Royden Harrison's portrait of Sidney and Beatrice Webb takes us beyond 1914, through the effects of the Russian Revolution, inter-war Labourism and 1945. While Harrison demonstrates that there were direct linkages between the Webbs' late-Victorian social engineering religion of socialism and their attraction to the Soviet Union of the 1930s, Stephen Yeo's 'Notes', on the other hand, demonstrate a connection between the pre-1914 *nouvelle couche sociale*, the term the Fabians used to describe the professional and white-collar classes of pre-1914 Britain, and the more recent products of university expansion and 'post-industrial' society. His notes are meant to stimulate discussion of problems particularly important to modern socialism, even if the focus of attention is upon the era before 1914.

David Beetham's contribution to this volume analyses the various theories of deradicalisation and 'bourgeoisification' proposed by socialists and syndicalists during the first decade of the twentieth century. Many of these, in one way or another, linked the growth of intellectual and white-collar influence to declining radical fervour in the socialist movement. As Beetham explains, the so-called 'revisionist' debate of these years can be associated with these fears, and with the universally noted growth of white-collar jobs due to the expansion of educational and state bureaucracies as well as of complex financial and bureaucratic institutions within industrial capitalism.

Critics of socialism as a vehicle for this 'New Class' included Bakunin, who apparently coined the phrase, and J. W. Machajski (1866–1926), an eccentric Russo-Polish Marxist theorist whose concept of intellectual capital Alvin Gouldner assimilated to recent theories of human, cultural and symbolic capitals.[40]

But other writers and activists dealt with similar concerns: William Morris (as Yeo shows in this volume), Peter Kropotkin, Gustav Landauer, Georges Sorel and other syndicalist theorists, the German *Jungen* (the ultra-left opposition within the SPD of the 1890s) and the Russian Economists – to name just a few examples.[41] Their interest, however, was more incidental, arising in the course of less focused criticisms of contemporary currents in European socialism which they believed argued for an educated elite to act as the organised vanguard of proletarian mass movements. Their targets, depending on national locations, were Lenin, Kautsky, Jaurès, the Fabians, Turati, etc.

The desire to explain the deradicalisation of socialism, Beetham concludes, begged an important question which still has a great deal of relevance for socialists in Western Europe in the 1980s. Deradicalisation theories presume the existence of a golden age of unsullied socialism before 'alien' social groups or conditions diverted it from its proper goals. But what must be explained is not the persistence of reformism within Second International or, for that matter, post-1945 social democracy, but why effective or 'flabby' reformisms have won out within specific national arenas.

A counterfactual history which investigated, for example, the

British case would analyse the failures of co-operation and of socialist Sunday schools, or the meaning of the metamorphosis of the noble *Daily Herald* into the appalling *Sun*. As Yeo puts it in this volume:[42] 'a social democratic politics which held the ring, at the level of the state, for wider, more-than-political working-class forms to exist and grow in civil society, never materialised. A working-class redefinition of politics never happened.'

But whether we can blame the failure of this alternative, grass-roots reformism on the educated middle-class social engineers, nationalisers or state idolaters is an entirely different matter. Both Yeo and Harrison demonstrate how ambivalent the notoriously centralising collectivist inhabitants of 'Webbville' could be. With all their abuse of 'primitive democracy' Sidney and Beatrice were stunned by the political capabilities of the British working class. 'The Trade Unions', they wrote in the famous conclusion to *The History of Trade Unionism*, 'offer the century-long experience of a thousand self-governing working class communities.'[43]

Beetham's insistence that theories of deradicalisation in their original political context were misconstrued is of course equally valid for the historian living seventy years later. One of the great obsessions of Marxist and non-Marxist labour, social and socialist historians since the 1950s has in fact just been their insistent attempts at identifying a stratum in civil society and/or within the organisational structure of the socialist and labour movements themselves – a labour aristocracy in the first case, a white-collar bureaucracy in the second – which, it is argued, somehow 'unnaturally' deradicalises or conversely radicalises working-class politics.

Much Marxist labour historiography has sought to explain the deradicalisation of Second International socialism by claiming that a labour aristocracy, controlling the proletariat's cultural, economic and political organisations, fostered working-class acceptance of the bourgeois nation-state. This has given rise to an extraordinarily rich debate, mostly concentrated upon the British working class, although some historians have sought to extend the explanatory framework to European examples.[44] However, opponents of the thesis, including its more subtle Gramscian variation, have cumulatively placed in doubt the very existence of a nationally identifiable labour aristocracy. It is now generally regarded as at best a heuristic device which in special cases may illuminate the class structures and associational life of local late-nineteenth- and early-twentieth-century British working-class communities.[45] Beyond this, as even one of its earliest academic advocates Eric Hobsbawm now asserts, there is no sure guide linking reformist or revolutionary political behaviour of groups of workers to their level of skill, cultural tasks or notions of respectability.[46]

Robert Michels's shifting series of theories is universally cited in discussions of the oligarchisation and deradicalisation of Second International parties by white-collar bureaucrats, and quite naturally his name appears in several of the essays in this volume.[47] In *Political Parties* (first published in German in 1911)[48] Michels, a disillusioned socialist, noted that even in socialist organisations with large manual working-class memberships, the specific weight of the educated middle class increased as one ascended the organisational hierarchy. He was one of the first students of the European socialist movement to examine systematically how, as party structures tended to become centralised, there was an apparent tendency for increasing involvement of educated middle-class individuals, and the simultaneous replacement of local initiatives by national machinery. He drew a highly suggestive portrait of a new composite stratum of liberal professionals, white-collar and self-educated ex-manual workers, drawn together through measures for a division of political labour which produced settled procedures and a permanent apparatus staffed by professional politicians and theorists.

In *Political Parties* Michels emphasised how socialist bureaucrats, of whatever class background, by mimicking the life-styles of the new middle classes, would deradicalise socialist politics. Later, however, during the final, Fascist phase of his intellectual and political evolution, Michels concentrated his energies on the psychology of the so-called revolutionary Bohemian intelligentsia and wrote about their need to establish a socialist political home so as to regularise status and employment.[49]

Michels's contradictory work gave rise to a sociological commonplace, which cold-war social science, assimilating Joseph Schumpeter's and Selig Perlman's variations upon the theme, generalised to post-war university students.[50] This argued that the motives of the educated middle class and the manual working class for membership of or support for socialist organisations are different: the educated emphasising more global and rationalistic projects for overall reforms or social revolution, manual workers more immediate concerns for short-term moderate improvements in daily life. In short, to paraphrase a famous turn in Lenin's political thought, the workers seemed to be economistic, but the intellectuals were capable of comprehending the general interest.[51]

The Michelsian legacy, with its undoubtedly interesting suggestions, is ultimately a highly confused and tendentious body of ideas. But it has affected the ways in which we view the SPD. The largest socialist party before 1914, indeed its membership in 1910 exceeded the combined total of other European *socialist* parties, has long been pictured as an organisation where a self-educated bureaucracy, undergoing a process of embourgeoisement, became the chief political actor. Since Michels we are accustomed to imagine the SPD as a great oligarchical machine, more recently the party has been described as a sub-culture in which the isolated urban working class created parallel institutions to those of Wilhelmine Germany's and was effectively 'negatively integrated' into broader German society.[52]

But this alleged deradicalisation of the SPD becomes meaningless if we assume that a reformist strategy was favoured from its beginnings even if certain ideologists wrestled over how the socialist revolt would come about. Furthermore, the party machine was never as monolithic as many commentators imagine. Recent work demonstrates that the party was a composite of locally rich regional and municipal groups; that trade union officials like their British contemporaries did not readily listen to socialist ideologists when their conclusions threatened daily practice; that in fact internal debate was vigorous, and finally (repeating a point made earlier), the working class rank and file and trade-union officialdom were largely unaffected by the Marxist texts produced by the intellectual elite. On the other hand, it was just this plodding social democratic and industrial reformism which the pre-war ruling class found so frightening; and as Wolfgang Mommsen shows in his contribution, placed reformist liberals such as Weber in a powerless position.[53]

Michels's theories were therefore founded on two untenable suppositions. First, the 'iron law of oligarchy' assumed the existence of inactive, gullible and indiscriminating 'masses'. Secondly, that socialist reformism caused by bureaucratic deradicalisation was functionally compatible with the German state. The tragic history of Germany after 1914 proves otherwise. Nevertheless, Michels retains a fascination because he did identify a certain grey area of former workers, journalists and skilful machine men who might have working-class roots but were born late enough to enter the first wave of new white-collar workers. Most were practitioners of labour journalism, combining a modern newspaper style copied from the American press with a socialist message.

I discuss some British examples in my contribution. Keir Hardie and Ramsay MacDonald inhabited this grey area. Both were Scottish and illegitimate, and eventually made their ways to the great metropolis; both came from great poverty; both sought respectability in their own ways, but were essentially individuals cast adrift in the urban hubbub. Hardie made his ascent from collier through self-taught journalism (a common avenue in Britain: Robert Blatchford was its master). MacDonald was a pioneer organisation man. He made his career *through* the first socialist organisations with the assistance of the Liberal Party, after gaining the requisite skills as a pupil teacher and Birkbeck night school student.

Grey area inhabitants were quintessentially social mediators; usually attracted to crowd psychology as a trick of their trade and as their vocational and personal philosophy. But their influence depended upon another group whom Michels, Weber and the Webbs found fascinating: trade-union officials.

This last group would not have made their ascent from manual labour if trade unions themselves did not need a political division of labour. They were the 'Legiens', 'Hendersons', 'Buozzis', 'Bondfields' and 'Jouhauxs'. They were generally reformists who knew how to control their rank and file, especially during periods of radicalisation, such as pre-war syndicalist revolts and post-war factory council or shop steward movements. They possessed a knowledge of industrial conditions and working-class life which most 'greys', lower middle-class or university socialists would never acquire. They therefore possessed an expertise, self-made intellectual capital, which made them formidable competitors for party influence against formally educated parliamentarians and newspaper editors. And they also possessed a direct linkage to the world of the autodidact to which I will now turn.

Education and the division of political labour

Almost without exception all socialist movements of the late nineteenth and early twentieth centuries were arenas of education, self-education and cultural activity in societies where the state and the 'culture industry' were just beginning to eradicate the popular voluntary sphere through substitution by national and corporate alternatives. Socialist movements, therefore, served as educational institutions in their own right, offering members a range of political and other instructions.[54]

Michels was perhaps one of the first observers to explain the weight of the educated middle class within socialist parties as due to an ability to supply and support this education. But it was the Webbs, Weber and Lenin who theorised how educational activities formed a 'filter' in which politically active workers were selected for leading roles. To a certain degree they were all forerunners of what Jonathan Rée describes as the modern advocates of the theory of 'educational systems'. His contribution in this volume can be considered a manifesto, a call to social historians to uncover the hidden non-systemised forms of education which tend to escape from functionalist histories of education.

Informal education received ambivalent responses from socialist politicians and theorists. It is not at all clear, for instance, where even such a sympathetic figure as Gramsci stood. He had a keen interest in popular learning, but sometimes one gets the feeling that he sought better to understand this uncharted experience so as to 'transcend' it.[55] For many educated middle-class socialist thinkers and politicians before 1914 education was envisaged both as pragmatic on-the-job training and as an appropriation of the best in bourgeois science and culture. And of course there is abundant damning evidence that 'universitarian' socialists (to employ Rée's apt description of the highly educated) were impatient with the do-it-yourself intellectuals in their midst. Karl Marx dismissed self-educated worker-philosophers with disguised contempt; the workers were meant to inherit German philosophy, not, like Proudhon, construct their own brand.[56] Similarly Lenin considered Bogdanov's, Gorki's and Lunarchasky's experiments with Bolshevik cultural party schools dangerous and foolish – not only because, like some Western reformists, he felt that worker graduates would be unsuited for tedious agitational work, but also perhaps more importantly because he suspected the very conception of 'proletarian culture' as it apparently threatened the knowledge 'bourgeois renegades' were supposed to provide.[57] But this tendency was not restricted to Bolsheviks. Filippo Turati, the great positivist intellectual leader of Italian reformist socialism, and Jean Jaurès, the *normalien* humanist parliamentary tribune, wanted workers to inherit good bourgeois lay schools, not proletarian universities, while leading German Social Democrats praised classical *Bildung*.[58]

The evidence, however, can mislead. Rée warns us in his contribution not to fall victim to the educated's love for a mythical virtuous worker anti-intellectualism. Studies which concentrate on educated middle-class socialist interference in hole-in-the-wall working-class practices can be drawn.

What particularly interests me as a historian are the self-educated, the new men and women of socialism's voluntary associations, those who most keenly felt the demands of both manual and mental work. I am particularly taken by their descriptions of the 'existential break' (and I discuss this in my contribution), a conversion process lovingly but unconsciously described in hundreds of triumphalist working-class autobiographies when workers enter (even at first semi-consciously) the white-collar world.[59] The party or trade-union organiser's salary (even if initially modest and accompanied by legal and physical dangers) replaces the precarious wage packet; work-time discipline is modified dramatically (even if long hours remain the rule); and perhaps most importantly one experiences geographical mobility and new circles of friends and colleagues.

The self-educated were not necessarily representative of the broader working class. They were not always skilled artisans, although their educational culture was largely refracted through the mores of artisanal life. They could appear queer and snobbish in their friends', colleagues' or relations' eyes. And the self-educated in turn might distance themselves unintentionally or consciously from popular custom. This education, however, was not conceived in an instrumental fashion. What the British self-educated had long called 'really useful knowledge' had no direct application to their working skills, nor did they believe it would result in their social elevation. Education was humanist not utilitarian; it opened the mind and body to a new symbolic order.[60] But whatever the self-educated set out to accomplish by studying, this process could produce paradoxical unintended results. While poetry or philosophy, the quintessence of classical education, rather than the basic skills of numeracy and literacy, were the highlight of their self-education, it was these basic skills that the self-educated employed to construct and maintain the pioneer socialist and trade-union organisations, even while the classics had stimulated their socialist imaginations.

The bureaucratisation of socialism before 1914 may have been accelerated by the emergence of a stratum of ex-worker officials. Yet this process was far more complex than either Michels or even Weber would allow.[61]

Self-educated socialists shared the common experience of constructing time budgets and undergoing the necessary self-policing of personal income so as to have financial and temporal resources for the pursuit of knowledge. Thus the political division of labour finds sustenance in a thousand obscure locations: in a quarry in northern England where a young man practises Roman orations; in a popular library in Milan where another reads Sué and De Amicis; or in Paris where men and women attempt to write poetry.

NOTES

1   For a recent European overview, see G. Grossick and H. G. Haupt (eds), *Shopkeepers and Master Artisans in Nineteenth Century Europe*, London, Methuen, 1984.

2   I review the literature in my Conclusion: see notes 1 to 5, pp. 282–4.

3   S. Collini, *Liberalism and Sociology*, Cambridge University Press, 1979, p. 59. See also D. Sutton, 'Liberalism, state collectivism and the social relations of citizenship', in M. Langan and B. Schwarz (eds), *Crises in the British State 1880–1930*, London, Hutchinson, 1985, pp. 63–79.

4   S. Clarke, *Marx, Marginalism and Modern Sociology*, London, Macmillan, 1982, pp. 186–96. Durkheim would also lend himself to such a comparison. See Yeo in this volume, pp. 221–2. See also my 'Socialism and the educated middle classes in Western Europe', in R. Eyerman, L. G. Svensson and T. Söderquist (eds), *Intellectuals, Universities, and the State in Modern Western Societies*, Berkeley, University of California Press, 1987, 154–91; L. Goldman, 'A Pecularity of the English? The Social Science

Association and the Absence of Sociology in Nineteenth-Century Britain', *Past and Present*, 114, 1987, pp. 133–71; J. T. Kloppenberg, *Uncertain Victory. Social Democracy and Progressivism in European and American Thought, 1870–1920*, Oxford University Press, 1987.

5 For comprehensive overviews, see G. Therborn, 'The rule of capital and rise of democracy', *New Left Review*, no. 103, 1977, pp. 3–41; A. Prezeworski, 'Social democracy as an historical phenomenon', *New Left Review*, no. 122, 1980, pp. 27–58; A. Prezeworski, *Capitalism and Social Democracy*, Cambridge University Press, 1985. A. Przeworski and J. Sprague, *Paper Stones. A History of Electoral Socialism*, University of Chicago Press, 1987. But also see the suggestive remarks of Val Lorwin many years ago. V. R. Lorwin, 'Working-class politics and economic development in Western Europe', *American Historical Review*, 63, 2, 1957, pp. 345–46.
Another study worth consulting is H. N. Mitchell and P. N. Stearns, *The European Labor Movement, the Working Classes and the Origins of Social Democracy 1890–1914*, Ithaca, Illinois, F. E. Peacock Publishers, 1971, pp. 204–6.

6 For surveys of municipal socialism, see M. J. McQuillen, 'The development of municipal socialism in France 1880–1914', Ph.D. thesis, University of Virginia, 1972; J. W. Scott, 'Social history and the history of socialism: French socialist municipalities in the 1890s', *Mouvement Social*, no. 111, 1980, pp. 145–54; J. W. Scott, 'Mayors versus police chiefs: socialist municipalities confront the French state', in J. W. Merriman (ed.), *French Cities in the Nineteenth Century*, London, Hutchinson, 1982, pp. 230–45; various essays in A. Agosti and G. M. Bravo (eds), *Storia del movimento operaio del socialismo delle lotte sociali in Piemonte*, Bari, De Donato, 1979; A. Riosa (ed.), *Il socialismo riformista a Milano al inizo del secolo*, Milan, Mondoperaio, 1981; J. D. Rolling, 'Liberals, socialists and city government in imperial Germany: the case of Frankfurt Am Main 1900–1918', Ph.D. thesis, University of Wisconsin-Madison, 1979; M. Nolan, *Social Democracy and Society*, Cambridge University Press, 1981; J. R. Kellett, 'Municipal socialism, enterprise and trading in the Victorian city', *Urban History Yearbook*, vol. 5, 1978, pp. 36–45; A. Offer, *Property and Politics 1870–1914: Landownership, Law, Ideology and Urban Development in England*, Cambridge University Press, 1981; S. Lawrence, 'Municipal socialism, municipal trading, and public utilities', *Bulletin of the Society for the Study of Labour History*, 51, 2, 1987. For the many alliances of socialists, left liberals and progressives, see R. I. McKibbin, *The Evolution of the Labour Party 1910–1924*, Oxford, Clarendon Press, 1974; H. C.

G. Matthews, R. I. McKibbin and J. H. Kay, 'The franchise factor in the rise of the Labour Party', *English Historical Review*, vol. 41, no. 361, 1976, pp. 723–52; D. Howell, *British Workers and the Independent Labour Party*, Manchester University Press, 1983; M. Reberioux, *La République radicale? 1848–1914*, Paris, Éditions du Seuil, 1975; B. Heckart, *From Basserman to Bebel. The 'Grand Bloc's' Quest for Reform in the Kaiserreich 1900–1914*, New Haven, Conn., Yale University Press, 1974.

7 G. Stedman Jones, *Languages of Class*, Cambridge University Press, 1983, pp. 22–3. For criticisms, see M. Sonenscher, 'The sans-culottes of the Year II: rethinking the language of labour in revolutionary France', *Social History*, vol. 3, no. 3, 1984, pp. 301–2; J. Foster, 'The declassing of language', *New Left Review*, no. 150, 1985, pp. 29–46. The importance of the educated middle classes as leaders and cadre within Second Internationalist socialism has often been noted. For a good summary of the argument, see Mitchell and Stearns, op. cit., p. 148: 'Most of the early Socialist leaders came from the middle classes. Liebknecht, Kautsky, Jaurès, Turati and many others were trained professional people, usually lawyers. Leading anarchists such as Bakunin were drawn from similar groups.'

8 The first seven paragraphs are a summary of earlier works. See: C. Levy, 1987, op. cit. For the Victorian principles of work and respectability, see G. Best, *Mid-Victorian Britain 1851–75*, London, Weidenfeld and Nicolson, 1979, pp. 74–81, 256–63. For productivism, see P. W. Stearns, 'The effort at continuity in working-class culture', *Journal of Modern History*, vol. 52, no. 4, 1980, pp. 626–55; R. Evans (ed.), *The Culture of the German Working Class 1848–1933*, London, Croom Helm, 1981; T. Shanin (ed.), *Late Marx and the Russian Road*, London, Routledge & Kegan Paul, 1984; A. Gouldner, *Against Fragmentation: The Origins of Marxism and the Sociology of Intellectuals*, New York, Oxford University Press, 1985; G. Bonacchi and A. Pescarolo, 'Cultura della communità' e cultura del mestière: alle origini della resistenza operaio italiana', *Movimento Operaio e Socialista*, vol. 3, no. 1, 1980, pp. 37–48. The most fully developed case for the persistence of pre-capitalist values in nineteenth- and early-twentieth-century Western Europe is found in A. J. Mayer, *The Persistence of the Old Regime*, London, Croom Helm, 1981. See also M. Wiener, *English Culture and the Decline of the Industrial Spirit 1850–1980*, Cambridge University Press, 1980. These approaches are criticised by P. Thane and J. Harris, 'British and European bankers 1800–1914: an "aristocratic bourgeoisie"', in *The Power of the Past*, Cambridge University Press, 1984, pp. 215–34; D. Blackbourn and G. Eley, *The Peculiarities of German*

History, Oxford University Press, 1984. For the German white-collar line, see the latest from Jürgen Kocka, 'Class formation, interest articulation and public policy: the origins of the German white-collar class', in S. D. Berger (ed.), *Organising Interests in Western Europe*, Cambridge University Press, 1981, pp. 63–81. For the persistence of the bucolic and romantic within socialism, see R. Williams, *Culture and Society 1780–1950*, London, Chatto & Windus, 1958; S. Pierson, *British Socialism: The Journey from Fantasy to Politics*, Cambridge, Mass., Harvard University Press, 1976 edn, pp. 763–816; M. Löwy, 'Marxism and revolutionary romanticism', *Telos*, no. 49, 1981, pp. 83–95; J. Mendilow, *The Romantic Tradition in British Political Thought*, London, Croom Helm, 1986.

The recent work of Raphael Samuel breaks new ground; see R. Samuel, 'The vision splendid', *New Socialist*, May 1985, pp. 24–8; R. Samuel, 'Enter the proletarian giant', *New Socialist*, July/August 1985, pp. 24–7; R. Samuel, 'The cult of planning', *New Socialist*, January 1986, pp. 26–9. In a similar vein, see M. Berra, *L'etica del lavoro nella cultura italiana dall'unità a Giolitti*, Milan, Franco Angeli, 1981; P. Audenino, 'Etica laica e rappresentazione della futura nella cultura socialista dei primi del novecento', *Storia e società*, vol. 5, no. 10, 1983, pp. 877–920; S. Privato, 'L'anticlericalismo "religioso" nel socialismo italiano fra otto e novecento', *Italia Contemporanea*, vol. 154, 1984, pp. 29–50. For the influence of artisan traditions on socialism see the suggestive remarks of John Breiully, 'Artisan Economy, Artisan Politics, Artisan Ideology: The Artisan Contribution to the Nineteenth-Century Labour Movement', in C. Emsley and J. Walvin (eds.), *Artisans, Peasants and Proletarians 1760–1860*, London, Croom Helm, 1985, pp. 187–225.

9 See O. W. Muller, *Intelligencija Untersuchungen zur Geschicte eines politischen Schagwortes*, Frankfurt, Athenaen Verlag, 1971; D. Berings, *Die Intellectuellen; Geschichte eines Schimpfwortes*, Stuttgart, Klett-Cotta, 1978, pp. 81–2. S.-E. Liedman, 'Institutions and ideas: Mandarins and non-mandarins in the German academic intelligentsia', *Comparative Studies in Society and History*, vol. 18, no. 1, 1986, pp. 119–44.

10 For the British 'intellectual' as sage or professional man/woman, see T. Heyck, *The Transformation of Intellectual Life in Victorian England*, London, Croom Helm, 1982. For would-be British *narodniki*, see S. Yeo 'A New Life: the religion of socialism in Britain 1883–1896', *History Workshop Journal*, no. 4, 1977, pp. 5–56.

11 E. J. Hobsbawm, 'La cultura europea e il marxismo', in E. J. Hobsbawm *et al.*, *Storia del marxismo*, vol. II, Turin, Einaudi, 1979,

pp. 81–2; A. Asor Rosa, 'La cultura', in R. Romano and C. Vivante (eds.), *Storia d'Italia*, vol. IV, part 2, Turin, Einaudi, 1975, p. 1010.

12 For the role of intellectuals and artists in French social movements, see D. L. Rader, *The Journalists and the July Revolutions*, The Hague, Nijhoff, 1973; T. Zeldin, *France 1848–1945: Politics and Anger, Intellect and Pride*, Oxford University Press, 1980; R. Debray, *Teachers, Writers, Celebrities*, London, Verso, 1981, pp. 17–59; L. Pinto, 'Les intellectuels vers 1900. Un nouvelle classe moyenne', in G. Lavau, G. Grunberg and N. Mayer (eds), *L'Univers politique des classes moyennes*, Paris, Presses de la Fondation Nationale des Sciences Politiques, 1983, pp. 140–55. On the politics of the École Normale, see T. Clarke, *Prophets and Patrons: The French University and the Emergence of the Social Sciences*, Cambridge, Mass., Harvard University Press, 1973; D. Lindenberg and P. A. Meyer, *Lucien Herr: le socialisme et son destin*, Paris, Calmann-Levy, 1977; R. J. Smith, *The École Normale Superieure and the Third Republic*, Albany, State University of New York Press, 1982.

13 E. J. Hobsbawm, 'The Fabians reconsidered', in *Labouring Men*, London, Weidenfeld & Nicolson, 1964, p. 267. The importance of the state has recently been reemphasised. For a summary of the arguments see, T. Skoopol, 'Bringing the State Back In: Strategies of Analysis in Current Research', in P. B. Evans, D. Rueschmeyer and T. Skoopol (eds.), *Bringing the State Back In*, Cambridge University Press, 1985, pp. 25–7. And for different national traditions of professionalism in relation to the state and law see, D. Rueschmeyer, 'Professional autonomy and the control of experts', in R. Dingwall and P. Lewis (eds.), *The Sociology of the Professions*, London, Macmillan, 1983, pp. 38–58. For an Anglo-American comparison see, M. Sarfatti Larson, *The Rise of Professionalism: A Sociological Analysis*, Berkeley, University of California Press, 1977, chapter 7.

14 For studies of British 'reformist professionals', see R. Harrison, 'The positivists: a study of Labour's intellectuals', in *Before the Socialists*, London, Routledge & Kegan Paul, 1965; H. Perkin, *The Origins of Modern English Society*, London, Routledge & Kegan Paul, 1969, pp. 252–70; C. Harvie, *The Lights of Liberalism*, London, Allen Lane, 1976; V. Kiernan, 'Labour and literate in nineteenth-century Britain', in D. E. Martin and D. Rubinstein (eds), *Ideology and the Labour Movement*, London, Croom Helm, 1979; Heyck, op. cit., (note 10).

15 Heyck, op. cit. (note 10); J. Goodie, *George Gissing: Ideology and Fiction*, London, Vision Press, 1978. A good portrait of the apolitical European intellectual 'dandy' is found in L. Graña,

Modernity and its Discontents, French Society and the French Men of Letters in the Nineteenth Century, New York, Harper, 1967.

16 J. J. Sheehan, *German Liberalism in the Nineteenth Century*, London, Methuen, 1982; P. Macry, 'Sulla storia sociale dell'Italia liberale: per una ricera sul "ceto di frontière"', *Quaderni Storici*, no. 35, 1977, pp. 521–50; C. Lovett, *The Democratic Movement in Italy 1830–1876*, Cambridge, Mass., Harvard University Press, 1982.

17 For the highly dubious thesis that unemployment and status incongruence radicalised Italian graduates, see M. Barbagli, *Educating for Unemployment: Politics, Labour Markets and the School System – Italy 1859–1973*, New York, Columbia University Press, 1982.

18 For the suppression of liberal or socialist currents within the Wilhelmine university, see F. Ringer, *The Decline of the German Mandarins: The German Academic Community, 1890–1922*, Cambridge, Mass., Harvard University Press, 1969; K. Jarausch, *Students, Society and Politics in Imperial Germany*, Princeton University Press, 1982. To this must be added the work of Sven Eric Leidman who demonstrates that, at least in the 1890s, socialist currents briefly made some headway within the German universities. Leidman, op. cit. For the Eastern European cases see, E. J. Hobsbawm, 'La cultura europea e il marxismo fra Otto e Novecento' in E. J. Hobsbawm *et al.*, *Storia del marxismo*, Vol. 2, *Il marxismo nell'età della Seconda Internazionale*, Turin, Einaudi, 1979, p. 77.

19 R. Michels, *Proletariato e borghesia nel movimento socialista italiano*, Turin, Bocca, p. 302; A. Hall, 'By other means: the legal struggle against the SPD in Wilhelmine Germany', *Historical Journal*, vol. 17, no. 2, 1974, pp. 365–85; A. Hall, *Scandal, Sensation and Social Democracy*, Cambridge University Press, 1977.

20 W. Guttsman, *The German Social Democratic Party, 1875–1933*, London, George Allen and Unwin, 1981, pp. 158–9; Hobsbawm, 1979, op. cit., p. 77.

21 C. Levy, 'Max Weber and Antonio Gramsci', in W. J. Mommsen, and J. Ostenhammel (eds), *Max Weber and his Contemporaries*, London, George Allen and Unwin, 1987. For the Jews see R. S. Wistrich, *Revolutionary Jews from Marx to Trotsky*, London, Harrap, 1976; N. Levin, *Jewish Socialist Movements, 1871–1917 While Messiah Tarried*, London, Routledge and Kegan Paul, 1978, pp. 20–37, 236–49; R. Brym, *The Jewish Intelligentsia and Russian Marxism: A Sociological Study of Intellectual Radicalism and Ideological Divergence*, London, Macmillan, 1978; for Spain see Hobsbawn, 1979, op. cit., p. 73.

22 For the role of intellectuals in French socialism, see G. Lefranc, *Jaurès et les socialisme des intellectuels*, Paris, Éditions Ouvrières, 1968; S. S. Gosch, 'Socialism and intellectual in France, 1880–1914', Ph.D. thesis, Rutgers University, 1971; Pinto, op. cit. (note 12). And for the importance of intellectuals in syndicalist and anarchist organisations, see J. Juillard, *Fernand Pelloutier*, Paris, François Maspero, 1971; J. Maitron, *Le Mouvement anarchiste en France*, Paris, François Maspero, 1975 edn, Vol. I, pp. 136–9. Others have discounted it; see P. N. Stearns, *Revolutionary Syndicalism and French Labor*, New Brunswick, NJ, Rutgers University Press, 1971; F. F. Ridley, *Revolutionary Syndicalism in France*, Cambridge University Press, 1970.

23 Besides Lefranc, op. cit. (note 22), see the magnificent biography by Harvey Goldberg, *The Life of Jean Jaurès*, Madison, University of Wisconsin Press, 1962; and M. Reberioux (ed.), *Jaurès et la classe ouvrière*, Paris, Éditions Ouvrières, 1981.

24 H. McLeod, 'Religion and the British and German Labour Movements. c. 1890–1914; A Comparison', *Bulletin of the Society for the Study of Labour History*, 51, 1, 1986, pp. 25–35. In general see, W. Elvander, *Skandinavsk arbetaröselse*, Stockholm, Liber-förlag, 1980.

25 P. N. Stearns, *Lives of Labour*, London, Croom Helm, 1975; Geary, op. cit. (note 18). J. Breuilly, 'Liberalism and social democracy: a comparison of British and German labour politics, c. 1850–1875', *European History Quarterly*, vol. 15, no. 1, 1985, pp. 3–42.

26 For an analysis of Labour Representation Committee MPs, see D. E. Martin, '"The instruments of the people": the Parliamentary Labour Party in 1906', in Martin and Rubinstein, op. cit. (note 14), pp. 125–46.

27 H.-U. Hesse, 'Il gruppo parlamentare del partito socialista, la sua composizione, e la sua funzione negli anni delle crisi del parlamentarismo', in L. Valiani and H. Wandruszka (eds), *Movimento operaio e socialista in Italia e in Germania dal 1870 al 1920*, Bologna, Il Mulino, 1978, p. 215.

28 On the ILP and the trade unions, see D. Howell, *British Workers and the Independent Labour Party 1893–1906*, Manchester University Press, 1983. For the French and the Italian examples, see the debate over trade unionism and revolutionary movements. On the grounds of low unionisation Stearns dismissed the importance of French anarcho-syndicalism. This, I believe, fails to notice the importance of local organisations in France and Italy, and is altogether too economistic; see Stearns, 1971, op. cit. (note 22). For more balanced accounts of French and Italian syndicalism, see B. Moss, *Origins of the French Labor Movement*, Berkeley,

University of California Press, 1976; R. McGraw, *France 1815–1914. The Bourgeois Century*, London, Fontana, 1983, pp. 300–12; A. Riosa, *Il sindacalismo rivoluzionario in Italia*, Bari, De Donato, 1976; various essays in *Richerche Storiche* (Florence) since 1976.

29 See note 27.

30 See Harrison in this volume, pp. 59–60.

31 For the best summary of this difficult subject, see F. Andreucci, 'La diffusione e la vulgarizzazione del marxismo', in E. J. Hobsbawm *et al.*, op. cit. (note 11), Vol. 2, pp. 5–58. We await a study of the dissemination of various socialisms.

32 P. Nettl, *Rosa Luxemburg*, Oxford University Press, 1969 abridged edn, pp. 262–7; N. Jacobs, 'The German Social Democratic Party school in Berlin', *History Workshop Journal*, no. 5, 1978, pp. 279–87; Lidtke, op. cit., pp. 173–4.

33 H.-J. Steinberg, *Sozialismus und deutsche Sozialdemokratie*, Hannover, Verlag für Literatur und Zeitgeschehen, 1967, pp. 129–42; Lidtke, op. cit., pp. 182–5. Also Lidtke shows that workers gained political information from newspapers, ibid., pp. 188–9; Guttsman, op. cit. (note 20), pp. 167–218.

34 Andreucci, op. cit. (note 31); R. Samuel, 'British Marxist historians, 1880–1980', *New Left Review*, no. 120, 1980, pp. 21–96; F. Turi, 'Aspetti dell' ideologia del PSI (1890–1910)', *Studi Storici*, vol. 21, no. 1, 1980, pp. 61–94. For Bellamy, see A. Lipow, *Authoritarian Socialism in America*, Berkeley, University of California Press, 1982.

35 R. Debray, *Teachers, Writers, Celebrities*, London, Verso, 1981; R. Williams, *Problems in Materialism and Culture*, London, Verso, 1980, pp. 148–69. An interesting application is hinted at in D. Sutton, 'Radical liberalism, Fabianism and social history', in R. Johnson, G. McLennan, B. Schwarz and D. Sutton (eds), *Making Histories*, London, Hutchinson, 1982, pp. 44–95. See Lidtke, op. cit., p. 55:

> Inns and pubs were also centers for the exchange of news, gossip and personal sentiment. They were for workers what 'coffee houses, salons and (elite) clubs' were for prosperous and educated Germans, succinctly stated in a phrase from a worker: 'The pub is the salon of the poor'.

36 Kocka, op. cit. (note 8).

37 D. Blackbourn, 'The "Mittelstand" in German society and politics 1871–1914', *Social History*, vol. 2, no. 4, 1977, pp. 409–33.

38 For the importance or insignificance of middle strata in various parties, see, for example, C. Willard, *Les Guesdistes*, Paris, Éditions Ouvrières, 1965; G. Melis, *Burocrazia e socialismo nell'Italia liberale*, Bologna, Il Mulino, 1982; Levy in this volume, pp. 137–43; Guttsman, op. cit. (note 20), pp. 106–8, 158–9, 251–9.

39 For the English case, see E. P. Thompson, *The Making of the English Working Class*, Harmondsworth, Penguin, 1968 edn, pp. 84–110; Stedman Jones, op. cit. (note 7), pp. 100–7. For the French case, see N. Birnbaum, *Le peuple et le gros: histoire d'un mythe*, Paris, Grasset, 1979. For a recent overview of the English lower middle class's ideology, see G. Crossick, 'The petit bourgeoisie in nineteenth-century Britain: the urban and liberal case', in Crossick and Haupt, op. cit. (note 1).

40 Gouldner, op. cit. (note 8). For Bakunin, see extracts from *Statism and Anarchy* (1873), in G. P. Maximoff (ed.), *The Political Philosophy of Bakunin: Scientific Anarchism*, London, Collier-Macmillan, 1964, pp. 288ff. For Makhajski, see A. D'Agostino, 'Intelligentsia socialism and the "workers' revolution": the views of J. W. Machajski', *International Review of Social History*, vol. 24, pt 1, 1969, pp. 54–89; J. W. Machajski, *Le socialisme des intellectuels. Textes choisis, traduits et présentés par Alexandre Skirda*, Paris, Le Seuil, 1979; David Beetham in this volume, pp. 113–14; Stephen Yeo in this volume, pp. 220. The fullest account is M. Shatz, 'Jan Waclaw Machajski and the "Makhaevshchina": 1866–1926. Anti-intellectualism and the Russian intelligentsia', Ph.D. thesis, Columbia University, 1968.

41 See David Beetham's essay in this volume; N. Berti, 'Anticipazioni anarchiche sui "nuovi padroni"', *Interrogations*, no. 6, 1976, pp. 70–104.

42 Yeo, p. 234. For further points, see R. Samuel and G. Stedman Jones, 'The Labour Party and social democracy' in R. Samuel and G. Stedman Jones (eds), *Culture, Ideology and Politics*, London, Routledge & Kegan Paul, 1983, pp. 320–9; G. Stedman Jones, op. cit. (note 7), pp. 239–56.

43 S. and B. Webb, *The History of Trade Unionism*, London, Longman, Green & Co., 1894, pp. 475–76.

44 For summaries of the debate in the 1950s, 1960s and 1970s, see R. Q. Gray, *The Aristocracy of Labour in 19th Century Britain, c. 1850–1914*, London, Macmillan, 1981; G. McLennan, *Marxism and the Methodologies of History*, London, Verso, 1981, pp. 206–32. For examples of German attempts to extend the thesis, see J. Breuilly, 'The labour aristocracy in Britain and Germany: a comparison', *Society for the Study of Labour History Bulletin*, no. 48, 1984, pp. 58–71. Paolo Spriano's work is representative of Italian attempts.

45 Breuilly, 1984, op. cit. (note 44).

46 E. J. Hobsbawm, *Worlds of Labour*, London, Weidenfeld & Nicolson, 1984, p. 222. For other recent criticisms, see A. Reid, 'Intelligent artisans and aristocrats of labour: the essays of Thomas Wright', in J. Winter (ed.), *The Working Class in Modern British*

History, Cambridge University Press, 1983, pp. 171–86; J. Zeitlin
and R. Harrison (eds), *Divisions of Labour*, Brighton, Harvester,
1985; J. Zeitlin and S. Tolliday (eds), *Shop Floor Bargaining and
the State. Historical and Comparative Perspectives*, Cambridge
University Press, 1985.

47 See Harrison, Mommsen, Beetham, Morris and Yeo.
48 R. Michels, *Zur Soziologie des Parteiwesens in der Modernen
Demokratie*, Leipzig, W. Klinkhardt, 1911. A good English
language edition with an interesting introduction by Seymour
Lipset is *Political Parties*, New York, Free Press, 1962.
49 R. Michels, 'La psicologia sociale della boheme e il proletariato
intelletuale', *Atti della Reale Accademia di Scienze Morali e
Politiche* (Naples), vol. LIV, 1931, pp. 181–99; R. Michels,
'Intellectuals', in E. Seligman and A. Johnson (eds), *Encyclopaedia
of the Social Sciences*, Vol. 8, New York, Macmillan, pp. 118–26.
50 S. Perlman, *A Theory of the Labour Movement*, New York,
Macmillan, 1928; J. Schumpeter, *Capitalism, Socialism and
Democracy*, London, George Allen and Unwin, 1943.
51 See the various works by Edward Shils and his followers. Another
example, a study of 'revolutionary elites', combines Machajski,
Michels and Parsons: H. Lasswell and D. Lerner (eds), *World
Revolutionary Elites: Studies in Coercive Ideological Movements*,
Cambridge, Mass, MIT, 1965. Finally, see J. Billington, *Fire in the
Minds of Men*, London, Temple Smith, 1980.
52 G. Roth, *The Social Democrats in Imperial Germany: A Study of
Working Class Isolation and National Integration*, Totowa, N.J.,
Metuchen Press; J. P. Nettl, 'The German Social Democratic Party
1890–1914 as a political model', *Past and Present*, 30; C.
Schorske, *German Social Democracy, 1905–1917*, Cambridge,
Mass., Harvard University Press, 1965; D. Groh, *Negative
Integration und revolutionärer Attentismus*, Frankfurt, Propylaen,
1973.
53 Guttsman, op. cit., G. D. Steenson, *'Not On Man, Not One
Penny'.: German Social Democracy, 1863–1914*, Pittsburgh,
University of Pennyslvania Press, 1981; Lidtke, op. cit.
54 For interesting examples see Kiernan, op. cit.; S. Macintyre, *A
Proletarian Science. Marxism in Britain 1917–1933*, Cambridge
University Press, 1980, chap. 1; Rée in this volume; V. Lidtke,
The Alternative Culture: Socialist Labor in Imperial Germany;
New York, Oxford University Press, 1985. M. G. Rosada,
'Biblioteche popolari e politica culturale del PSI tra ottocento e
novecento', *Movimento Operaio e Socialista*, vol. 23, nos. 2/3,
1977, pp. 259–88; M. G. Rosada, *L'Università popolari*, Rome,
Riuniti, 1975; C. G. Lacaita, 'Socialismo, istruzione e cultura
popolare tra l'800 e il '900', in A. Riosa (ed.), 1981, op. cit., M.

Carl Levy

Reberioux, 'Critique litteraire et socialisme au tournant du siecle', *Mouvement Social*, no. 59, 1967, pp. 3–28; S. Lebenstein, 'French Libertarian Education Theory and Experiments, 1895–1915', University of Wisconsin Ph.D., 1972. G. Turi, 'Socialismo e cultura', *Movimento Operaio e Socialista*, 3, 2/3, 1980, pp. 143–52.

55 H. Entwistle, *Antonio Gramsci: Conservative Schooling for Radical Politics*, London, Routledge & Kegan Paul, 1979; A. M. Cirese, 'Gramsci's observations on folklore', in A. Showstack Sassoon (ed.), *Approaches to Gramsci*, London, Writers & Readers, 1982.

56 For the era of Proudhon, see J. Rancière, *La nuit des proletaires*, Paris, Fayard, 1981. For self-educated philosophers in Britain, see J. Rée, *Proletarian Philosophers*, Oxford, Clarendon Press, 1984.

57 J. Schurrer, 'Bogdanov e Lenin: bolscevismo al bivio', in Hobsbawm, 1979, op. cit. (note 11), pp. 445–546.

58 Rosada, 1977, op. cit. (note 54); Lidtke, op. cit. (note 54), pp. 144, 187, 196, 198.

59 I discuss some British examples; see pp. 165–73.

60 D. Vincent, *Bread, Knowledge and Freedom*, London, Europa, 1981.

61 See Mommsen's contribution for a discussion of the bureaucratisation of the SPD.

2
Sidney and Beatrice Webb
Royden Harrison

INTRODUCTION

In 1935 Sidney and Beatrice Webb published an enormous book entitled *Soviet Communism: A New Civilisation?*. When the second edition appeared two years later they removed the interrogation mark. In private, the Webbs – who were childless – referred to this work as their 'last and biggest baby'. In public, they described it as an act of 'supererogation' a theological expression meaning a service performed beyond the call of duty: something fit to be ignored or criticised, but not anything which might warrant blame.

In describing *Soviet Communism* in this way, the Webbs were claiming that they had done enough to secure their reputation without adding this last offering to the total of their accomplishment. After all, in the course of almost half a century they had published well over one hundred books, pamphlets and substantial articles. Their literary output, if allowance be made for what they wrote separately as well as in collaboration, certainly exceeded one thousand items, and at least some of these items were of enduring importance.[1] Together they had written the standard history of trade unionism and a companion volume, *Industrial Democracy*, which is still noted as the greatest study ever produced in the English language of the theory and practice of trade unionism. They were – and they remain – the greatest authorities on the history of English local government. As contributors to socialist thought they belong with Robert Owen and William Morris as the only English writers in the very highest rank. The achievements of their literary partnership were, indeed, sufficient to ensure their lasting fame even without reference to their astonishing record as founders of new and enduring institutions or as prophets of new directions in social policy and public administration.

When *Soviet Communism* first appeared the combined age of the Webbs was 155. Why did these two aged mortals visit the vast Soviet land? Why did they dare to undertake a work of such magnitude as that involved in interpreting this 'new civilisation' to a Western public? Were they being true to themselves as socialists and as scholars when they wrote about that civilisation in such favourable terms?

Perhaps Beatrice's choice of the term 'a work of supererogation' is to be understood as a slightly defensive response to these questions. Unlike Sidney, she was prone to the torments of self-criticism and self-doubt. In public she always appeared to be arrogantly self-possessed and completely self-confident. In fact, she never managed to arrive at any permanent settlement concerning her opinions about either herself or the world. She employed a Cartesian regard for the method of universal doubt together with a Rousseauesque intuition into the mysteries of the human psyche. Just as Sidney, at well over seventy, was ready to try to learn Russian, Beatrice was so far distant from senility that she could continually alert herself against the disabilities of old age. The old, as she repeatedly observed, are either scatter-brained or obsessed. And then she went on to ask, Which are we? The question could hardly be put by anyone who had completely succumbed to either of these afflictions – as, of course, she very well knew when she asked herself that question!

Yet few were prepared to allow *Soviet Communism* the status which its authors wished it to have. For the leading British Communist theoretician, R. Palme Dutt, it was to be considered not as a work of supererogation, but of contrition. What was Sidney Webb if he was not what H. G. Wells had called him – the 'prevailing Fabian'? And what was Fabianism if it was not a completely honest and conscious expression of the fight against Marxism? For Dutt, the Webbs' favourable estimate of the USSR constituted a massive blow against reformism, gradualism, parliamentarianism and everything which scaled down or diminished revolutionary socialism. The Webbs were the architects of 'revisionism' – the teachers of Bernstein – but they themselves were guiltless of the pretence of ever having been the disciples of Marx. If the world's most distinguished anti-Marxians went over to the Soviet Union that was 'a definite landmark in the history of the British Labour Movement'. Even more, it was 'a definite victory on the front of the world revolution'.[2]

Was it?

This essay attempts to answer that question. It aims to show that there was far more continuity between the established position of the Webbs and their admiration for the USSR than Dutt appreciated. It aims to establish that there was a correspondence between the value system of certain late-Victorian professional people and the 'strange syndrome of Soviet Marxism under Stalin'.[3] It attempts to identify those strengths and weaknesses of Fabian thought which went into the making of the Webbs' estimate of the new civilisation. But such a critique of the authors cannot avoid becoming a critique of the USSR itself. It cannot avoid reference to the grand fact about human consciousness in the 1930s; only Marxism could enter into an understanding of the Soviet experience, but Marxism was disabled from doing so because it had become, so largely, a mere form of false consciousness arising from the reality which it was required to interpret.[4]

ENTER SIDNEY

Sidney Webb was born the son of a hairdresser in the heart of London in 1859.[5] His father was an unqualified man who appears to have done odd jobs as an accountant or business consultant. While his mother had strong religious impulses which no existing church or chapel seemed capable of satisfying, his father was an admirer of John Stuart Mill and the tradition of philosophic radicalism. While the young Webb never himself experienced poverty, he witnessed it on all sides, and the fear of its coming spoiled an otherwise happy childhood. It also gave him the strongest incentive to enter the new and rising world of professional men which was at many points overtaking the old world of the professional gentlemen. The lower-middle-class boy who aspired to security and to self-respect could find these experiences in such burgeoning professions as teaching, accountancy, architecture and, pre-eminently, the Civil Service, which after 1870 began to become professionalised in accordance with the recommendations of the Northcote-Trevelyan Report.

Sidney chose the Civil Service as the most secure of all occupations and the one most open to men of talent as measured by examination performance. And even by the most exacting standards set by Chinese mandarins there was never a more wonderful examinee than Sidney Webb! He came only to conquer: only to be first. It made little difference whether the subject was geology or political economy, mathematics or foreign languages; Webb was in the habit of enrolling himself in whatever classes there might be available and passing out of them with whatever prizes or high honours there were. In those rare cases in which distinction fell short of outstanding excellence and undisputable ascendancy, he calmly enrolled in the course for a second time until his triumph was past any possible qualification. Thus, he passed his time after concluding his full-time education at around the age of fifteen. He proceeded up the Civil Service by a remorseless process of examination success, until in the early 1880s he had arrived at the highest position attainable by merit unaided by social or political preferment: that of a first division clerk in the Colonial Office. By 1885 he had also qualified as a barrister, but he only once accepted a brief.

The young Webb was not, however, merely an accomplished 'swot'. He made himself felt in student societies and at Birkbeck College he organised a revolt which championed the claims of women to equal rights with men. While still in his early twenties he was becoming a 'big man in a small way' in local 'parliaments', debating societies and philosophical discussion groups. In literature he was an admirer of George Eliot; in philosophy a follower of J. S. Mill – 'corrected' to take account of the advances in biology and Herbert Spencer's concept of 'organic development'; in politics he was a Gladstonian. Such were the principal characteristics of his intellectual condition when he first met George Bernard Shaw at the meetings of the Zeitetical Society in 1881.

Shaw was quite unknown at the time, but armed with gaiety, brilliant wit and immense personal charm he forced his friendship upon Webb. At least, this was how Shaw himself described the beginning of their relationship.[6] The Irishman needed the Londoner's encyclopedic knowledge and capacity for sustained analysis if he was to give a grounding to his imagination, and consequence and direction to his purpose. Sidney, for his part, was bound to recognise that a committee of Webb and Shaw was sure to add up to more than the sum of their powers taken separately. Shaw had a great presence, while Sidney – small, rotund and myopic – made little impression upon first acquaintance. Shaw was the extravagant and daring extrovert, while the young Webb thought of himself as a hypersensitive introvert. Shaw was unequalled in debate, but Sidney, who spoke with a cockney accent and a faint lisp, found the committee room more congenial than the platform.

In 1885 Shaw persuaded Webb to join the Fabian Society. This body was one of the three major organisations that contributed to the revival of socialism in England in the 1880s.[7] It took its name from the Roman general Fabius and had for its motto the words 'For the right moment you must wait, as Fabius did most patiently, when warring against Hannibal, though many censured his delays: but when the time comes you must strike hard, as Fabius did, or your waiting will be vain and fruitless.' According to the best authorities Fabius never did strike hard, and it is certain that the young Webb had no intention of doing so. Indeed, when he first addressed the society his position was much closer to that of a positivist looking to the moralisation of capitalism than of a socialist anxious to destroy the existing system root and branch. By temperament and training Sidney was averse to destruction. He had a profound loathing of capitalist competition, which he had already come to regard as unjust and untidy, but anything which suggested anarchism or violence or chaos would be still worse. He saw his problem as how to develop a socialism which would be constructive, practicable and ultimately acceptable to all classes. By 1887 he was already well on the way to this objective; by 1889 the presence of this kind of socialism was being felt, and its leading characteristics could have been discerned by an intelligent observer.

Fabianism announced its independence from Marxism no matter whether it was the Marxism of H. M. Hyndman's Social Democratic Federation or that of William Morris's Socialist League.[8] Ultimately the difference stemmed from two distinct conceptions of human nature. All major social and political doctrines contain an 'organising insight' into these grand questions. At first sight such an insight may look like a hypothesis of great generality, but still one to be tested by the facts. In practice, it does not function like an ordinary hypothesis and it is not tested by the facts. It serves, rather, to conjure hitherto neglected facts out of the ground and bring them into fresh and surprising relationship with facts that are already familiar. It is characteristic of those who discover such an organising insight, or who become possessed by one, that it closes up the distance between the world of fact and the world of value. Those who cannot see the world anew after having been shown its transforming power tend to be dismissed as blind or wicked or hopelessly conditioned.

For Marx, man was an animal whose defining characteristic was that he continuously changed his own nature in the course of his conscious transformation of nature. It was through work that man transformed the world and himself at the same time. It was through the changes which men made in their material powers of production – and through the changing relations to each other that they entered into around these changing powers – that the conditions of alienation and liberation were equally to be understood. For the Fabians, on the other hand, the dialectic – if there was one – lay in man as a being whose uniqueness consisted in his being moulded by institutions even while he was the maker of them. What was decisive was the institutional 'superstructure' rather than the economic 'base'. Man was an animal who formed committees! The wealth, health and happiness of mankind depended, to a large degree, upon the adequacy or otherwise of the structure of public administration and the scope which was allotted to it.

This contrast is real and important, but it favours the Fabians in so far as it suggests a greater preoccupation with first principles or major premises in social philosophy than they usually showed. In practice, Webb displayed little interest in major premises, preferring to occupy himself with formulating minor ones. To the disgust of philosophers like Bertrand Russell, he boasted that if he could insert a minor premise in a political syllogism he could always take his opponent to the right conclusion. Sidney was not in favour of delaying matters with debates about the essential nature of man or the purpose of life. For practical purposes, he would accept virtually any of the usual assumptions concerning happiness, freedom or progress, so long as he was allowed to demonstrate that these general ideals could be brought to any particular effect only through a specific proposal for institutional changes that would involve the extension of social provision, social control and social ownership.

The second characteristic of Fabianism which separated it from Marxism was that it appealed, more or less self-consciously, to a distinctively English political and philosophical tradition. In the first half of the nineteenth century the philosophic radicals (Bentham, Mill, Chadwick and others) had established that a small group of original, clear-headed and well-placed thinkers might exercise a great influence upon the development of law and opinion. In the third quarter of the nineteenth century the English Positivists (E. S. Beesly, Frederic Harrison and others) had continued this tradition, albeit with less distinction and success. Webb thought of himself as the successor to J. S. Mill in English public life and, like his fellow Fabian, Graham Wallas, he was an attentive student and admirer of Jeremy Bentham.[9] He was also, as was noticed, influenced by positivism, as were many other Fabian leaders. Thus, it was not for nothing that the Fabians were referred to as 'the new utilitarians' and seen to take their place in the English tradition which accorded influence, if not power, to a succession of politico-philosophic ginger groups which prided themselves on the independence and community of their intellectual life and, upon the advanced and radical character which brought them into harmony with the still inchoate aspirations of 'the Democracy'.[10]

By contrast, the tradition out of which Marxism arose was not a merely national one. Deeply as it was indebted to British historical experience and to British political economy, it drew upon the entire West European tradition of class struggle from 1789 onwards. Sidney Webb, although he spoke fluent French and German, did not place himself in that tradition – beyond remarking that he was a Girondist who had no time for the metaphysical cobwebs of Germanic philosophers.

It was precisely in relation to the class struggle that the Fabians appeared most remote from Marx. Sidney did not deny its reality. In 1887 he produced one of the most successful and influential pamphlets in the history of British labour, entitled *Facts for Socialists*. A whole section was devoted to 'the Class Struggle'. But Webb saw that struggle as one of the faults and wastes of capitalism rather than as the agency by which capitalism itself would be transformed. Engels greatly respected the quality of this type of Fabian propaganda, but complained that it was spoiled by trying to hush up or

evade the need for a class struggle.[11] Webb expected the progress
of socialism to result from other agencies. The class war was useful
only in so far as it might, under certain circumstances, promote
the growth of 'social compunction'. Socialism would advance, so
he expected, through a growing consensus in its favour: one which
was to develop around existing institutions and their developing
concerns. In other words, socialists must learn to use the institutions of local and central government and get what they wanted
from the great departments of state. Unconsciously, town councillors and statesmen, civil servants and political economists, church-
men and university teachers were becoming socialists as they found
themselves obliged to deal with the problems posed by modern
industry set within the framework of an expanding democracy. He
made his point very effectively in a small book, *Socialism in
England*, first published in the United States in 1889:

> The Individualist Town Councillor will walk along the municipal pave-
> ment, lit by municipal gas and cleansed by municipal brooms with
> municipal water, and seeing by the municipal clock in the municipal
> market, that he is too early to meet his children coming from the
> municipal school hard by the county lunatic asylum and municipal
> hospital, will use the national telegraph system to tell them not to walk
> through the municipal park but to come to the municipal tramway, to
> meet him in the municipal reading room, by the municipal art gallery,
> museum and library, where he intends to consult some of the national
> publications in order to prepare his next speech in the municipal town-
> hall, in favour of the nationalisation of canals and the increase of the
> government control over the railway system. 'Socialism, sir,' he will
> say, 'don't waste the time of a practical man by your fantastic absurdities.
> Self-help, sir, individual self-help, that's what's made our city what it
> is!'[12]

The Fabians, unlike the Marxists organised within the Social
Democratic Federation or the Socialist League, neither wished nor
expected to recruit many proletarians. Webb and his friends saw
themselves for what they were: a contingent recruited from *la
nouvelle couche sociale*, the rising stratum of modestly placed
professional men, civil servants, journalists, teachers, scientists and
technicians. This social formation developed relatively late in
England as compared with other European countries, and such
'intellectuals' were far less likely to feel outcasts in their own

country utterly alienated from the existing order of things than were their counterparts in the continental intelligentsia. Indeed, the Russian word 'intelligentsia' could not be applied without embarrassment or reservation to such exceedingly practical people as the Fabians took themselves to be.[13] Men like Webb wanted to enlarge the sphere of their own existing usefulness: to change the world so as to give greater scope to the disinterested expert and the professional administrator at the expense of backward politicians and selfish industrialists. They thought of socialism in terms of the gradual eradication of injustice and waste in favour of order and progress: of diminished inequality and of discreetly regulated freedom. Unlike William Morris they did not identify socialism with a world renewed in which man would be wholly remade. Their highest ideal was to generalise their own modest life-style and to make it possible for all to achieve their own sure sense of social usefulness.

This does not mean that the Fabians failed to appeal to the working class. They did so with considerable effect. But their object was to stir them into action within the labour movement rather than to persuade them to join the Fabian Society. As unashamedly lower-middle-class men and women, they preferred the surroundings of the drawing-room, the lecture hall or the relatively orderly arrangements of a working men's club to addressing open-air meetings at street corners or attempting to lead mass demonstrations of the unemployed. This respectability and self-consciousness about their own social position was no obstacle when Webb and his friends appealed to the organised workers of London. On the contrary, it was Fabian socialism rather than Marxism which tended to make the most headway among them after 1887.[14]

To fully understand the reasons for this it would be necessary to make a detailed reappraisal of the whole socialist revival of the 1880s. For present purposes it will suffice to draw attention to certain limited aspects of it.

Webb and his friends made a detailed study of Marx' *Capital* in so far as it had become available in German and French. By 1887 they had clearly rejected the labour theory of value. Under Webb's leadership they began to develop an alternative theory of exploitation in which exploitation was accounted for through an extension of the Ricardian theory of rent.[15] This theory had the merit of confronting and apparently explaining the gross inequality of income as between the owners of land and capital on the one hand and the mass of the workers on the other. It had the still greater merit, from an agitational point of view, of appearing to be in accord with the recognised and approved teachings of political economy. Moreover, London workers had been taught to think of rent as a peculiarly unjustifiable category of income. By demonstrating that 'profit' was merely 'rent' under another name, the Fabians found it easier than the Marxists to get workers to advance from radicalism to socialism.

In taking their socialism to the London workers' clubs the Fabians were much more fortunate than the Marxists. Hyndman had made his major effort in 1881–3 before the club movement had entered upon a period of rapid growth and before it had generally succeeded in throwing off the grip of the wealthy patrons who had controlled it. The Fabians made their major effort from 1887 to 1889, after these events had occurred. Not only was their socialism expressed in a much more familiar vocabulary, but it was linked in a much more acceptable way to a programme of immediate demands and tactical devices. All the then existing forms of British Marxism failed to resolve the difficult problem of how to relate the immediate demand to the ultimate end. If capitalism was leading inexorably to increasing immiseration and final collapse, what good was there in encouraging the workers to fight for palliatives or to engage in mere trade-union struggles? On the other hand, how was it possible to reach the workers and develop a socialist consciousness among them unless one started from their immediate problems and concerns? For Webb and his friends this whole problem or complex of problems was removed, since every extension of social provision, social control and social ownership was regarded as a further instalment of socialism. Sidney carried this argument to such extreme lengths that even his fellow Fabians complained about being asked to treat the introduction of hawkers' licences as evidence of 'The Progress of Socialism'![16] But for every convinced socialist like William Morris or Hubert Bland who complained that 'although socialism involves state control, state control does not imply socialism', there were a hundred men in the workers' clubs ready to acknowledge that socialism had been introduced to them in a much more practicable, intelligible and English fashion. After all, one might mock at hawkers' licences, but was it absurd to suggest that a legally enforceable eight-hour day was both desirable in its own right and a step in the direction of regulating production in the interests of the producer instead of regulating the producer in the interests of production for someone else's profit?

In the second half of the 1880s Fabianism grew strong through its influence upon the London workers' clubs. The clubs numbered their politically conscious members in thousands when the socialist societies numbered theirs in a few hundred. And behind every politically conscious club member there stood ten others who went to the club for beer or conviviality, who could be drawn into political action as the occasion required. By systematically working the club circuit, Webb and his fellow Fabians secured a mass basis which those who sought recruitment to Marxist organisations failed to obtain. A socialism which presented itself as continuous with, rather than discontinuous from, the traditions of middle-class radicalism was much more marketable than any other variety. Besides, Sidney was happy to make the most of common ground. On the land question, taxation, free speech and the reform of the peculiarly archaic system of London government the Fabian appeared as a whole-hearted Radical – and something more. He did not dismiss the old battle-cries with contempt, as the Marxists tended to do, but documented, clarified and extended them. He did not ask workers to break from their traditional allegiance to Radicalism or Liberalism; he asked them to improve upon it. Sidney's tactic was to reject a clean break with the Liberal Party in favour of 'permeating' it from within while occasionally pressuring it from without. No one was asked to break from his moorings – only to untie, cast off and float upon the tide. If the Fabians were taken on board, why then, there would be accomplished pilots who might navigate the ship past the unseen rocks and out into the open sea!

Thus, when Sidney Webb first met Beatrice Potter in January 1890 he was already well on the way to celebrity. He was recognised as the prevailing Fabian and the moving spirit of such influential publications as *Facts for Socialists* and *Essays in Fabian Socialism*. His friend Graham Wallas had emerged as the leader of the Metropolitan Radical Association, and the Fabians had largely succeeded in getting this important proletarian body – formed out of the most advanced workers' clubs – to adopt some of the leading features of their own policy on the eight-hour day, free school meals, the destruction of monopoly and privilege in London government and other matters. Webb's name already occasioned hope among the younger Liberals in search of ways of rejuvenating their party, even while it occasioned fear among the more established figures, who were afraid that they might be compelled to adopt his 'wild' schemes for an advanced social policy.[17] He was not exactly respectable; but he was respected. He was not a dangerous revolutionary, but he was arguably the most dangerous socialist in England.

ENTER BEATRICE

Beatrice Potter was, at the time of their first meeting, neither a socialist nor dangerous.[18] She was born in Gloucestershire in 1858, the eighth daughter of a great railway magnate. It is tempting to see in her family history the mirror of the history of a whole class. Her grandfathers had been energetic and intelligent men who made their fortunes in textiles. They had been dissenters in religion and Radicals in politics. They had been for the first Reform Act, but opposed to Chartism. They had been against the corn laws but in favour of the severities of the New Poor Law.

Beatrice's father, Richard, had been inclined to exchange the North of England for the South: the hard life of action in business and politics for the leisurely pursuits of a gentleman. The financial crisis of 1847 and the revolutions of 1848 destroyed his independence, but he was cushioned against complete disaster by the network of social ties that grew up among those who had been rich long enough for them no longer to count as parvenus. Richard was helped into the timber trade in Gloucester and then went on into railways. By the time Beatrice was born, his capital was so great that he was virtually beyond the reach of commercial crises. His family lived in the highest style in London or else occupied one of their three immense houses scattered about different parts of the country. Dissent was soon exchanged for Anglicanism. In 1867 the Potters broke with Radicalism and became identified with the Tories. However, the household remained open-minded and cultivated. Beatrice's father encouraged her to read whatever books she liked without restriction of any kind. Her mother spoke most European languages and tried her hand at writing a serious novel.

Despite all these advantages, Beatrice Potter (unlike Sidney Webb) had an unhappy childhood and youth. Her mother valued what she took to be 'masculine' qualities of mind and she considered that Beatrice was the least able of all her children. The ninth Potter child had been the long awaited boy, but he died in his early childhood. While he lived he drew love and attention away from Beatrice; when he died he may well have left her with a hidden sense of guilt and remorse about her own equivocal feelings towards him.

From her earliest years she was unable to be herself for striving to be the sort of person she would have to become if she was to win the love and respect of her mother. She became moody and introspective. She was chronically out of sorts and suffered from a whole series of illnesses mostly of a rather trivial and ill-defined kind. From her adolescence onwards she kept a journal which served a number of purposes. It was a record of notable trips abroad, of public and family happenings, of visits to the household of such great men as the sociologist Herbert Spencer, who was the only adult – or so she suspected – who loved her or interested himself in her thoughts and activities. (Ironically, Beatrice came to see her greatest debt to Spencer in his having taught her to think about human institutions 'just like animals or plants'.) The journal was intended also to be an exercise yard in which she might develop those literary skills which, following her mother, she admired and wanted to cultivate. But the journal's most important function was to serve as a form of therapy for the anguish of her 'divided self'.[19]

After her mother's death in 1882, Beatrice reflected that her mother had been a divided personality: one who had spent her life repressing her humanity out of deference to the teachings of political economy and out of a regard for what she took to be the responsibilities of her own social class. Beatrice persuaded herself that she too was a 'duplex' being. She referred to 'the nether being in me: the despondent, vain grasping person – the Heyworth – doomed to failure. Linked to this nethermost being was the phantom of Mother – the gloomy religious [one] affecting asceticism and dominated by superstition.'

The second self was

essentially a realist in intellectual questions, a rationalist in metaphysics and therefore a sceptic of religion. This is the happiest and perhaps the highest expression of my Ego. But alas! This being has its life and origin in my sensual nature: it springs from vigorous senses and keen perception. If I were a man this creature would be free, though not dissolute in its morals; a lover of women. These feelings would be subordinate to the intellectual and practical interests, but still the strong physical nature upon which the intellectual is based, would be satisfied. And as I am a woman; these feelings – unless fulfilled in marriage (which would mean the destruction of the intellectual being) – must remain controlled and unsatisfied, finding their only vent in one quality of the phantom companion of the nethermost personality – religious exaltation.[20]

This passage points to many of the features of Beatrice's life which made it so difficult for her to be herself. Deeply influenced as she was by Herbert Spencer and his approach to sociology, she could never take any permanent comfort in his solution of the problem of how to reconcile science and religion, knowledge and purpose. When she published the first volume of her autobiography she took as her organising principle the conflict between an ego that affirmed and an ego that denied.[21] She described herself as one who was perpetually torn between affirming and denying the possibility of social science. Assuming that social science was possible, then she became divided once more about how the conclusions of such a science might be related to the affirmation of her moral and religious experience. For Beatrice was a religious person in a way that Sidney Webb was not. She believed in the efficacy of what she called 'prayer' and she derived solace from religious music and architecture. At the same time she was unable to accept theological dogmas. When in Rome she meditated a conversion to Catholicism, but she turned away from it as equivalent to 'intellectual suicide'.

By 1883 all Beatrice's elder sisters had highly successful marriages. Their husbands were squires, ship-owners, bankers, distinguished lawyers or surgeons and two of them, Courtney and Hobhouse, were Members of Parliament. In that year Beatrice met and fell in love with one of the most powerful politicians of the day, Joseph Chamberlain. As mayor of Birmingham, Chamberlain had been responsible for many measures of municipal ownership and control, of gas-and-water socialism. He was now in the Cabinet as its most 'advanced' leader, proclaiming far and wide the need to extend democracy and to force the rich to pay a 'ransom' to the poor.[22] In short, he had pioneered many of the policies which Sidney Webb and the Fabians were to expound in a more systematic and philosophic form. Unlike Sidney, he was immensely rich – having acquired a monopolist position in the Birmingham nut-and-bolt trade – and he had a commanding presence. Beatrice was fascinated by his arrogant assurance of power, even if she was uncertain as to whether he was making a sincerely felt and legitimate use of the power he was acquiring.

In a sense it was Herbert Spencer who stood between Beatrice and Chamberlain. Spencer thought of Beatrice almost as if she were his own daughter and he regarded her as the most promising of his disciples.[23] At almost exactly the moment of the meeting between Chamberlain and Beatrice, Spencer was writing a series of essays against the advance of socialism which he entitled *The Man versus the State*. He anticipated Webb in identifying every increase in state regulation, provision and ownership as an instalment of socialism – not excepting the opening, free of charge, of museums and libraries. The difference was, of course, that Spencer regarded this tendency as thoroughly pernicious, calculated to undermine the sense of individual independence and responsibility, to retard the progress of trade and industry and generally to stop the advance of civilisation which he had confidently predicted in all his works since the appearance of *Social Statics* in 1850. Near the beginning of their relationship, Chamberlain made occasion to remark that if she was a disciple of Mr Spencer's she could not be a follower of his nor an admirer of his style of politics.[24]

Beatrice, with her eyes set upon a great marriage to a handsome public figure, was ready to be modest about her own opinions and to show herself open to conviction. What she could not bring herself to do was to pretend to hold convictions which were not her own. Had Spencer's influence over her been confined to a debate about the merits of state intervention as against *laissez-faire* she might have emancipated herself from them easily enough, but it went far deeper than that. Spencer had taught her that women had as much intelligence as men and that they ought to use it. When their governess had given orders to the Potter girls to attend to their lessons, Spencer had been in the habit of shouting out, 'Submission not desirable!' and then of taking them all out to learn through play in the countryside. The governess had her revenge when she reminded Beatrice that if she went with Mr Spencer she should abide by his teachings and do exactly what she liked!

This libertarian education was a poor preparation for life with Joseph Chamberlain, who expected women to comfort, encourage and obey their husbands. Beatrice made every concession that she could. She discovered and publicly announced that women ought not to have political equality with men and that they were not suited by their natures or their upbringing for the strenuous and often demoralising rough-and-tumble of politics. She subjected Spencer's arguments to renewed critical examination and began to make shrewd and telling objections to aspects of his methods and conclusions.[25] She went into the East End of London and to a northern factory town to observe at first hand the conditions of life of the working class, the better to join effectively in the debate about the causes and extent of poverty.

In so far as she was prompted to do these things in the hope that they might lead her to an eventual marriage with Chamberlain, Beatrice was to be disappointed. Doubtless he sensed that she was too powerful and demanding a spirit to make the kind of wife he was looking for. He seemed to her to be playing with her affections: first encouraging her hopes, then dashing them to the ground. He was the dominant figure in her emotional life throughout the 1880s. Twice she took the unbecoming step of telling him that she loved him, and on each occasion it left her only with a deeper sense of humiliation. She also discovered that keeping pace with Mr Chamberlain's changing social and political opinions and allegiances was a difficult matter. In 1886 he broke with Gladstone on the question of home rule for Ireland and joined forces with the Tories. Overnight the interests of the poor and the homeless were replaced by a concern to maintain the United Kingdom and the advancement of the Empire. He who had been seen as a kind of Robespierre at once became the hero of high society. Beatrice was bored by high society and in her journal she never once attempted to discuss the Irish question.

Between 1883 and 1890 Beatrice served her apprenticeship as a social investigator. She began by working as a visitor for the Charity Organisation Society – a body which sought, by careful casework, to distinguish the 'deserving' from the 'undeserving' poor and thus to stop an indiscriminate philanthropy from demoralising both categories.[26] She then became a rent collector in a working-class tenement near the London docks. Finally, she began to work with her cousin Charles Booth on an exhaustive inquiry into the extent and nature of poverty in London. From 1887 onwards she began to publish a series of essays on the dock workers, the tailoring trade and the Jewish community of East London, which gradually came to establish her as an authority on the social question. She attracted particular attention by her pioneering use of the technique of participant observation. In other words, she became a Jewish emigrant tailoress in a London sweat shop and a farmer's daughter visiting distant working-class relatives in the mill town of Bacup. In 1888 she was sufficiently well known to be called to give evidence before the House of Lords committee on the sweating system.

When she looked back upon these seven years Beatrice saw in them a succession of experiences and understanding taking her inevitably towards Fabian socialism. First, her studies of East End life had persuaded her of the need for an all-pervading control, in the interests of the community, of the economic activities of the landlord and the capitalist. She then came to recognise that no amount of control could avert cyclical crises or ensure for every citizen a national minimum standard of life below which none should be allowed to fall. She then – so she said – began to reflect upon the morally corrupting effects of a society divided between the rich and the powerful on the one hand and the poor and the weak on the other. She had rejected Marx because he seemed to ignore the necessary activities of the profit-making employer and she could see no alternative to capitalist authority. In the last stage of her apprenticeship, however, she began to study the co-operative movement. In this movement with its production for use and its elimination of the profit-taker she began to perceive a possible alternative to existing business enterprise.[27]

This is tidy and intelligible, but also misleading and inaccurate. She was slow to recognise the need to curtail competition and still slower to suggest that it was something that had to be done by promoting public ownership and not just hoping for the advent of big business. In her evidence given in 1888 to the Lords committee on the sweating system she suggested that most of the Jewish workers in the sweated tailoring trades did not seem to find life too objectionable. She also expressed the gravest doubts about whether anything could be done about conditions in the East End of London and considered that trying to impose restrictions on landlords and capitalists might lead to more evil than it removed.[28] In her determination to appear as a *professional* social investigator she studiously avoided anything that might suggest 'feminine sentimentality'. She also gave a most misleading impression of the amount of time she had spent as a work-girl in a sweat shop. It had been much less than she had suggested. In private she acknowledged that she could not have endured the sheer physical strain of more than a single day's labour in such a place. Had she made this admission in public it would have told against much of her testimony and the complacency which it encouraged.

There was a certain 'hardness' about Beatrice. Sidney detected it in her writings even before he met her. It was also matched by ruthlessness. She boasted that when she worked for the Charity Organisation Society she helped to hasten the death of a drug addict whose presence she considered to be a burden to his wife and children.[29] She was ashamed of her own more compassionate acts and suspected that she was being weak and immoral when she helped one of her tenants who had been injured at work. In retrospect, Beatrice thought that the development of a middle-class sense of guilt had been one of the leading characteristics of the 1880s. If so, she herself gave little evidence of it. On the contrary, she exhibited a sang-froid attitude. She told herself that she felt envy, rather than pity, for the half-starved casual labourers and their families. Out of work more often than in it, she came to see them as the 'leisured class' at the foot of society. They were economically unfit to live, but they had positive qualities. She acknowledged their warm-heartedness and the generosity of their 'practical communism', their readiness to share what little they had.

Such pity as she had she reserved for the working-class elite, for those few of brains and character who were struggling to lift themselves and their class out of the morass. How could they succeed? She did come to see that unregulated competition was at the root of the evil, but in 1889 she was still very doubtful about whether that competition could be regulated either by trade unionism or by legislation. Since 1886 she had begun to doubt the scientific character of that political economy which made hard-heartedness the leading virtue of the rich. But she had little to put in its place, and she remained persuaded that if anything was done for the unemployed, the low paid, the sick or the homeless, it would have to be accompanied by draconian measures against the idle, the thriftless, the scroungers and the roughs. If the latter were not effectively dealt with in the workhouse or the labour camp, then those who were prepared to work would be demoralised and become idlers themselves. Beatrice was convinced that, if socialism ever became possible, the discipline and rigours of the workhouse would have to be many times more terrible than they were already.[30] Even in 1889 Beatrice was so far from being a socialist that she could contemplate collaborating on a novel with the aristocratic anarchist Auberon Herbert, which would have had an individualist moral.

If the first step in Beatrice's conversion to socialism had been so imperfectly accomplished before she met Sidney, so had the others. She was not impressed by the need for public ownership to avert cyclical crises. She rightly saw the problem of the East End of London as one of a chronic over-supply of labour. She was, indeed, becoming critical of capitalist acquisitiveness as well as of aristocratic idleness. She observed that her father – loving and considerate in family relations – was harsh and ruthless in business. She began to complain that some of her sisters were not sufficiently exercised by the problems of the poor. But she took much in class society for granted. She knew that she belonged to the class that gave orders rather than received them. Although she developed a certain camaraderie with some working-class leaders, she never forgot her own social position and she took a great pride in her family. She showed a particularly haughty and contemptuous attitude towards the lower middle class and she was never surprised when she found members of it lacking in self-control or in true refinement of manners. Finally, although she began in 1889 to make a serious study of the co-operative movement she certainly did not discern in it an alternative to capitalist *production*. What she tried to demonstrate was that it provided an alternative to capitalist *distribution*. She was convinced that co-operation succeeded in serving the working-class *consumer*, but that it deluded itself in supposing that it had anything to offer the working-class *producer*. All her life she remained persuaded that worker control was a utopian fantasy and that modern industry required to be directed by authority from above: if not the authority of the capitalist then the authority of the managerial expert.

Beatrice failed to do justice to two teachers from whom she

learned much between the summer of 1889 and the winter of 1890. The first was the organised British working class. She was developing a growing respect for its capacity for self-government as a result of her investigation of the co-operative movement. She was deeply impressed by many of its leaders, who successfully managed millions of pounds of capital while limiting their own salaries to £3 per week.[31] There then occurred a marvellous awakening in the East End of London. The dockers whom she had sadly written off as incorrigible sensualists, incapable of self-discipline and virtually devoid of hope or ambition, organised themselves into a trade union and staged one of the most triumphant strikes in the history of British labour.[32] The achievement was not diminished by the fact that they were led by Tom Mann and John Burns, who were skilled engineers by trade, and by Will Thorne, who had been taught to read and write by one of Beatrice's acquaintances, Eleanor Marx. This was a high point in the rise of the 'new unionism' which demonstrated that organisation was not necessarily the monopoly of the labour aristocracy.[33] Beatrice was enormously encouraged by the way in which East End people showed a capacity for an orderly and well-disciplined strike as opposed to the kind of riot which had hitherto been the limit of their collective action.

In January of 1890 a mutual friend introduced her to Sidney Webb.[34] With his vast knowledge of existing legislation and his fertility in projecting extensions of it, he quickly persuaded her that the unrestrained competition which led to sweating in the East End could be subdued. It was not until she met him that she was able to declare, 'At last I am a socialist', and Fabian socialism was the only sort of socialism which she could have avowed. To be a Fabian did not involve unmeasured denunciations of civilisation and putting oneself outside decent society. It did not make one a revolutionary. It was not a scandal and disgrace, even if it was daring and bold. It was practicable, peaceable and well documented. It was middle class, even if only lower middle class.

Moreover, the 'prevailing Fabian' was entirely in love with her and prepared to make all kinds of sacrifices for her sake. She was merciless in her dealings with him. He had to stop wearing grubby shirts, stop dropping his *h*'s, stop talking about what he would do when he was Prime Minister. He had also to stop writing to her in terms which suggested anything remotely of lust! Later on –

during their engagement – she was willing enough to allow what she described as 'intervals for human nature', but from the beginning to the end she insisted that any permanent relationship had to be based upon her terms. She advised him that in a marriage the man should take the important decisions and the woman the unimportant decisions, but she added that she would determine which were which!

Miss Potter's reasons for marrying Mr Webb were characteristically complicated. She made no secret of the fact that she was on the look-out for a research associate. Their marriage, she made clear, must be childless. They would produce books instead of children and, in the first instance, serious studies of the labour movement. Second, Beatrice, with candour unusual in late-Victorian middle-class women, acknowledged that chastity was as irksome to one sex as it was to the other. She could never feel the passion for Sidney which she had felt for Joseph Chamberlain, but other women had found Sidney attractive. For Beatrice he had a special attraction which she was apt to misdescribe as his disinterestedness.

To quite a peculiar degree he cultivated self-deadness. He too had suffered the pains of unrequited love and had forgotten them by learning to live vicariously in committees. Like his hero, J. S. Mill, he abandoned the vain pursuit of happiness and discovered it *en passant* in working for the happiness of others.[35] He spoke of marriage as 'the ultimate committee'. If she would allow him the happiness of being her husband he would renounce all claims to personal life. He would never be sick or depressed or moody or at all egotistical. It was a promise which he kept, so that when he was seventy he could say that he could never write his autobiography since he had 'no inside'.[36]

To marry one's research associate in the hope that together it would be possible to move the world was an intelligible, if unromantic, motive. Their enemies made mocking references to the Webbs as 'two type-writers beating as one'. Yet Beatrice had enough self-understanding to acknowledge that it was partly the assurance of such mockery which persuaded her to marry Sidney. A strange mixture of masochism and exhibitionism went into her consent. Having failed to make a 'great marriage' with Chamberlain, she would astonish the world by accepting this plebeian little man. Having brought 'humiliation' upon herself once, she would make her penance. In the murky region inhabited by these strange considerations the Webb partnership was born; it was a brilliant success. And it was a success not only by the standards of what D. H. Lawrence called the 'bitch goddess'; it brought to them both happiness and achievement on a scale unequalled in English history.

POLITICAL AND INTELLECTUAL PROJECTS, *1890–1914*

Up until the years preceding the First World War the Webb achievement might be described as 'cultural' rather than political.[37] At any rate, the young Beatrice would have been pleased and flattered to think that such a description was accurate. She made it plain to Sidney that, while she would allow him to interest himself in the government of London, she was not prepared to be the wife of a Member of Parliament. He might, she conceded, usefully employ his mornings as a member of the London County Council, which he did. He was not to have parliamentary ambitions. Such ambitions would draw him away from the research work necessary if they were to write the books that mattered. And those books were not to be about economic theory but about social institutions: trade unions and co-operative societies rather than the theory of rent.

Beatrice gave Sidney to understand that politics was a very suspect area; the topography of politics was distinguished by great mountain ranges identified as 'vulgarity', 'fickleness' and 'deceit'. It was, she insisted, better to persuade than to coerce – better to discover and win conviction than to trick or bully the bourgeoisie into submission. Moreover, Beatrice had all the right connections with the established controllers. She suggested prospects of an influence which would be wider and more efficacious than the crude devices that might be available to those who sought power. In short, she encouraged Fabianism into the occupation of certain retreats on the pretence that they were redoubts. Admittedly this was not the sort of confusion against which Fabians might be expected to mount a considerable resistance. It was half-way to these capitulations before her arrival set the seal upon them.

Yet 'capitulation' is an odd word to employ about the Webbs. They may have been opportunists taking no clear and consistent side in the class struggle, but they were heroic opportunists who worked tirelessly for what they understood to be socialism and for the development of a new learning and new culture which would be appropriate to it. Moreover, they got results – even if these were not always quite what they had intended.

They never claimed themselves to be advancing towards a 'third culture'.[38] They themselves recognised that they lacked the round-ness of mind and the order of sensibility required. Sidney happily conceded that he was fully occupied in what he termed 'the kitchen of life'.[39] Beatrice was always inclined to think in terms of their specialisms and to dismiss many important problems as 'not our subject'. Their philistinism about the arts, other than literature, soon became legendary.[40] Yet, in retrospect, the Webbs can be seen as pressing beyond the limitations of the two cultures which held sway in Victorian England. They clearly rejected the tradition of classical, literary and aristocratic culture which still largely ruled in Oxford and Cambridge. The lowest, but not the least important, function of a classical education was that it was seen to be useless and therefore was the distinguishing mark of a gentleman. Sidney made himself master of this tradition in his spare time and proceeded to present a fresh view of the inheritance of Rome:

> In every age of Roman history the individual is ruthlessly sacrificed to the mass, and the whole generation to the Commonwealth. . . . Even Roman excesses are often ennobled by their unselfish end and the cruelties of Emperors are forgotten in the patriotic splendour of their careers. This supreme devotion has been a beacon light to all successive ages and is beyond all question our most important heritage from Rome.[41]

Webb's remarkable conclusion that 'the desire to lead an indi-vidual life is the survival of the brute in man' distanced him even further from the second great English cultural tradition, which might be described as provincial bourgeois culture. This tradition was nourished in the Scottish universities, but in England it flourished in the philosophical and literary societies of great indus-trial towns such as Manchester and Birmingham. It emphasised scientific, practical and useful knowledge, including, of course, political economy. It valued dissent and open competition against the claims of the established church with its tests and the landed oligarchy with its restraints upon free trade in land.[42]

Webb's own career was, at first sight, a model of that industrious self-advancement which was so highly praised by this cultural tradition. But the condition of Sidney's progress had not been the accumulation of diplomas taken in the course of professional training. When Webb recommended the words of Goethe, 'Renounce, renounce, renounce!', he was expressing in an extreme form the ethic of the professional man as against the businessman. He was seeking to magnify an ideal of professionalism in which the ruling motive was service rather than profit and where advancement depended upon measured knowledge and ability, not upon greed or luck. Professionalism implies some measure of collective control of the conditions of entry into an occupation which will be exercised through objective tests of fitness. It implies collective regulation and, for Webb at least, it pointed to the end of individualism: to a world in which men would never aspire to act alone.

Thus, the third culture saw the service of man as something which would not be attained by a reliance on *noblesse oblige*, nor as the incidental outcome of everyone being allowed to pursue their own selfish interests in an open market. 'Man ought to be cultivated like a favourite fruit-tree.' The minimum standard of civilised existence would not be established by aristocratic paternalism, nor would it come about of its own accord thanks to the free operation of market forces. Rather, it had to be made the object of policy, and policy had to be shaped by experts who were professionally trained for their work.

The Webbs and other enlightened late Victorians accordingly argued that the provision of social services such as old-age pensions, working-class housing schemes and improved free educational facilities ought not to be thought of as costs to productive industry.[43] There ought to be an advance towards planned production for community consumption. Workers had to be persuaded to make this ideal their own. Business men must be brought to see that increased social provision was the condition of national efficiency. In the end both classes must be taught to renounce politics and economics in favour of public administration – but the administrators themselves must study the people with whom they had to deal so that they might mobilise that consciousness of consent to the plans of the professional expert. In modern societies the expert had to face the fact that he could not impose his programme upon an ignorant or hostile population.

Between 1892 and 1914 the Webbs went to work to establish the intellectual and institutional conditions for the eventual ascendancy of this new culture. They began by studying the organised working class, since its history was virtually *terra incognita* to the established cultural traditions. The new culture required a profound understanding of the working people and needed to take the measure of their receptivity, creativity and political capacity. The Webbs accomplished this task in their books on the co-operative and trade-union movements, all of which appeared before the end of the nineteenth century. These works established labour historiography as a new branch of learning in England, while their translation into foreign languages ensured that the Webbs acquired an international reputation as scholars of the first order. Both Edward Bernstein and V. I. Lenin attached the highest importance to their great book *Industrial Democracy* (1897). This work took to a conclusion ten years of reflection on labour history, trade-union practice and the possible future of the working class. Bernstein valued it particularly for its emphasis upon the trade union as the primary and essential organisation of the class and because of its insistence that the trade union was not an institution which could be expected to die with capitalism. The Webbs held that the worker as producer would still need to have his interests protected from managers and consumers under socialism.

Lenin, who translated this book while in exile in Siberia, made a close and critical use of it when he was writing his own highly important monograph *What Is to Be Done?* (1902). The Webbs gave him ammunition in his fight against 'primitivism' in organisational questions, since they demonstrated that ultra-democracy had been tried and had failed in the British labour movement. They also lent support – albeit in a strange way – to Lenin's conviction that the working class would not spontaneously find its way to socialism. Without the help of a contingent from a radicalised or revolutionary intelligentsia, trade-union consciousness would never become socialist consciousness. Moreover, the Webbs argued the case for a new, professionalised labour leader who would be more than a delegate, without having the autonomy of a representative. They urged the need for a labour leader who would shape the opinions of his constituents while abiding by them in the last resort. Between the Webbs' professional labour leader and Lenin's professional revolutionary there lay a world of difference, but there was also a notable area of common ground.[44]

At the same time as the Webbs were making an independent contribution to learning of a high order, they were concerning themselves with the possibility of a new organisation of learning. In 1893 Sidney had been elected the first chairman of the London Technical Education Board. With consummate political skill he used this toe-hold to greatly extend educational opportunity to the children of Londoners, to establish a new centre of learning in the social sciences, to use that, in turn, as a way into the complete reorganisation of London University, and to make all these measures tell in favour of his plans for the extension of secondary education throughout Great Britain.

As chairman of the Technical Education Board, Sidney Webb commanded a considerable amount of money, which he constantly augmented. He put it to use in supplying scholarships to increasing numbers of lower-middle- and upper-working-class children, to enable them to continue their schooling beyond the age of twelve or thirteen. He then used some of the money to support the London School of Economics and Political Science, an institution which he had founded in 1894.

In that year an eccentric but wealthy Fabian had taken his own life and left £10,000 for the purpose of promoting Fabian socialism. The Webbs decided not to use this money for ordinary propaganda work, but to create an institution for teaching and research in the social sciences. With an astonishing, if characteristic, sleight of hand Sidney managed to persuade the Fabians that a realistic social science was bound to make socialists, while he simultaneously convinced his non-socialist colleagues on the Technical Education Board and in the world of business that the new institution had nothing to do with socialism and was no more 'political' than the Massachusetts Institute of Technology or L'École des Sciences Politiques in Paris! Even Bernard Shaw was shocked by such audacity. However, the Webbs saw to it that Shaw's wealthy wife became one of the principal benefactors of their new school.

The prophets of provincial bourgeois culture had, more than half a century earlier, established University College in Gower Street, London, as a centre for the dissemination of their own opposition to the prevailing classical and aristocratic culture. Webb speedily outdistanced them in the teaching of social science, so that the old 'infidel' institution in Gower Street was quite overtaken by the new 'socialistic' one near by in Clare Market. The difference lay in the fact that, whereas the philosophical radicals commanded the resources to promote their kind of learning, Webb was obliged to exploit the credulity of all and sundry.

However, the LSE was established during a decade in which economists and other social scientists strongly felt the need to protect their disciplines through a secure professionalism. It flourished and achieved an international repute within a remarkably short space of time. This allowed Webb to use it as yet another base from which to extend his lines, and he rapidly emerged as one of the most influential figures in the reshaping of London University which transformed it into a teaching, as distinct from a merely examining, institution. In this matter of the reorganisation of London University, Sidney once more displayed – or rather concealed – his consummate political artistry. He wanted to establish a centre of new learning suited to what he took to be the needs of the lower middle and the upper working class, which would contribute the trained personnel for the socialist society of the future. However, he concealed his idea of a university behind a logic of administration which appeared to be disinterested to the point of perfect ideological neutrality.[45]

Having made himself into a celebrated educationalist, it was only to be expected that he would play some part in the reorganisation of secondary education, which had long been pressing itself upon the agenda of government. At the heart of the problem of extending the educational experience of more academically inclined children lay the competition between the popularly elected school boards, financed with public money, and the voluntary church schools, which tended to be much inferior in scholastic achievement. Instead of taking the popular Liberal and Labour view, which looked to the extinction of church schools, Sidney collaborated with the Tory leaders in planning to endow them with public money so that they could be brought up to the required standard of efficiency. Sidney took care that public money for the church schools should be matched by public control over their teachers and curriculum. But this did not prevent him from being regarded as a renegade and an unprincipled opportunist by both nonconformists and socialists.

By 1902–3 the Webbs had much to show for themselves in terms of practical achievement, but they had largely forfeited the confidence of 'the left'.[46] At almost every point they appeared to have been fobbed off with illusions rather than realities. Thus, if they had extended educational opportunity for the children of London, they had done so at the expense of the ideal of secondary education for all. By providing a ladder for the 'bright' girl or boy they had made the claims of all the children of the less well off seem less urgent. Similarly, to maintain their School of Economics as a respectable academic institution worthy of university status they had had to bend over backwards in the matter of key appointments. Not one of the academic directors was a socialist. On the contrary, all the early directors were imperialists who looked to the state for an expansion of Empire before they considered it as a possible provider of social services. One of these directors, Sir Sydney Caine, has asserted that the London School of Economics on balance did more to promote the interests of anti-socialists or non-socialists than anything else. It is a debatable assertion, but he may well have been right.

For all their undeniable achievements and for all their remarkable cleverness – not to say deviousness – there remains in the end a suspicion that the Webbs outsmarted everybody including themselves. They certainly cut themselves off from Labour and the left. The Liberal Party appeared to them to be bent on self-destruction. Accordingly, the Webbs concentrated their energies upon winning over its imperialist wing and, as had been shown, did not hesitate to work with the Tories when this seemed expedient. The imperialists necessarily wanted to enlarge the powers of the state, and the Webbs naïvely imagined that this would make them as ready to assert state power at home as it made them ready to assert it abroad. Sidney and Beatrice became imperialists, partly because they were sincerely persuaded that English civilisation was superior to any other, more significantly because they thought that those who wanted an Empire upon which the sun would never set would also want to do away with the streets upon which the sun never rose.

They deluded themselves into supposing that those who believed in Britain's imperial destiny would be persuaded that this required the establishment of that minimum standard of life without which there could be no imperial race. It was considerations of this kind which led to the formation of one of the most bizarre dining clubs in modern British history: the Co-efficients.[47] Here Sidney tried to cement an alliance between imperialism and social reform, consorting with a future Foreign Secretary (Grey) and a future Secretary of State for War (Haldane). Imperialism was further reinforced by the presence of present and future directors of the London School of Economics. Bertrand Russell and H. G. Wells represented philosophy and popular education, but neither of them had any clear idea of what Sidney was up to.

It all ended badly for the Webbs. The political and social forces upon which they had come to rely were all but destroyed by a great Liberal victory in the general election of 1906. The 'little Englanders', whom they had dismissed as behind the times, seemed to be back in the saddle. The nonconformists who had been outraged by the Education Act, which the Webbs had helped to shape, seemed to be restored to their old power. The Labour Party, which they had tended to ignore, had made great gains. Ironically, this last great Liberal government in British history was destined – thanks to the efforts of Winston Churchill and Lloyd George – to lay the foundations of the Welfare State.[48] It embarked on a great programme of social reform, which owed much to the Webbs by way of general inspiration and through an altered climate of opinion, but which resolutely refused to accept them for its friends and advisers. Cabinet ministers like John Burns and Winston Churchill took a peculiar pleasure in *not* following any advice which came from 41 Grosvenor Road – the London home of the Webbs and the celebrated salon where Beatrice tried to bewitch the great and the powerful with her wit, learning and charm.

Beatrice had, however, established one strong vantage-point for herself. She had been made a member of the Royal Commission charged with inquiring into the working of the Poor Law. The Poor Law of 1834 was one of the most clear-cut consequences of the victory won by the industrial and commercial bourgeoisie thanks to the Reform Act of 1832. It perfectly expressed their ideal of rationality, efficiency and economy. All who were unable to support themselves – the old and infirm, the unemployed and the destitute – were cared for under the conditions of 'less eligibility'. In other words, they were sent to the workhouse, where they subsisted on a standard of life below that enjoyed by the least-well-off person in gainful employment. Husbands were separated from wives and parents were separated from their children within a regime universally feared and hated by the working people. The Webbs set out to demolish this system, which had been designed and inspired by their predecessors, the Philosophical Radicals. Instead of dealing with the problem of the poor, they proposed to eliminate poverty. Instead of an indiscriminate mixing of all classes of the destitute, they proposed methods of ameliorating the sufferings of all the distinct sections of the poor. Instead of accepting and enforcing a minimum standard of life determined by capitalist market forces, they proposed to enforce a minimum standard of national life by reference to considerations of humanity, scientifically ascertained needs and the requirements of national efficiency.

If they secured victory in this great enterprise that victory was moral rather than immediate. The proposals of the minority report of the commission, drafted by the Webbs, may have been a landmark in English social thought, but for the time being their recommendations were dismissed or ignored. On many grounds the Webbs were entitled to count Winston Churchill as one of their pupils, but when it came to the crunch Churchill preferred the principle of national insurance against unemployment to the prescriptions suggested to him by Sidney and Beatrice.[49] The Webbs rejected the principle of insurance against unemployment because it took no account of the capacity to pay – it involved a regressive poll tax – or of the character of the unemployed. It was a position which pointed up their character as equalitarians and their inadequacy as libertarians. As Beatrice remarked: 'The *unconditionality* of all payments under insurance schemes constitutes a grave defect. The state gets nothing for its money in the way of conduct and it may even encourage malingerers.'[50]

The failure of the Webbs to get the minority report adopted by government, and the Poor Law abolished at a stroke, drove them away from the politics of permeation and backstage intrigue to a return to the almost forgotten method of mass pressure from without. To this end they attempted to organise a vast popular campaign for the prevention of destitution, and it was in the context of this campaign that they founded the *New Statesman*.

It was during the years just preceding the outbreak of the First World War that Beatrice joined the Independent Labour Party. The Webbs were beginning to effect a *rapprochement* with the labour movement. Thus it was that when the war came Sidney was well placed to move into a decisive position in the Labour leadership which allowed all his old compromises with Liberal and Tory to be almost forgotten.

THE WAR

The Webbs sided with the great majority in the British labour movement in supporting the war effort. Beatrice was sickened by it, but could see no alternative to going through with it. After all, neither foreign policy nor war were among the Webbs' 'specialities'. Until 1917 she was reduced to ineffectual, anguished questioning about the 'metaphysic of violence': a concept which allowed her to relate the militant syndicalism of the pre-war years to the phenomenon of Prussian militarism. Sidney did not waste his time with such high speculation, but advised her that they must not be paralysed by the horror. Their duty, he said, was to copy the French peasants and carry on with their work even if it was directly behind the firing line.[51]

This meant in practice using the war as an opportunity for advancing the claims of Fabian socialism. On the very day upon which war broke out, there was established a War Emergency Workers' National Committee, of which Sidney became a leading member.[52] The committee had originally been convened to concert action against war, but in a characteristically British way it accepted the war as a *fait accompli*. It directed its attention to the defence of working-class interests during the hostility and here again it demonstrated a peculiarly British characteristic. The most violent chauvinists, the more level-headed patriots, pacifists and ostriches who had decided to ignore the war, active opponents of the bloodshed who longed for a peace by negotiation, as well as a small minority who came close to the position of 'revolutionary defeatism': all managed to submerge their differences in the interests of labour unity. It was superb or absurd according to one's point of view. But it marked a definite stage forward in the concept of the unity of the labour movement as Sidney and Beatrice had conceived of it twenty years or so earlier. As with so many other concepts, the Webbs had succeeded in impressing upon all observers their own notion of the labour movement as a tripartite institutional affair in which trade unionism, co-operation and a Labour Party all sustained and complemented each other. In these terms the War Emergency Committee, as Beatrice noticed, was the highest expression of labour unity to date.

Not only was the War Emergency Committee a great advance organisationally; it also came to be associated with great strides forward programmatically and ideologically. Sidney was continually pressing for new measures of social provision, control and ownership. By 1915 he formulated a demand for the 'conscription of riches', and the committee mounted a very effective campaign around it. Sidney argued that government control must be extended and systematised so that all the main branches of the economy became subject to central direction. As capitalist management was deprived of its function, so it ought also to be deprived of its profits. Profiteering in wartime was a scandal which must be put down. It was hard for old-fashioned Liberals to resist this campaign, for Mr Asquith's Cabinet was being forced by the requirements of the war effort to leave less and less to be determined by market forces. Asquith was most reluctant to be drawn further along the road to which Webb and his friends were pointing, but that reluctance contributed to his own eventual undoing. At the end of 1916 Lloyd George replaced him as prime minister and took the Labour leader, Arthur Henderson, into his War Cabinet. Henceforth, the advance towards collectivism was greatly accelerated.

It would be hard to overestimate the impact of war upon the British labour movement.[53] 'The conscription of riches' was seen to be a thoroughly practical demand, whereas a few months earlier it would have been dismissed as rooted in nothing but dreams or nightmares. The experience of the War Emergency Workers' National Committee gave to organised labour a satisfactory sense that its proposals were influential and 'correct' in that governments were forced to adopt more and more of them as time went on. For the first time, 'socialism' in England had become real politics. Trade unionists, fearful of plans to introduce industrial or military conscription, saw that the socialist slogan of 'the conscription of riches' was an effective bargaining counter. Patriots increasingly came to see that 'socialism' was the condition of national efficiency and survival. To those preoccupied with moral issues and anxious for equality of sacrifice, the conscription of riches had an equally compelling appeal. Finally, to those socialists who opposed the war and who did not put themselves at the standpoint of the interests of the state, the slogan was also entirely acceptable. They imagined that it could never be conceded by the ruling class and that this would lead to growing disillusionment with the war and give rise to a demand for a negotiated peace.

At the end of 1915 Sidney became the representative of the Fabian Society on the National Executive Committee of the Labour Party. A year later the Liberals were hopelessly divided in consequence of the conflict between Asquith and Lloyd George. Webb saw that there was now an opportunity for Labour to replace the Liberals after the war and to make that party the principal carrier of the claims of Fabian socialism. As usual, he declined to act alone and began to build up a close working relationship with Arthur Henderson. Henderson was sent to Russia in the summer of 1917 and he came back convinced that the British government would have to clarify its war aims and allow the possibility of peace by negotiation if the eastern front was to be maintained. He wanted the government to allow representatives of British labour to participate in a conference of socialists from all countries, neutral and belligerent, which was to be held in Stockholm. Lloyd George and his colleagues in the War Cabinet refused to countenance this idea. They humiliated Henderson and forced his resignation.[54] This left him free to devote all his time to collaborating with Sidney and building a Labour Party with which he might hope to secure his political revenge after the war.

Webb worked with his usual furious energy. The first task was to draft a statement of war aims acceptable to the Labour Party and the socialists of Allied countries, and perhaps eventually fit to be taken as the basis of a negotiated peace. Sidney brought essentially the same skill and purpose into preparing Labour's foreign policy as he had shown in shaping its 'conscription of riches' campaign. He wanted to maintain Labour's independence from the government without leading it into opposition to the interests of the state. Indeed, in trying to steal the initiative from the former institution he fancied that he was serving the interests of the latter. He anticipated President Wilson's 'fourteen points', but in adopting what looked like a principled line against annexations and indemnities he took care to maintain the interests of British imperialism. The right to national self-determination was confined to Europe. There was no suggestion that it should be applied to British possessions in Asia or Africa. Given the reality of war-weariness and the radicalising effect of the February Revolution in Russia, the best way of maintaining British labour's support for the war was to assert a measure of independence in criticising the ends and means used by the government in conducting it. This was also the best way of preparing for the advent of a new and much more powerful Labour Party after the war.

The Bolshevik Revolution exposed the sharp contrast between appearance and reality. To H. G. Wells, Lenin appeared as 'just a Russian Sidney Webb; a rotten little incessant egotistical intriguer. He and the Kaiser ought to be killed by some moral sanitary authority.'[55] It adds to the absurdity of this comparison that Sidney and Beatrice were in favour of putting Lenin down by fire and sword. Webb belonged to the minority on the Labour Party's National Executive which favoured armed intervention against the Bolsheviks. They saw in Bolshevism a strange mix of anarchism and elitism. They distrusted Lenin because they thought he was no democrat and they alleged that he thought it more important to be one of the elect than to be one of the elected! While his intentions were thought to be authoritarian, the result of his presence was anarchy and chaos. He meant the end of the eastern front and the possibility that there would be a German victory and an imperialist peace at the expense of Russia. They expected that that would be a severe set-back for the British Empire and for Fabian socialism. (As we have seen, they were accustomed to the suggestion that the interests of the two were fully compatible.)

The second task of the newly established partnership of Webb–Henderson was to reconstruct the policy and structure of the Labour Party so as to make it fit for office in the post-war world. Sidney saw the problems of structure and policy as being closely interconnected. Until he devised a new constitution for it in 1918, the Labour Party had been a federal organisation with an 'indirect' membership. One joined it by way of membership of an affiliated trade union or socialist society. It was Webb who was primarily responsible for the establishment of constituency Labour Parties which recruited members directly. The effect of this change was to widen the door through which members of the middle class might enter the party. It was also calculated to diminish the importance of the Independent Labour Party, which had hitherto been the most customary body for socialists to join. The power of the ILP was further diminished by increasing the strength of the trade unions by allowing them increased representation upon the party's National Executive.[56] However, Webb offset this concession to labourism at the expense of socialism by writing the socialist objective into the fundamental rules of the party for the first time. In the celebrated words of clause (iv) of the new constitution the declared aim of the party became:

> To secure for the workers by hand or by brain the full fruits of their industry and the most equitable distribution thereof that may be possible, upon the basis of the common ownership of the means of production and distribution and the best obtainable system of popular administration and control of each industry or service.[57]

This was properly regarded as a decided shift leftwards. Yet its importance was limited by enlarging trade-union power and by the fact that it could be endorsed by different elements with widely different purposes in exactly the same way as the 'conscription of riches' slogan had made its appeal to widely different people and interests.

One of Sidney's objectives in drafting clause (iv) had been to take the wind out of the sails of the revolutionary left. Certainly British admirers of Bolshevism found in Webb one of their most skilful and determined opponents. When Lenin told British Communists that they must overcome the 'infantile disorder' of left-wing communism and join the Labour Party, Sidney successfully led the resistance to this manoeuvre.[58] When in 1922 Beatrice allowed Sidney to enter Parliament as the Labour MP for Seaham Harbour she told the women of that constituency that the Bolshevik Revolution would be regarded as the biggest disaster for the British labour movement since the French Revolution. This was a rather curious view of British labour history, since working-class consciousness had been heightened by the events in France, but it pointed to the profound hostility which the Webbs felt towards all things Bolshevik.

LABOUR IN POWER

Up until 1929 there was only one event which disturbed the intense dislike the Webbs felt for Russia, the Russian Revolution and the Russian temperament. (As Beatrice noticed, Sidney did not care for temperament at the best of times and he cared for what he took to be the Russian temperament least of all.) The one exception to this rule was a bizarre encounter at a summer school between the

Webbs and the Fabians, on the one hand, and two Bolshevik emissaries, Kamenev and Krassin, on the other. Beatrice formed a poor opinion of Kamenev, but Krassin made a speech which captured her imagination. He held out a vision of a new Russia:

> *Working to a plan*, elaborated by scientific experts, under the instructions of the Communist Party . . . In a splendid peroration, which excited the most enthusiastic applause from all those assembled Fabians who understood German, (Krassin used this language rather than Russian), he asserted that Soviet Russia alone among nations had discovered the 'philosopher's stone' of increased productivity in the consciousness, on the part of each individual communist, that he was serving the whole community of the Russian people – a consciousness which would transform toil into the only true religion – the service of mankind.[59]

Until 1929 this – it must be insisted – was the one occasion upon which the Webbs showed any sympathetic interest in Soviet society. They gave to their own socialism a sharper expression and a more systematic form than it had had before the war; yet there was an almost ostentatious neglect of Russian experience. Thus, in their projected *Constitution for the Socialist Commonwealth of Great Britain* (1920) the Webbs made only a passing and dismissive reference to the Russian attempt to make a socialist constitution, not merely in theory but in practice.[60] In the *Decay of Capitalist Civilisation* (1923) they showed little inclination to point to an alternative civilisation in Russia. On the contrary, they suggested that there was a profound identity between the destruction of the rights of pre-industrial craftsmen and agriculturalists by the bourgeoisie in England between 1750 and 1850 and what the Bolsheviks had been doing since 1918. The difference was that the Russians had no capacity for democratic institutions. The Webbs proclaimed that the dogmas of Russian communism were little more than the other side of the dogmas of capitalism; both were irrelevant to a sane reconstruction of the industrial order.[61] Unfortunately, the experience of the first two Labour governments in Britain suggested that democratic socialism was scarcely more relevant.[62]

Sidney was a Cabinet minister in both the first and the second Labour governments. But what ought to have been the glorious climax to a brilliant career began as a disappointment and culminated in a disaster. In 1924, at the age of sixty-five, he served as President of the Board of Trade. He had Ramsay Macdonald as the Prime Minister. Macdonald was a long-established acquaintance of the Webbs. They regarded him as a quite unfit person to hold a junior lectureship in the London School of Economics, but thought that he made a 'magnificent substitute for a leader' so far as the Labour Party was concerned! Sidney was a wholly loyal and uncritical supporter of Macdonald, who at once set out, not to build socialism, but to establish that Labour was 'fit to govern'. This meant observing every constitutional convention and propriety and giving no offence to the monarchy, the House of Lords, the established heads of departments of state or the leaders of organised business. Predictably, the government fell because it was charged – falsely – with being soft on communism. The Tories supported this charge with the aid of a forged letter which was attributed to Zinoviev, one of the leaders of the Communist International.

The second Labour government, which took office in 1929, was even more calamitous than the first. This time Sidney took office as Colonial Secretary. He reminded his civil servants that he himself had begun life as a clerk in that very department. They ought not to fear the advent of Labour rule. He knew from experience who made the decisions, adding, with a smile, 'Carry on!' This summed up much of the essential spirit of the second Labour government. It had no intention of challenging the established controllers and it secretly rejoiced that it had no majority of its own in the House of Commons.

The great advantage of minority government is that it can explain away its weaknesses – which stem from flaws in its understanding and its character – as the results of the precarious nature of its parliamentary situation. Beatrice looked down upon the government with an expression of sadness mingled with contempt. It was a pity that 'the Other One' (meaning Sidney) was mixed up in it. As the great crisis advanced throughout world capitalism, she recognised that the Labour leaders were nothing but 'flies on the wheel of world welter'.

When the New York bankers made further loans to the government conditional upon a balanced budget and savage reductions in the 'dole' paid to the unemployed, Henderson and the leaders of the TUC finally decided that it was unacceptable and that they could no longer support the government on such terms. Sidney had buried himself so deeply beneath the responsibilities of his own department that he could no longer recognise reality. He described the trade-union leaders as 'pigheaded' for not agreeing to the imposition of further sacrifices upon their own people.[63] However, when Macdonald agreed to form a coalition with the Tory and Liberal leaders in the alleged interests of maintaining business confidence and the stability of the system, Webb decided to go with the majority of his Cabinet colleagues in denouncing their former leader as a traitor and a renegade.

Once the Labour Party had been split, Macdonald instantly adopted the policy of taking Britain off the gold standard. Sidney was flabbergasted by this audacity. He had been given to understand that cuts at the expense of the unemployed and public employees were the only way to restore confidence. He turned to Beatrice and asked, rather plaintively, 'Why didn't they tell us that we might do that?'[64] 'They' – the financial authorities – had controlled the government instead of being controlled by it.[65]

This dismal experience of Labour government certainly played its part in sending the Webbs towards Soviet communism. Yet, no more than the rise of Fascism, did it constitute the principal explanation of their turn to the 'left' or to the 'East'. In 1929 they had visited Trotsky in exile in Prinkipo. The revolutionary had played the prophet and had foretold a second world war in which the main antagonists would be Great Britain on the one side and the United States of America on the other. The future of socialism, he told the Webbs, was to be found somewhere within such apocalyptic forecasts rather than in the pedestrian programme of Stalin. Understandably, Sidney and Beatrice were driven into resistance to a hypothesis so foreign to the kind of tradition to which they themselves adhered. 'Socialism in one country' conformed to the requirements of Webbian insularity, even if the country in question did not. The inauguration of the first Five-Year Plan in 1929 may have endorsed many of them. In combating the reasoning of Trotsky, the Webbs were being forced into sharing assumptions with Stalin.[66]

When they returned home Sidney went straight into the second Labour government – not as Member of Parliament for Seaham Harbour, but as Lord Passfield. He had relinquished a safe Labour seat to his leader, Ramsay Macdonald. He had become a peer but only because of the Labour Party undertaking to form an administration. It was short of experience. He was needed within it and could serve only by being a member of the House of Lords. Beatrice recognised that this might be expedient as well as ironic, but she insisted that she was not to be known as 'Lady Passfield'. She had changed her name once for Sidney's sake; she could not be expected to do so again. Socialist convictions conspired with haughty bourgeois pride to make her despise aristocratic titles. Despite taking a certain pleasure in the fact that 'the Other One' occupied a position in the Cabinet that had once been held by Joseph Chamberlain, she preferred the society of the Soviet ambassador, Sokolnikov, to that of Court circles.[67]

A NEW CIVILISATION

After the downfall of the government and his release from ministerial responsibility, Sidney found Beatrice engaging in 'revolutionary chatter'. He pointed out to her that she had no intention of spending her old age living the life of a revolutionary. She accepted this rebuke while confessing that she was uncertain about what it meant. However, the new Soviet ambassador to the United Kingdom, Ivan Maisky, suggested that there were ways of being on the side of the revolution without experiencing too large a revolution in one's own life-style. He urged the Webbs to visit his country. They had received and declined such invitations in the past – fearing that they would be held as hostages. In 1932 the invitation was accepted. The Webbs spent some months in the Soviet Union, and Sidney returned alone for a second visit in 1934.

However, they felt that they learned more from talking to Maisky in their own home at Passfield Corner than they managed to assimilate from their Russian tours. Maisky was the least 'buttoned up' of Soviet officials. They took, in their traditional manner, all kinds of testimony from all kinds of witnesses: ardent Bolsheviks, White Russian *émigrés*, disillusioned left-wing intellectuals and fellow Fabians who anticipated their own enthusiasm. Yet Maisky was more valuable to them than all these put together. Perhaps, one should remember Ivan Maisky as one whose collaboration – as much as his witness – went into the making of the Webbs' last and most commercially successful book: *Soviet Communism:*

A New Civilisation?. Certainly, they consulted him at every point, and a whole chapter was written under his guidance.[68] It seems highly probable that the Soviet ambassador was killing two birds with one stone. First, he could take part of the credit for having won over to 'communism' the leading protagonists of parliamentary socialism. Second, by arranging a Russian translation of their work, he could introduce criticism of Soviet society into Stalin's Russia at a time when no other criticism was permissible or possible.

The Webbs went to Russia in the expectation that it would meet with their approval. But, equally, their admiration for the 'new civilisation' was qualified. They singled out for criticism what came to be called 'the cult of the individual'. They complained about the 'disease of orthodoxy' – the nonsense which gave rise to dialectical-materialist interpretations of the fishing industry. They drew attention to what they termed the 'contradictory tendencies in Soviet foreign policy'. By this they meant the alleged opposition between the line of the Soviet state in favour of peace and collective security and the line of the party according to which the Soviet Union was still to be thought of as the motherland of world revolution. They devoted a whole chapter to 'liquidations', acknowledging the reality of terror and lawlessness as well as the immeasurable suffering which they knew to have been associated with the destruction of the kulak.[69] The hostile reader might argue that they made far too little of these and other 'shortcomings'; he could not – without the aid of ignorance or dishonesty – maintain that the Webbs failed to refer to them at all.[70]

A few shrewd observers, such as G. D. H. Cole, guessed that the Webbs would be 'converted' as a result of their research into Soviet Russia. Cole once cleverly remarked that 'Sidney Webb is never in transition.' The fact that he had been a member of an ultra-respectable and constitutional British government would not, accordingly, prevent him from suddenly emerging as the friend-in-chief of the USSR. This was a good hunch. With the benefit of hindsight it is not difficult to grasp why Sidney and Beatrice became pro-Soviet. As against the judgment of R. P. Dutt it spoke more for the steady continuity of their values than for any sudden change in them. Far from their experience of Russia persuading them that they had been wrong all along, it convinced them that they had been right all along! 'Granted the need for violent revolution,' wrote Beatrice,

Soviet Communism embodies Fabian policy: Fabian consumers' economics and Fabian emphasis upon the application of science to social institutions, and Fabian dislike for emotional and libertarian utopias. Indeed, the followers of Lenin have outplanned the Webbs: and it was our belief in a planned social order that was caricatured in the Webbville and damned and derided by the anarchist revolutionary movement of 1910–1914.[71]

If a society claimed to constitute a new civilisation then it must, Sidney and Beatrice thought, give proof of its novelty at three levels. First, it must propose a new structure of institutions. They concluded that Soviet society did this because within it man was represented as a producer and a consumer as well as a citizen. It had effected and improved upon the pluralistic arrangements which they themselves had recommended in a *Constitution for the Socialist Commonwealth of Great Britain*. The fact that it had added a new institution, the Communist Party, by no means diminished its healthiness. On the contrary, the Communist Party, they decided, was just what they needed, but had not thought of. It represented the 'vocation of leadership': a phrase which excellently expressed their faith in a quasi-religious notion of professionalism and their exalted view of a Civil Service come into its own.

Second, a new civilisation must constitute property relations on radically new lines. Manifestly the Soviet Union had met this requirement. With collectivisation the finishing touches were being put to a world without landlords or capitalists. Given the exceptional readiness of the Webbs to equate ownership and control by the state with socialism, it is easy to understand how impressed they were by this circumstance.

Third, a new civilisation meant a transformation of religious beliefs. Soviet communism, by substituting the service of man for the service of God, evidently met this requirement. The Russians, as they replaced the pursuit of profit by the planning of production for community consumption, discarded a religious authority which set itself above men for a social science which served their ascertained needs.

It is hard to resist the conclusion that the Webbs, in this last great journey abroad, were really coming home. Unable and unwilling to penetrate the world of appearances in Stalin's Russia, they became enchanted with landmarks that seemed reminiscent of the sought-for country of their youth. Here was the new Rome in which – in the words of Sidney's sermon on the old Rome – the individual was ruthlessly sacrificed to the mass.[72] Here was a world in which the renunciation of self and a vicarious living through the collective became the highest good. Here was a world in which the old Adam of competitiveness – economic and political – gave place to the rationality of the public administrator who took his decisions unfettered by the whims of a few rich, busy men or by a slavish submission to the requirements of the 'average sensual man'.

Soviet Russia, the Webbs decided, was to be described in terms neither of autocratic government nor of government by consent. Rather, it was government by disinterested professional experts who were clever enough to recognise the importance of the 'consciousness of consent'. This Soviet democracy seemed to them to express the best hopes of the 'third culture' which they had tried to encourage. It meant that social services were taken to be the condition of national efficiency rather than as costs incurred at the expense of economic growth. It meant equality, but not a mindless equality which would sentence an intellectual or a Stakhanovite to share a single room with ten tramps. It meant the emancipation of women, but it also meant a welcome absence of cuddling in the Parks of Culture and Rest. It meant – as they had always known it would – opportunity for those who wanted to work and severity for those who would not take advantage of the opportunity. While strenuously denying extravagant accounts of the extent and purpose of forced labour in Russia, the Webbs could see nothing incongruous about labour camps under socialism.

Sidney wisely observed that the commonest source of error in sociology was to try to interpret the present in terms of categories and definitions shaped in the past. He was also well aware of the temptation to applaud whatever could be construed as conforming to what the observer had himself proposed in other times and other circumstances. Beatrice frequently recognised the connection between the late-Victorian preoccupation with the possibility of secular religion and what was going on in the USSR.[73] Similarly, repeatedly remarking that the old are either scatter-brained or obsessed, she went on to admit that she was obsessed with Soviet communism. All this tells against the contemptuous suggestion that Sidney and Beatrice were senile when they went to Russia. At the same time, one of the most insidious forms of self-deception consists in assuming that by clearly marking a pitfall one ensures that one will not fall into the pit. Thus, while the Webbs were well aware of the need to distinguish between simulacra and *arcanna imperii* they failed to make that distinction in relation to Soviet society.

The Webbs exposed the 'errors and mistakes' of Stalin's Russia twenty years before Krushchev. What limited this achievement was that the vocabulary of 'errors and mistakes' was impoverished from the standpoint of moral standards and intellectual integrity. Of course, before the publication of the Smolensk archive it was virtually impossible to discover any hard documentary evidence about the working of the Soviet political system.[74] Due allowance must be made for this. Yet the fact remains that the Webbs knew that there were many warts on the face of Soviet society, and Beatrice sometimes suspected the presence of a more deep-seated rottenness. Consideration of tactical expediency and a sincerely felt obligation to solidarity help to explain – but cannot justify – the Webbs' readiness to go so far towards accepting the USSR in terms of its own assessment of itself.

Sidney and Beatrice were at fault in treating Russia's industrial revolution as an extenuating circumstance rather than as a key to interpretation. The dark side of Soviet reality was excused by reference to its need to catch up with the industrialised world. They followed the Soviet leaders in assuming that solving pre-capitalist economic problems was simply an additional difficulty put in the way of the main task, which was identified as the liberation, not the creation, of a proletariat.

The Webbs' 'organising insight', the belief in the primary importance of institutions and institutional arrangements, led them astray. Marx's contention that we should no more judge an epoch of social revolution by its own consciousness than we should judge an individual by his opinion of himself was no part of the Webbs' intellectual baggage. Since his marriage to Beatrice, Sidney had put aside economic theory in favour of the study of social and political institutions. Accordingly, he could dwell lovingly upon the elaborate organisational details of Gosplan without once asking himself about the criteria which the planners consulted when they distributed scarce resources between competing uses. Since they were accomplished historians and strongly impressed with the importance of historical method it is harder to explain the almost total indifference which they showed in Soviet Communism to the history of the revolution. Yet it was profoundly in character for them to be attracted to a study of the fruits of the revolution in ongoing institutional concerns rather than to dwell upon the possible relevance of the pre-revolutionary controversy between Bolsheviks and Mensheviks. They cheerfully assumed that the issue between Bolsheviks and Mensheviks had been finally settled by the victory of the former. Accordingly, they uncritically accepted the claim of the regime to be one of planned production for community consumption, without ever even noticing Preobrachevsky's warning: 'We don't live in a society with planned production for community consumption; we live under the iron heel of primitive socialist accumulation.'[75]

Today it is arguable that the later an industrial revolution occurs the greater must be the proportion of national income devoted to saving and investment as opposed to consumption.[76] This follows from the altered character of the productive forces themselves: from the fact that industrialisation no longer means the spinning jenny, but the hydroelectric power-station. The efficient utilisation of twentieth-century technology means planning indivisibilities and complementaries which formerly established themselves through the working of market forces. Above all, twentieth-century industrialisation involves investing in human beings. It means the conquest of the illiteracy, innumeracy and mindless traditionalism which appear, at every point, as fetters upon the progress of modern industry. Given the altered character of the productive forces involved in the new, or second-generation, industrial revolution, it was hardly to be expected that it could be accomplished within the property relations and forms of state power which had been appropriate to the first. What was wanted now was not the enterprising innovator who would conjure up new techniques, so much as the rational planner who would organise an international transfer of an achieved technology.

The task was beyond the reach of private saving and investment. It wanted a comprehensive expropriation of the available surplus far beyond the wildest dreams of primitive accumulation under capitalism. Private accumulation of capital had to give pride of place to public thrift and planned production. But the immense sufferings involved could be legitimised only by reference to the most advanced ideals and exalted purposes. It was not in terms of the rhetoric of a failed bourgeoisie that one could make this revolution. On the contrary, it was only under cover of the language of a class that came to supersede a failed bourgeoisie that this essential work could be done. Thus, pre-capitalist problems were solved in the pretence that they were post-capitalist ones. The Webbs, enchanted as ever with institutional arrangements, were illplaced to consider Soviet experience in this light.

The reception accorded to the Webbs' book on 'the new civilisation' fluctuated over time. The first edition was widely acclaimed in England even by critics who were not disposed to be sympathetic to the USSR. The second edition, coming out in 1937, coincided with the trial of the 'parallel centre':[77] a high point in the history of the Stalinist purges. The fact that the Webbs chose this moment to remove the interrogation mark from the title of their work did not help matters. Some of their firmest friends and admirers, such as Harold Laski, Professor of Political Science at the LSE, expressed strong disapproval of such unregulated enthusiasm. In the privacy of her journal, Beatrice admitted to her own anguished doubts. Indeed, she and Sidney tried to intervene on behalf of their old friend Sokolnikov who was one of the principal figures among those accused in 1937. She fancied she had done something to save his life when he was sentenced to ten years' imprisonment; in fact he was secretly shot immediately after his trial. In public, Beatrice continued to express her immense confidence in Russia. In private she reeled under the successive shocks of the Russo–German pact and the Finnish war.[78]

Of course, everything seemed to come right in the end. Before her death in 1943 the Soviet army won its decisive victory at the battle of Stalingrad. The third edition of *Soviet Communism* saw the Webbs hailed as prophets who had been proved correct by events. Sidney died in 1947, the acknowledged father of the first majority Labour government, which greatly extended the public sector of the mixed economy and inaugurated the Welfare State. In fact, the old man spent the last two years of his life criticising British Labour's foreign policy rather than expressing pleasure at seeing so many of his projected reforms carried into practice.

CONCLUSION

The Webbs' greatness lay in describing institutions like those of the British labour movement and of British local government. Still more, it lay in their ability to found or to reshape institutions themselves: the Fabian Society, the London School of Economics and the Labour Party. They saw themselves as constructive social- ists, never as revolutionary ones. This settled disposition, associated as it was with a profound distaste for anything resembling anarchy or chaos, explained the timing of their turn towards the USSR. The institutions which they built and those which they celebrated did not always work towards ends that they intended or approved. The Webbs wisely reconciled themselves to such disappointments so long as they could feel that something important was happening. They both loved Goethe, and it was Goethe who remarked: 'To think is easy: to act is difficult: to act in accordance with one's thoughts is the most difficult thing in the world.'

SIDNEY AND BEATRICE WEBB: CHRONOLOGY

1858: Birth of Beatrice Potter.

1859: Birth of Sidney Webb.

1881: Webb appointed first division clerk in the Colonial Office. S.W. meets George Bernard Shaw at the Zeitetical Society.

1883: Beatrice Potter visits working-class family at Bacup disguised as a farmer's daughter. Falls in love with Rt Hon. Joseph Chamberlain MP.

1885: Sidney joins Fabian Society.

1886: Independently of each other, Sidney and Beatrice write unpublished essays on Karl Marx.

1887: Sidney prepares *Facts for Socialists* for Fabian Society. Beatrice publishes the first of her essays on working-class life in the East End of London.

1888: Beatrice gives evidence to the House of Lords Committee on the Sweating System.

1889: *Fabian Essays*. The Great Dock Strike.

1890: First meeting between Sidney and Beatrice.

1891: Beatrice publishes her *The Co-operative Movement in Great Britain*.

1892: Death of Richard Potter. Sidney resigns from the Civil Service and is elected as Progressive and Fabian candidate to the London County Council for the division of Deptford. Marriage of Sidney and Beatrice.

1893: Sidney becomes chairman of the London Technical Education Board.

1894: Webbs publish *History of Trade Unionism*.

1895: Foundation of the London School of Economics and Political Science.

1897: Webbs publish *Industrial Democracy*.

1898: Webbs embark on a tour of the English-speaking world.

1899: Webbs begin their research into the history of English local government.

1901: Sidney publishes, in *Nineteenth Century*, 'Lord Rosebery's Escape from Houndsditch', debunking Gladstonian liberalism and fostering union between imperialism and Fabian collectivism.

1902: Education Act passed with Sidney's help and blessing.

1903: London Education Act, largely drafted by Sidney, carried into law.

1905: Beatrice appointed to the Royal Commission on the Poor Law and the Relief of Distress.

1906: Great Liberal victory at general election. Emergence of Parliamentary Labour Party.

1909: Beatrice presents minority report on the Poor Law.

1910: The Webbs plunge into propaganda and attempt to organise a popular campaign for the prevention of destitution.

1911: Webbs embark upon a tour of the Orient.

1912: Foundation of *New Statesman*.

1914: Webb elected to War Emergency Workers' National Committee.

1915: Sidney becomes Fabian representative on the National Executive Committee of the Labour Party.

1916: Campaign for 'the conscription of riches' makes headway.

1917: Sidney drafts Labour Party's Memorandum on War Aims. Beatrice becomes member of the (Haldane) Machinery of Government Committee.

1918: With Arthur Henderson, Sidney prepares the new constitution of the Labour Party. Sidney unsuccessfully contests London University as a Labour candidate.

1919: Sidney appointed to the Sankey Commission. With the majority, he calls for the nationalisation of the coal mines.

1920: Webbs publish *A Constitution for the Socialist Commonwealth of Great Britain.*

1922: Sidney elected as Labour Member of Parliament for the mining constituency of Seaham Harbour.

1923: Webbs publish *The Decay of Capitalist Civilisation.*

1924: First Labour government under J. R. Macdonald. Sidney enters Cabinet as President of the Board of Trade. Government falls within the year.

1925: Webbs leave their famous salon, 41 Grosvenor Road.

1926: General Strike in defence of the coalminers. Webbs disinclined to support strike. Beatrice publishes first volume of autobiography, *My Apprenticeship.*

1927: Webbs publish *English Poor Law History*, Vol. 1, Part 1.

1929: Webbs visit Trotsky in exile. Formation of the second Labour government under J. R. Macdonald. Webb – as Lord Passfield – enters Cabinet as Secretary of State for the Dominions and Colonies.

1931: Fall of the second Labour government. J. R. Macdonald and other Labour leaders form coalition with Conservatives and Liberals. Massive defeat of the Labour Party in the general election. Webb effectively retires from parliamentary life.

1932: Webbs' first tour of the Soviet Union.

1934: Sidney returns alone to the Soviet Union for further tour.

1935: Webbs publish *Soviet Communism: A New Civilisation?*.

1937: Webbs publish second edition with the interrogation mark removed.

1941: Webbs publish third edition.

1943: Death of Beatrice Webb.

1945: Third Labour government: 229 Fabians in House of Commons; ten in Cabinet.

1947: Death of Sidney Webb (Lord Passfield).

12 December 1947: On G. B. Shaw's suggestion the ashes are taken to Westminster Abbey: the first occasion in nine hundred years in which a man and wife had been buried at the same ceremony.

BIBLIOGRAPHY

Primary sources

The Passfield Papers, London School of Economics and Political Science.

Autobiographical sources

Webb, B., *Beatrice Webb's Diaries 1924–1932*, edited by M. Cole, London, Longmans, Green & Co., 1956.
Webb, B., *Our Partnership*, Cambridge University Press, 1975 edn.
Webb, B., *My Apprenticeship*, Cambridge University Press, 1979 edn.
Webb, B., *The Diary of Beatrice Webb*, edited by N. and J. MacKenzie, London, Virago (in association with the London School of Economics and Political Science), Vol. I: *1873–1892 Glitter and Darkness Within* (1982), Vol. II: *1892–1905 All the Good Things of Life* (1982), Vol. III: *1905–1924 The Power to Alter Things* (1984), Vol. IV: *The Wheel of Life* (1985).
Webb, S., and Webb, B., *The Letters of Sidney and Beatrice Webb*, edited by N. MacKenzie, Cambridge University Press (in co-operation with the London School of Economics and Political Science), 1978, Vol. I: *Apprenticeships 1873–1892*, Vol. II: *Partnership 1892–1922*, Vol. III: *Pilgrimage 1912–1947*.

About the Webbs (in chronological order)

Cole, M. (ed.), *The Webbs and their Work*, London, Frederick Muller, 1949.
Liebman, M., 'Fabianisme et communisme: les Webbs et l'union sovietique', *International Review of Social History*, vol. 5, pt 3, 1960, pp. 49–73.
McBriar, A. M., *Fabian Socialism and English Politics: 1884 to 1918*, Cambridge University Press, 1962.
Hobsbawm, E. J., 'The Fabians reconsidered', in *Labouring Men*, London, Weidenfeld & Nicolson, 1964, pp. 250–71.

Muggeridge, K., and Ruth, A., *Beatrice Webb: A Life 1858–1943*, London, Secker & Warburg, 1967.

Harrison, R., 'The War Emergency Workers' National Committee: 1914–1920', in A. Briggs and J. Saville (eds), *Essays in Labour History*, London, Macmillan, 1971, pp. 211–59.

Winter, J., *Socialism and the Challenge of War. Ideas and Politics in Britain, 1912–18*, London, Routledge & Kegan Paul, 1974.

Wolfe, W., *From Radicalism to Socialism*, New Haven, Conn., Yale University Press, 1975.

MacKenzie, N., and MacKenzie, J., *The First Fabians*, London, Weidenfeld & Nicolson, 1977.

MacKenzie, J., *A Victorian Courtship: The Story of Beatrice Potter and Sidney Webb*, London, Weidenfeld & Nicolson, 1979.

Harrison, R., 'The Webbs as historians of trade unions', in R. Samuel (ed.), *People's History and Socialist Theory*, London, Routledge & Kegan Paul, 1981, pp. 322–6.

Cane, B., 'Beatrice Webb and the "woman question" ', *History Workshop Journal*, vol. 14 (Autumn), 1982, pp. 23–43.

Britain, I., *Fabianism and Culture*, Cambridge University Press, 1983.

Radice, L., *Beatrice and Sidney Webb*, London, Macmillan, 1984.

Nord, D. F., *The Apprenticeship of Beatrice Webb*, London, Macmillan, 1985.

NOTES

This chapter was first published in *Nihon Rōdō Kyōkai Zassi* (monthly journal of the Japan Institute of Labour), nos. 298/299, February/March 1985, Tokyo.

1 British Library of Political and Economic Science, *Publications of Sidney and Beatrice Webb. An Interim Checklist*, London School of Economics and Political Science, 1973, p. 36.

2 R. P. Dutt, 'Notes of the month', *Labour Monthly*, vol. 18, no. 1, 1936, pp. 3–26.

3 H. Marcuse, *Soviet Marxism, A Critical Analysis*, London, Routledge & Kegan Paul, 1958.

4 R. Harrison, 'Marxism as nineteenth-century critique and twentieth-century ideology', *History*, vol. 66, no. 217, 1981, pp. 208–20.

5 For Sidney Webb's early life, see W. Wolfe, *From Radicalism to Socialism*, New Haven, Conn., Yale University Press, 1975, pp. 183–205; N. and J. MacKenzie, *The First Fabians*, London, Weidenfeld & Nicolson, 1977, pp. 56–72.

6 G. B. Shaw, *Sixteen Self-Sketches*, London, Constable, 1949, p. 6.
   For G. B. Shaw's early life, see Wolfe, op. cit. (note 5), pp. 113–
   50; N. and J. MacKenzie, op. cit. (note 5), pp. 30–44.

7 Two interesting accounts of socialist revival are S. Pierson, *The
   Origins of British Socialism*, Ithaca, NY, Cornell University Press,
   1973; S. Yeo, '"A new life": the religion of socialism in Britain,
   1883–1896', *History Workshop Journal*, no 4 (Autumn), 1977,
   pp. 5–56.

8 C. Tsuzuki, *H. M. Hyndman and British Socialism*, Oxford
   University Press, 1961; E. P. Thompson, *William Morris*,
   London, Merlin Press, 2nd edn, 1977; D. Howell, *British Workers
   and the Independent Labour Party*, Manchester University Press,
   1983.

9 On Graham Wallas, see M. J. Wiener, *Between Two Worlds*,
   Oxford, Clarendon Press, 1971; T. H. Qualter, *Graham Wallas
   and the Great Society*, London, Macmillan, 1981.

10 For some studies of these 'reformist professionals', see R. Harrison,
   'The positivists: a study of labour's intellectuals', in *Before the
   Socialists*, London, Routledge & Kegan Paul, 1965, pp. 251–342;
   H. Perkin, *The Origins of Modern English Society 1780–1880*,
   London, Routledge & Kegan Paul, pp. 257–70; P. Hollis (ed.),
   Pressure from Without, London, Edward Arnold, 1974; C.
   Harvie, *The Lights of Liberalism*, London, Allen Lane, 1976; C.
   Kent, *Brains and Numbers: Elitism, Comteism and Democracy in
   Mid-Victorian England*, University of Toronto Press, 1978; V.
   Kiernan, 'Labour and the literate in nineteenth-century Britain', in
   D. E. Martin and D. Rubinstein (eds), *Ideology and the Labour
   Movement*, London, Croom Helm, 1979, pp. 32–61; H. Perkin,
   'Land reform and class conflict in Victorian Britain', *The Structured
   Crowd*, Brighton, Harvester Press, 1981, pp. 100–35; T. Heyck,
   The Transformation of Intellectual Life in Victorian England,
   London, Croom Helm, 1982; K. Kumar, 'Class and political
   action in nineteenth-century England', *European Journal of
   Sociology*, vol. 24, no 1, 1983, pp. 3–43.

11 F. Engels to Sorge, 18 January 1893, in D. Torr (ed.), *Marx and
   Engels: Selected Correspondence*, London, Lawrence, 1934,
   p. 504.

12 S. Webb, *Socialism in England*, London, Swan Sonnenshein, 1890,
   pp. 116–17.

13 E. J. Hobsbawm, 'The Fabians reconsidered', in *Labouring Men*,
   London, Weidenfeld & Nicolson, 1964, pp. 251–71.

14 On Fabianism and the London labour movement after 1887, see P.
   Thompson, *Socialists, Liberals and Labour*, London, Routledge &
   Kegan Paul, 1967, p. 154.

15 On the Fabian theory of rent, see D. M. Ricci, 'Fabian socialism:

a theory of rent as exploitation', *Journal of British Studies*, vol. 9, no. 1, 1969, pp. 105–21; S. Clarke, *Marx, Marginalism and Modern Sociology*, London, Macmillan, 1982, pp. 190–1.

16 H. Bland, 'The outlook', in G. B. Shaw (ed.), *Fabian Essays in Socialism*, London, Fabian Society, 1889, p. 212.

17 On the New Liberalism, see H. V. Emy, *Liberals, Radicals and Social Politics 1892–1914*, Cambridge University Press, 1973; M. Freeden, *The New Liberalism and Social Politics 1892–1914*, Oxford, Clarendon Press, 1978; S. A. Collini, *Liberalism and Sociology: L. T. Hobhouse and Political Argument in England 1880–1914*, Cambridge University Press, 1979.

18 On Beatrice Potter's early life, see N. and J. MacKenzie, op. cit. (note 5), pp. 119–65; J. MacKenzie, *A Victorian Courtship: The Story of Beatrice Potter and Sidney Webb*, London, Weidenfeld & Nicolson, 1979; B. Cane, 'Beatrice Webb and "the woman question"', *History Workshop Journal*, no. 14 (Autumn), pp. 23–43; D. E. Nord, *The Apprenticeship of Beatrice Webb*, London, Macmillan, 1985.

19 This phase of my argument owes much to R. D. Laing, *The Divided Self*, London, Tavistock, 1960.

20 B. Webb, *The Diary of Beatrice Webb, Volume I: 1872–1892 Glitter and Darkness Within*, edited by N. and J. MacKenzie, London, Virago (in association with the London School of Economics and Political Science), 1982, pp. 188–9.

21 B. Webb, *My Apprenticeship*, Cambridge University Press, 1979, p. xliv.

22 R. Jay, *Joseph Chamberlain: A Political Study*, Oxford, Clarendon Press, 1981.

23 D. Wiltshire, *The Social and Political Thought of Herbert Spencer*, Oxford University Press, 1978.

24 B. Webb, 1982, op. cit. (note 20), p. 102.

25 B. Webb, 1979, op. cit. (note 21), pp. 191–3.

26 For the 'discovery' of poverty, see G. Stedman Jones, *Outcast London*, Oxford, Clarendon Press, 1971; J. Harris, *Unemployment and Politics*, Oxford, Clarendon Press, 1972; H. Bosanquet, *Social Work in London 1869–1922*, Brighton, Harvester Press, 1973.

27 B. Webb, 1979, op. cit. (note 21), pp. 391–5.

28 *First Report from the Select Committee of the House of Lords on the Sweating System: 30 July 1888* (Beatrice's evidence, 11 May 1888).

29 Private source, 1880s.

30 B. Potter, 'The dock life of the East London', *Nineteenth Century*, October 1887, p. 499.

31 See S. Yeo's contribution to this volume, pp. 228–34.

32 For Beatrice's first reactions, see her diary entry for 31 August 1889, B. Webb, 1979, op. cit. (note 21), p. 396.

33 On the dock strike and the new unionism, see Hobsbawm, op. cit. (note 13), pp. 179–203.

34 On their courtship, see J. MacKenzie, op. cit. (note 18).

35 J. S. Mill, *Autobiography*, London, Longmans, Green, Reader & Dyer, 1873, p. 100.

36 S. Webb, 'Reminiscences', *St Martin's Review*, no. 452, October 1928, p. 478.

37 A summary of their activities before 1914 is found in N. and J. MacKenzie, op. cit. (note 5), pp. 179–395.

38 C. P. Snow, *The Two Cultures and the Scientific Revolution*, Cambridge University Press, 1959.

39 S. and B. Webb, *The Letters of Sidney and Beatrice Webb*, edited by N. MacKenzie, *Vol. I: Apprenticeships 1873–1892*, Cambridge University Press (in co-operation with the London School of Economics and Political Science), 1978, p. 345.

40 A recent interesting, if unsuccessful, attempt to revise this opinion can be found in I. Britain, *Fabianism and Culture*, Cambridge University Press, 1983.

41 S. Webb, 'Rome: a sermon in sociology', *Our Corner*, vol. 12, 1888, pp. 53–64, 79–89.

42 E. P. Thompson, 'Peculiarities of the English', in *The Poverty of Theory*, London, Merlin Press, 1977, p. 59 (originally published 1965).

43 Collini, op. cit. (note 17), pp. 13–50.

44 S. and B. Webb, *Industrial Democracy*, London, Longmans, Green & Co., 1897, p. 70. For the comparisons with Lenin and Bernstein, see R. Harrison, 'The Webbs as historians of trade unions', in R. Samuel (ed.), *People's History and Socialist Theory*, London, Routledge & Kegan Paul, 1981, pp. 322–6.

45 S. Webb, *London Education*, London, Longmans, Green & Co., 1904. On the Webbs and the foundation of the LSE, see N. and J. MacKenzie, op. cit. (note 5), pp. 214–17, 220.

46 On the Webbs' problems with the left, see P. Thompson, op. cit. (note 14), p. 147.

47 For the Webbs and social imperialism, see B. Semmel, *Imperialism and Social Reform: English Social-Imperial Thought, 1895–1914*, Cambridge, Mass., Harvard University Press, 1960; B. Porter, *Critics of Empire*, London, Macmillan, 1968; G. R. Searle, *The Quest for National Efficiency*, Berkeley, University of California Press, 1971; A. Davin, 'Imperialism and motherhood', *History Workshop Journal*, no. 5 (Spring), 1978, pp. 9–65.

48 Harris, op. cit. (note 26).

49 On Churchill and welfare measures, see B. B. Gilbert, 'Winston

Churchill versus the Webbs: the origins of British unemployment insurance', *American Historical Review*, vol. 71, no. 3, 1966, pp. 846–62.

50　B. Webb, *Our Partnership*, Cambridge University Press, 1975, p. 430.

51　B. Webb, Diary (unpublished), 12 October 1915.

52　R. Harrison, 'The War Emergency Workers' National Committee: 1914–1920', in A. Briggs and J. Saville (eds), *Essays in Labour History*, London, Macmillan, 1971, pp. 11–59.

53　A. Marwick, *The Deluge*, London, Bodley Head, 1967.

54　On Henderson, see R. I. McKibbin, 'Arthur Henderson as labour leader', *International Review of Social History*, vol. 33, pt 1, 1978, pp. 79–101. On Henderson and the ill-fated Stockholm conference, see A. Mayer, *Wilson vs Lenin*, Cleveland, Meridan Books, 1967, pp. 218–24, 237.

55　H. G. Wells to U. Sinclair, cited by B. Webb, *The Diary of Beatrice Webb, Vol. III: 1905–1924 The Power to Alter Things*, edited by N. and J. MacKenzie, London, Virago (in association with the London School of Economics and Political Science), 1984, p. 311.

56　G. D. H. Cole, *History of the Labour Party from 1914*, London, Routledge & Kegan Paul, 1948, pp. 44–81.

57　Ibid., p. 72.

58　V. I. Lenin, 'Left-wing communism: an infantile disorder', in *Collected Works*, Vol. 31, Moscow, Progress Publishers, 1966, pp. 77–89.

59　B. Webb, op. cit. (note 55), 1984, p. 366.

60　S. and B. Webb, *A Constitution for the Socialist Commonwealth*, London, Longmans, Green & Co., 1920.

61　S. and B. Webb, *Decay of Capitalist Civilisation*, London, Fabian Society and Allen & Unwin, 1923, pp. 77–8.

62　On these two Labour governments, see R. Lyman, *The First Labour Government*, London, Chapman & Hall, 1957; R. Skidelsky, *Politicians and the Slump. The Labour Government 1929–31*, London, Macmillan, 1967; D. Marquand, *Ramsay MacDonald*, London, Cape, 1977; B. Pimlott, *Labour and the Left in the 1930s*, Cambridge University Press, 1977, pp. 1–70.

63　B. Webb, *Beatrice Webb's Diaries 1924–1932*, edited by M. Cole, London, Longmans, Green & Co., 1956, p. 281.

64　B. Webb, Diary (unpublished), 20 September 1931.

65　Skidelsky, op. cit. (note 62).

66　B. Webb, 1956, op. cit. (note 63), p. 223.

67　N. and J. MacKenzie, op. cit. (note 5), pp. 401–6.

68　Ivan Maisky granted the author an interview which took place in Moscow in the summer of 1966. Mr Maisky claimed a special responsibility for the chapters on 'liquidations'.

69   S. and B. Webb, *Soviet Communism: A New Civilisation?*, London, private subscription edition, Labour Party, 1935, pt II, ch. VII: 'The liquidation of the landlord and the capitalist'.

70   Three recent studies which deal with intellectuals and Stalinist Russia are D. Caute, *The Fellow Travellers*, London, Weidenfeld & Nicolson, 1973; P. Hollander, *Political Pilgrims*, New York, Oxford University Press, 1981; E. J. Hobsbawm, 'Gli intellettuali e l'antifascismo', in E. J. Hobsbawm *et al.*, *Storia del Marxismo*, Vol. 3, Turin, Einaudi, 1981, pt 2, pp. 443–90.

71   B. Webb, Diary (unpublished), 3 May 1934.

72   S. Webb, 1888, op. cit. (note 41).

73   B. Webb, 1956, op. cit. (note 63), p. 299, 4 January 1932: 'It is the invention of the religious order, as the determining factor in the life of a great nation, that is the magnet which attracts me to Russia. Practically that religion is Comteism – the religion of Humanity!'

74   M. Fainsod, *Smolensk under Soviet Rule*, Cambridge, Mass., Harvard University Press, 1958. For recent work on similar themes, see M. Lewin, *The Making of the Soviet System*, London, Methuen, 1985; S. Cohen, *Rethinking the Soviet Experience*, New York, Oxford University Press, 1985.

75   E. Preobrazhensky, *The New Economics*, Oxford University Press, 1965, pp. 79ff; see also S. Cohen, *Bukharin and the Bolshevik Revolution*, New York, Knopf, 1975, pp. 160–212.

76   For recent statements on this theme with the Soviet experience in mind, see Cohen, 1985, op. cit. (note 74); Lewin, op. cit. (note 74); T. Shanin (ed.), *Late Marx and the Russian Road*, London, Routledge & Kegan Paul, 1984; T. Shanin, *The Roots of Otherness: Russia's Turn of the Century*, London, Macmillan, 1985.

77   Cohen, 1975, op. cit. (note 75), pp. 364–81; R. Conquest, *The Great Terror: Stalin's Purges of the Thirties*, London, Macmillan, 1968.

78   S. and B. Webb, *The Letters of Sidney and Beatrice Webb, Vol. III Pilgrimage 1912–1947*, edited by N. MacKenzie, Cambridge University Press (in co-operation with the London School of Economics and Political Science), 1978, pp. 430–1, 433–4; B. Webb, *The Diary of Beatrice Webb Vol IV: The Wheel of Life*, edited by N. and J. MacKenzie, London, Virago (in association with the London School of Economics and Political Science), 1985, pp. 438–9, 441–2.

3
Max Weber and German Social Democracy

Wolfgang J. Mommsen

Max Weber was undoubtedly one of the seminal political thinkers of the early twentieth century. His views on the character and role of the German Social Democratic Party in Wilhelmine Germany are of interest in many respects. He considered the Social Democratic Party to be one of the most advanced examples of the bureaucratic mass party which in his opinion was about to become dominant in modern parliamentary government. More importantly, he was interested in the Social Democrats as a socialist movement which had tied its political fortunes to a considerable degree to the Marxist theory of historical materialism. But paramount in his views about Social Democracy were considerations concerning the concrete role which the Social Democrats played within Wilhelmine politics. Above all he concentrated on one issue, namely whether their policies were likely to promote or retard the political system's democratisation. In his opinion an alliance of the middle and the working classes ought to end aristocratic dominance of the state. Weber believed this to be necessary on liberal grounds, but also for national reasons; only an Imperial Germany whose policies enjoyed the full support of all the nation's classes would be able to play a major role in the world politics of the future.[1] It is this viewpoint which was all important in Weber's assessment of German Social Democracy.

WEBER AND MARXISM

However, before we turn to this crucial aspect of Weber's attitude to Social Democracy, his views on Marxism as a political philosophy should be briefly outlined.[2] Weber was quick to admit that these were largely conditioned by his own personal class status. He pointed out that he was (quite literally) a member of the bourgeoisie, since his wife Marianne drew an income from her co-ownership of a small family-owned textile mill in Westphalia.[3] Nevertheless, his views on Marx and Marxism were not as biased as he imagined them to be. Though a radical critic of Marx even to the point that he has been called his bourgeois counterpart, Weber's own sociology was to no small degree developed under the influence of and in intellectual debate with Marx and his theories. In his earlier years he perhaps tended to identify with contemporary vulgar anti-Marxist arguments which were based on a rather superficial reading of Marx. But in his mature works he displayed a full command of Marxist theory and discussed its implications with many of his Marxist students, not the least of them Georg Lukács.

Weber dismissed the Marxist theory of history more or less out of hand, since he believed neither that laws in history could ever be established, nor that the historical process in its entirety could ever be reconstructed solely along scientific lines. The most that was possible were ideal-typical reconstructions of segments of historical development as seen from a particular vantage-point. But such ideal-typical models could not claim to be objective in either the Hegelian or the Marxist sense – they were merely hypothetical models. As a substantive theory of history Weber rejected Marxism totally. As a system of ideal-typical hypotheses, or theoretical models of social reality, particularly of modern capitalism, however, it had indeed to be taken seriously.[4] Though strongly opposed to the spirit and the letter of the *Communist Manifesto* as a political pronunciamento, Weber considered it as a scholarly achievement of the first order.[5]

Indeed, it can be shown – and I have done so elsewhere[6] – that Weber integrated important elements of Marx's theories into his own 'interpretative sociology'. For instance, the ideal-typical analysis of the capitalist system in its pure form which we find in *Economy and Society* in many respects parallels Marx's own analysis half a century earlier. Weber's 'formal rationality' and Marx's 'alienation' are rather similar concepts describing the effects of the separation of the means of production from the proletariat. Furthermore, both men employed similar language to document the human costs of factory discipline upon workers. According to Weber, labour contracts entered into by 'formally free labour' were tantamount to its subjugation by capitalist entrepreneurs. The modern industrial system, he concluded, was based upon authoritarian domination, and the fact that it arose from the formally independent decisions of free individuals within the market-place, rather than by physical coercion, did not mitigate his judgment. Hence, Weber did not hesitate to assimilate Marx's usage of the notion of 'class', though he came to differentiate this concept far more than Marx ever thought necessary. In any case, Weber found little difficulty in describing the conditions of modern industrial labour as determined by class situation.

These few remarks may indicate that a large area of mutual consensus is to be found in the theoretical thought of Marx and Weber, so far as their assessment of the nature of the modern industrial system is concerned. However, while there are striking similarities in their diagnoses of the evils of capitalism, Weber did not in the least consider Marx's suggested cures valid. His lectures on 'Socialism', given in 1918 before Austro-Hungarian army officers,[7] presents a critical account of the main tenets of Marxist theory: (a) concentration of capital; (b) accumulation of economic crises; (c) polarisation of the population into classes. In his opinion they were neither theoretically sound nor suitable bases for a programme of practical political action.

While there might be many varieties of socialism, the only viable one, compatible with modern civilisation, was bound to be some type of centrally directed 'planned economy'. Rather than socially elevating workers, nationalisation would make social control even more extensive and oppressive. It would not matter to them whether these were private capitalists or a state managerial class. On the contrary, their chances of resisting the latter would be considerably reduced compared with conditions under a market-oriented capitalist system with an independent government. Any centrally organised socialist society would merely give a further boost to the process of bureaucratisation which Weber considered the greatest danger to humanity in the age of industrial capitalism.

WEBER AND THE SPD

However strong Weber's objections to Marxist theory were on scientific grounds, he was prepared to pay tribute to 'pioneer' Marxism as a heroic, albeit utopian, creed which had stimulated the workers' movement within a society that utterly rejected their claims to a fair share of the social product and a decent living. Furthermore, he considered the *Communist Manifesto* and the so-called *Katastrophentheorien*, both of which predicted an inevitable early demise of capitalism, as prophecies with considerable suggestive power. In his view they provided the backbone to the early socialists' fervent semi-religious creed.

In his own day, however, Weber noted that this socialist creed had deteriorated into a self-perpetuating mechanistic ideology. In his view it had become mere ritualistic abuse of existing social institutions, summarily dismissed as bourgeois but left without critical examination. In other words, what in the early days had been a heroic creed had become mere radical rhetoric devoid of any rational assessment of social reality. This refers in particular, of course, to the Social Democrats in Imperial Germany. To put it in a nutshell: the Social Democrats had failed to rid themselves of the ideological modes of thought typical of a political sect which were unsuitable for a modern political party. Hence they were incapable of facing reality and unwilling to work for the improvement of the workers' lot on the bases of a realistic assessment of existing conditions, possible chances of success in specific areas and suitable political alliances.

Already in his Inaugural Lecture in 1895 Weber mentioned (though characteristically as an aside) that, however advanced it had become in economic terms, the working class was in no way ready for political leadership: 'Politically the German working class is infinitely less mature than is maintained by a clique of journalists who aspire to monopolise its leadership.'[8] It was above all the lack of any sense of power which he considered the most critical deficiency of the German working class, in marked contrast, as he pointed out, to the British and French working classes. In this respect he referred to the support given to British imperialism by important sections of the British working class who, unlike their German counterpart, allegedly understood the need for empire and power politics. For the leaders of the Social Democratic Party –

'those declassed bourgeois' – he felt little more than contempt: 'They are pathetic experts in political triviality: they lack the deep instinct for power that a class which is called to take over the political leadership in a society ought to possess.'[9]

After the turn of the century Weber's imperialist convictions were no longer so vehement that they determined his opinion of the Social Democrats. But, in principle, neither his views nor the state of the Social Democratic Party had changed significantly. In his view it was pursuing an orthodox Marxist strategy devoid of any real revolutionary spirit. Social Democratic agitation, according to Weber, amounted to mere verbal radicalism, in sharp contrast to, if I may put it this way, the anarchists' propaganda by deed.

WEBER AND MICHELS

Between 1906 and 1909 Weber discussed these issues at considerable length with Robert Michels. He had attracted his interest as a young scholar of remarkable gifts, but equally because he was a devoted left-wing socialist with strong syndicalist leanings, as well as being a convert from a wealthy bourgeois family.[10] Weber took considerable interest in Michels's work on socialism and socialist parties, and it is significant that Michels published widely in the *Archiv für Sozialwissenschaft und Sozialpolitik*, even though he could not have been considered an established scholar. Michels's famous book on the 'sociology of modern parties' – *Political Parties* – was based on a series of essays, all of which had first been published in the *Archiv*.

Michels belonged to a dissident group of left-wing socialists with moderate anarchist views. Though a convinced socialist, he soon became a bitter critic of the German Social Democratic Party. This may be partly attributed to the fact that he felt ostracised being an intellectual from a bourgeois background. Indeed, Michels was never fully at home within German Social Democracy, even though he remained a party member until 1907. His passionately moralistic approach to socialism, combining an ethical imperative with deep-rooted fundamentalist democratic principles, was not shared by the bulk of Social Democrats. Neither were his leanings towards anarchist views well received in a party in which pragmatic attitudes prevailed and solidarity, discipline, and subservience to the party leaders were considered sacrosanct.

Michels was a *Gesinnungsethiker* (conviction politician): a syndicalist rather than an ordinary socialist. Both of these aspects of Michels's personality fascinated Max Weber. In some ways he identified in Michels an *alter ego*, following paths which he forbade himself to enter, but which he would none the less have liked to walk. Hence a lifelong though asymmetrical partnership developed between the two men. Of the many disputes they conducted either in their correspondence or during Weber's frequent visits to Heidelberg or Turin (where Michels moved after his habilitation at a German university had come to nought), socialism and the state of the German Social Democratic Party enjoyed pride of place.

Weber's and Michels's initial assessments of German Social Democracy were not all that different. In 1906 Weber attended the Social Democratic Party congress in Mannheim. His account to Michels of the proceedings was utterly devastating:

> Mannheim was very depressing. I heard Bebel and Legien refer at least ten times to 'our weakness'. Furthermore this extremely petty-bourgeois habit of mind, all these portly publicans' faces, the lack of dynamism and resolution, and at the same time the unwillingness to embark upon a rightist policy now that the way for a 'leftist policy' is blocked, or is considered to be so. These gentlemen won't frighten anybody any more.[11]

With considerable acuteness Weber observed how under the prevailing circumstances the German Social Democratic Party was not a serious political force. In his view the Social Democrats had only two mutually exclusive strategies available:

(1) a reformist strategy which should aim at attaining gradual changes in social and constitutional matters; this would have required ending meaningless repetitions of ritualistic formulas concerning the socialist *Endziel* (the final goal);
(2) anarchist struggle against the established system, regardless of the immediate consequences; this amounted to a radical *gesinnungsethisch* (utopian fundamentalist) approach, which, though perhaps impracticable, was at least honest and straightforward.

It goes without saying that, while Weber respected the second alternative as plausible for those who sincerely believed in socialism, he supported a reformist policy, and sought to establish personal contacts with such leading 'revisionists' as Eduard Bernstein.

From his vantage-point the Social Democrats' avoidance of making clear-cut decisions regarding the two policy options open to them was disastrous. They immersed themselves in a socialist Utopia, merely reiterating the traditional determinist socialist liturgy. This quietist policy, masked by verbal radicalism and revolutionary rhetoric, effectively forestalled constitutional reforms in Imperial Germany by causing the Social Democrats' potential allies to unite against them. Weber pointed this out perhaps most effectively in his essay on the Russian Revolution of 1905, written in 1906:

> There is not a shadow of plausibility in the view that the economic development of society, as such, must nurture the growth either of inwardly 'free' personalities or of 'altruistic' ideals. Do we find the slightest hint of anything of that kind in those who, in their own opinion, are borne forward by 'material development' to inevitable triumph? Among the masses, the 'respectable' Social Democrats drill the spiritual parade, and instead of directing their thoughts to an other-worldly paradise (which according to Puritanism should *also* inspire respectable achievements in the service of this worldly 'freedom'), they turn their minds to a paradise in this world, and thereby make of it a kind of vaccination for the vested interests of the existing order. They accustom their pupils to a submissive attitude towards dogmas and party authorities, or to indulgence in the fruitless play-acting of mass strikes or the idle enjoyment of the enervating howls of their hired journalists, which are as harmless as they are, in the end, laughable in the eyes of their enemies. In short, they accustom them to a 'hysterical wallowing in emotion', which replaces and inhibits economic and political thought and action. The only plant which can grow on this infertile soil, once the 'eschatological' age of the movement has passed and generation after generation has vainly clenched its fists in its pockets or bared its teeth towards heaven, is that of spiritual apathy.[12]

Weber's intensive correspondence with Robert Michels concerning parties and party organisations, and in particular the German Social Democratic Party, occurred when Michels was working on what was later to become *Political Parties*. Naturally, Michels bitterly criticised the Social Democratic Party for having become an oligarchical and undemocratic organisation. Weber took a radically different line. He thought it useless to criticise this development (which was apparently inevitable and irreversible) from the vantage-point of Michels's fundamentalist position. And he lectured the latter about his seemingly utopian views on socialism and democracy:

> How much resignation will you still have to put up with? Such notions as 'will of the people', 'genuine will of the people', have long-since ceased to exist for me, they are fictions. . . . All ideas for getting rid of the domination of men over men by whatever sophisticated forms of democracy and socialism are utterly utopian.[13]

Referring to Ostrogorski's examination of politics in the United States, Weber predicted that the German Social Democratic Party would turn into a *ganz kommune Parteimaschine* – a common party machine. As a bureaucratic mass party, it would no longer be a threat to the existing social order. In due course it would become a pragmatic working-class party pursuing reformist policies. He even contemplated, though entirely along theoretical lines, actually joining such a party himself: 'only the credo of the Social Democrats I would not be able to share honestly and this might prevent me from joining them . . . even though it is after all merely a lip-service much like the *Apostolicum*'.[14]

WEBER AND BOURGEOIS REFORMISM

Weber's assessment of the character of the Social Democratic Party in Imperial Germany was matched by his contempt for bourgeois fears about an alleged 'red danger'. On the contrary, Weber pleaded for the Social Democrats to be given a fair share of influence and power in the political arena, whether in local government, in the federal states or at the Reich level. He welcomed the participation of Social Democrats in local government. Likewise he wanted the Free Trade Unions to be acknowledged as equal partners of management and as the legitimate representatives of the workers' interests in all matters regarding industrial relations. He strongly condemned paragraph 15 of the *Reichsgewerbeordnung* (the German industrial and commercial legal code) which made any intimidation of strike-breakers, even of an entirely peaceful nature,

97

a legal offence.[15] On many occasions he polemicised against the paternalistic rule of management in heavy industry. He would have nothing to do with the *Herr im Haus* attitude of many German entrepreneurs and condemned 'yellow' unions. Neither did he support semi-official arbitration boards designed to restrain strike action. It was the state's duty to provide a fair legal framework within which unions and entrepreneurs could freely conduct struggles over wages and working conditions.

Weber considered the official policy of hampering the growth of trade unionism through a gamut of legal and administrative measures to be most harmful for the development of relatively harmonious industrial relations in an advanced industrial society such as Imperial Germany. Instead he wanted a liberal system of industrial relations in which the trade unions would not be subjected to rigid governmental control but would be left to carry on the fight for workers' economic and social interests as best they could, as was the case in contemporary Great Britain.

In late 1912 Weber participated in the formation of a group of progressive academics interested in social reform.[16] He planned to launch a *Socialpolitische Vereinigung* outside the *Verein für Socialpolitik*, which by then was dominated by conservative academics. This new association was intended to revive public interest in social reform and halt the trends towards reducing or even scrapping parts of the social welfare system which had come into being during the previous decades.

In the end this effort failed, largely due to a personal rift with Lujo Brentano over whether or not Social Democrats should be asked to join in its initial stages, with Weber (for purely tactical reasons) negatively disposed. This was all the more regrettable as Weber had consistently denounced discrimination against scholars holding socialist convictions, widely practised by the German academic community and the educational authorities. He made his position known when Michels was refused the chance to qualify as a university lecturer due to his membership in the SPD, demanding that the ban on the habilitation of socialist scholars be lifted. He had also opened the pages of the *Archiv für Sozialwissenschaft* to socialist scholars wherever possible, though with limited success since there were but few of them prepared to publish in a bourgeois journal.

Weber's attitude was straightforward enough. He wanted Social

Democrats to be treated on an equal basis in all spheres of public activity and he surely would have welcomed a policy 'from Bassermann to Bebel', as Friedrich Naumann put it at the time, namely the formation of a parliamentary coalition of all progressive forces in German society, Social Democratic and liberal alike.

WEBER AND THE WORLD WAR

After the outbreak of the First World War, Weber initially became a staunch supporter of Bethmann Hollweg's policy of 'reorientation' which proposed even-handed co-operation with the Social Democrats and envisaged constitutional reforms when peace returned. Weber welcomed the loyal attitude of the Social Democrats, who rallied behind the government and joined other classes in the common war effort. He strongly favoured a policy placing the Social Democrats on an equal footing with the other political parties rather than treating them as outcasts, as had been official policy before the outbreak of war, thereby strengthening the fragile partnership between the working class and the government which had developed as a consequence of the Social Democrats' new position.

However, he soon recognised the weaknesses of the official policy of 'reorientation', which merely held out vague promises of concessions to the working class after the war as a quid pro quo for proper conduct in matters relating to the war effort. By the spring of 1916 Weber had become one of the most outspoken critics of Prussian three-class suffrage, and supported the Social Democrats' increasingly insistent demands for immediate electoral reform. Weber's public campaign against the existing limited suffrage in Prussia culminated in an article in the *Frankfurter Zeitung* late in 1917 where he argued that come what may suffrage had to be given to the soldiers returning from the war, echoing similar arguments which led in Great Britain to the Electoral Act of 1918.[17]

The second issue on which he joined forces with the Social Democrats was his determined opposition to all extreme annexationist policies. Unlike the Social Democrats, Weber did not oppose annexations in principle; in Eastern Europe he was in favour of establishing a number of autonomous nation-states under the loosely defined overlordship of Imperial Germany. But he agreed

99

with the Social Democrats that the war should be conducted on defensive grounds and not be extended by a single day for annexationist purposes. He also rejected unrestricted submarine warfare, which the German government had been considering since March 1916 and instituted in January 1917, thereby provoking the United States to declare war and ending all hopes of a speedy conclusion of a negotiated peace. By 1917 Weber dropped his reservations about co-operating directly with the Social Democrats in order to counteract the extremist propaganda of the German Fatherland Party and on 5 November he spoke jointly with the Social Democratic deputy Wolfgang Heine – albeit a member of the right wing of the party – at a public rally in Munich, 'for a peace of conciliation and against the Pan–German danger'.[18]

During the war years Weber increased his confidence in the Social Democrats' reliability on matters of national interest. On the occasion of the Stockholm Peace Conference, called by the Second International in May 1917, Weber even considered assisting (however indirectly) the head of the German delegation, Gustav Scheidemann.[19] He suggested that Scheidemann be accompanied by one of his Russian friends, Dr Gutmann. Admittedly Weber hoped thereby to put his view across that 'if German Social Democracy were to conclude a *bad* peace, we will have the reactionary rule of the Pan–Germans after the war, and they [the Social Democrats] will lose all influence'.[20]

Weber was increasingly concerned that the Social Democrats might, under the impact of the Russian February Revolution, gradually drift leftwards. His essays on the events in Russia were to a large degree addressed to the Social Democrats in an attempt to immunise them against the revolutionary slogans emanating from Petrograd. Weber eventually went so far as to argue that the Soviet regime was nothing more than a rather ordinary military dictatorship and that Russian imperialism would soon resurface once again. He pleaded with both the Social Democrats and trade-union leaders to remain loyal to the national cause, publicly condemning the mass strikes of April 1917, and even more so those of January 1918, though personally furious about the outrageous conduct of the German peace negotiators at Brest-Litovsk which had stimulated the last strike. On the other hand, he had some personal sympathy for the strikers' motives and even defended the conduct of the leaders of the Social Democratic Party when they joined the central strike committee in Berlin in January 1918, thereby publicly demonstrating solidarity with the strikers and concluding the strike without further fuelling public unrest. During these weeks he confided privately that revolutionary developments were likely if the war was not brought rapidly to an end, especially as there was still no sign that long-overdue constitutional reforms would be implemented in the near future.

WEBER AND REVOLUTION

Weber was aware of how difficult it had been for the Social Democrats to sustain their policy of national loyalty under conditions that were steadily deteriorating both internally and externally. The crucial test for his views on the Social Democrats came, however, with the outbreak of revolution in November 1918.

Weber's initial reaction was negative in the extreme. In a violent emotional outburst he called the revolution an irresponsible 'bloody carnival' which had dealt a death blow to Germany's few remaining chances of obtaining reasonable peace conditions. He also raged against the utter chaos allegedly created by the Workers' and Soldiers' Councils. Only after he joined the Heidelberg Workers' and Soldiers' Council as a representative of the middle classes did he begin to appreciate their position. Likewise he found nothing favourable to say about the *Rät der Volksbeauftragten* (Council of Peoples' Representatives), even though he had nearly become secretary of state for the interior and had been considered for the post of German ambassador to Vienna. Somewhat later he restrained his polemics against the revolutionary regime, especially after the Independent Socialists had left the government. He conceded that while they were, in his view, either irresponsible demagogues or at best romantics harbouring revolutionary dreams of a pacifist Utopia, the Majority Socialists were 'honest people' operating under difficult circumstances.

Within weeks of the November Revolution, Max Weber spoke publicly in favour of creating a new democratic party. He became actively involved in preparations for its establishment in Frankfurt and also played a part in founding the *Deutsche Demokratische Partei* (the first initiative for which had been taken in early December 1918 by Theodor Wolff and some prominent liberals in

Berlin, including his brother Alfred). In a widely publicised speech at a rally in Frankfurt on 1 December 1918 Weber pleaded for the middle classes to shake off the political apathy to which they had succumbed in the initial stages of the revolution and participate in the establishment of a new democratic order in conjunction with the Majority Socialists.[21] Under the circumstances whole-hearted co-operation with the Majority Socialists appeared to be the only viable course of action for progressive liberals, and indeed for the middle classes as a whole. In the same speech Weber declared emphatically: 'All honest, unreservedly pacifist and radical bourgeois democrats and Social Democrats could work side by side for decades to come until their ways might eventually have to part again.'[22]

During the following weeks Weber became deeply involved in the electoral campaign of the German Democratic Party for the National Assembly. He spoke at more than twenty public rallies, and argued for the implementation of a Majority Socialist/Liberal alliance.[23] He went so far as to suggest that, under the prevailing conditions, some degree of nationalisation of the means of production might be unavoidable and perhaps even welcome. In principle, however, he always stuck to his conviction that only dynamic capitalism could rescue Germany from utter economic ruin. He considered the half-hearted and ill-considered nationalisation policies of the *Rat der Volksbeauftragten* absolutely futile, since they would endanger a desperately needed economic recovery and equally play into the hands of the Allied powers, which might find it easier to extract reparations from state, rather than privately owned, industries.

Weber continued to object to nationalisation, though for tactical reasons in his campaign speeches he had made statements to the contrary. His last public statement on this issue occurred in June 1920 when he was invited to join the Second Commission on Nationalisation as a representative of the German Democratic Party. He refused with unaccustomed harshness:

Everywhere, at all gatherings, private or public, I have declared that socialisation as it is presently understood is utter 'nonsense'. We are in need of entrepreneurs like Herr Stinnes, or others of his calibre. I have said about the Shop Stewards' Law (*Betriebsverfassungsgesetz*) 'Ecraser l'infame' for it is most disastrous if seen from the vantage-point of a possible future socialist order.[24]

Weber had planned to give a lecture course on socialism at the University of Munich during the following summer term. His premature death deprived us of a comprehensive assessment of socialism and Social Democratic policies which might have wound up his lifelong intellectual dialogue with Marx and his followers. It was not to be. One thing, however, is sure; he was always a fair antagonist of the socialist movement, prepared to respect those socialists who fought honestly for their cause, however wrong he considered it to be.

NOTES

1 See for the general context W. J. Mommsen, *Max Weber und die deutsche Politik 1890–1920*, 2nd edn, Tübingen, J. C. B. Mohr (Paul Siebeck), 1974, pp. 73ff. *passim* (English trans. *Max Weber and German Politics, 1890–1920*, Chicago University Press, 1985). Henceforth quoted: Mommsen, *Max Weber*.

2 For a more detailed assessment of Weber's relationship with Marx, see W. J. Mommsen, 'Kapitalismus und Sozialismus. Die Auseinandersetzung mit Karl Marx', in *Max Weber. Gesellschaft, Politik und Geschichte*, Frankfurt, Suhrkamp, 1974, pp. 144–207 (English transl. in R. J. Antonio and R. M. Glassman (eds), *A Weber–Marx Dialogue*, Lawrence, University of Kansas Press, 1985). See also G. Roth, 'Das historische Verhältnis der Weberschen Soziologie zum Marxismus', *Kölner Zeitschrift für Soziologie und Sozialpsychologie*, vol. 20, 1968, pp. 432ff. (English trans. in R. Bendix and G. Roth, *Scholarship and Partisanship. Essays on Max Weber*, Berkeley, University of California Press, 1971, pp. 227–52). See also Jürgen Kocka's essay 'Social science between dogmatism and decisionism: a comparison of Karl Marx and Max Weber', in R. J. Antonio and R. M. Glassman, op. cit. (note 2); W. J. Mommsen, *The Age of Bureaucracy. Perspectives on the Political Sociology of Max Weber*, Oxford, Blackwell, 1974, pp. 47ff.

3 Letter to Robert Michels, 6 November 1907, Fondazione Luigi Einaudi, Turin. Cf. W. J. Mommsen, *Max Weber*, p. 116, n. 84.

4 See *inter alia Gesammelte Aufsätze zur Wissenschaftslehre*, 3rd edn, Tübingen, J. C. B. Mohr (Paul Siebeck), 1968, pp. 166ff., 204ff.

5 'Der Sozialismus', in W. J. Mommsen with G. Hübinger (eds),

Max Weber. Zur Politik im Weltkrieg. Schriften und Reden 1914–1918, *Max Weber Gesamtausgabe*, Vol. 1, 15, Tübingen, J. C. B. Mohr (Paul Siebeck), 1984, p. 616. Henceforth quoted *MWG* 1/15.

6 See Mommsen, 1974, op. cit. (note 3), pp. 58–70.

7 *MWG* 1/15, pp. 597–633.

8 *Gesammelte Politische Schriften*, 2nd edn, Tübingen, J. C. B. Mohr (Paul Siebeck), 1958, p. 22.

9 Ibid., pp. 22ff.

10 The following analysis is based upon W. J. Mommsen, 'Max Weber and Roberto Michels. An asymmetrical partnership', *Archives Européennes de Sociologie*, vol. XXII, 1981, pp. 100–16, and W. J. Mommsen, 'Roberto Michels und Max Weber: gesinnungsethischer Fundamentalismus versus verantwortungsethischer Pragmatismus', in W. J. Mommsen, and J. Osterhammel (eds), *Max Weber and his Contemporaries*, London, Allen & Unwin, 1987. See also W. Röhrich, *Robert Michels. Vom sozialistischsyndikalistischen zum faschistischen Credo*, Berlin, Duncker & Humblot, 1972; D. Beetham, 'From socialism to fascism: the relation between theory and practice in the work of Robert Michels', *Political Studies*, vol. 25, 1977, pp. 3–24, 161–81; and L. A. Scaff, 'Max Weber and Robert Michels', *American Journal of Sociology*, vol. 96, 1981, pp. 1269ff. See further Guenther Roth's short assessment of the attitudes of Weber and Michels to socialism, in R. Bendix and G. Roth, op. cit. (note 2), pp. 247–52.

11 Letter to Michels, 8 October 1906, Fondazione Luigi Einaudi, Turin. Cf. Mommsen, *Max Weber*, p. 114.

12 'Zur Lage der bürgerlichen Demokratie in Rußland', *Archiv für Socialwissenschaft und Socialpolitik*, vol. XXII, Beilage, pp. 120ff.

13 Letter to Roberto Michels, 4 August 1908, Fondazione Luigi Einaudi, Turin.

14 See ibid.: 'the reason why I would become a Social Democrat . . . only if everything goes by the board – a mutilation of the suffrage – is first my absolute scepticism regarding its credo, second my low estimation of the political qualifications of the "leaders"'. See also letter to Toennies of 9 May 1909, quoted in Mommsen, *Max Weber*, p. 137, n. 152.

15 See W. J. Mommsen, *Max Weber*, pp. 125ff.

16 Ibid., pp. 127ff., and also B. Schäfers, 'Ein Rundschreiben Max Webers zur Sozialpolitik', *Soziale Welt*, vol. 18, 1967, pp. 261–72.

17 'Das preußische Wahlrecht', *MWG* 1/15, pp. 222ff.

18 *MWG* 1/15, pp. 720ff.

19 See Mommsen, *Max Weber*, pp. 273ff.

20 Ibid., p. 274.

21 'Das neue Deutschland', Speech on 4 December 1918 in Frankfurt, in W. J. Mommsen with W. Schwentker (eds), *Max Weber. Zur Neuordnung Deutschlands. Schriften und Reden 1918–1920, Max Weber Gesamutausgabe*, Vol. 1/16, Tübingen, 1988 (henceforth quoted *MWG* 1/16), pp. 207–13.
22 Ibid., p. 312.
23 For a comprehensive collection of reports on Max Weber's public speeches in 1918–19 at various election campaign rallies of the German Democratic Party, see *MWG* 1/16, pp. 293ff.
24 Letter to Karl Petersen, 14 April 1920, quoted in Mommsen, *Max Weber*, p. 333, n. 105.

4
Reformism and the 'Bourgeoisification' of the Labour Movement

David Beetham

It is a commonplace of historiography that not only the kind of explanation we give of historical events and processes, but also what we define as significant and deserving of explanation in the first place, depends upon a set of prior assumptions that may be unstated or only barely articulated. In particular, the identification of a historical outcome as significant because *unexpected*, and therefore as raising a special problem for explanation, depends upon assumptions about what could reasonably have been expected, about what a typical course of events would have been. Such counterfactual assumptions are no mere idle fancy or speculation, but constitute one of the standard bases for the selection of historical problems. It is a task of historical theory, though by no means an uncontroversial one, to render the assumptions underlying such processes of selection explicit, so that they can be subjected to examination and, where possible, made more secure.

Ever since Marx and Engels set out in the *Communist Manifesto* a scenario of the working-class movement growing ever stronger despite all its set-backs, eventually winning the 'battle of democracy' and using its political supremacy to wrest the ownership of capital from the bourgeoisie, their followers have seen the reformist and accommodationist tendencies of the European labour movements as constituting not only a deviation to be combated, but a problem requiring explanation. That scenario was to be sure a prospective one, and comprised a synthesis of historical elements drawn from the experience of different countries – British industrial development, French revolutionary experience, the German philosophical tradition – in a way that was not true of any one alone. Yet the expectations it embodied were subsequently reinforced by the analysis of *Capital,* which provided a theoretical explanation for the antithesis between the interests of capital and labour and for the incapacity of the capitalist system to meet the basic needs of the working class despite temporary alleviations, an incapacity which could be expected to be abundantly confirmed over time by the workers' own experience.

As is well attested, Marx himself did not expect a socialist consciousness to arise automatically from the process of capitalist development, nor to lead directly to revolutionary politics. His correspondence with Engels is full of regrets at the absence of a revolutionary temper among the British working class, which he attributed variously to its internal divisions and to its lack of theoretical sophistication or revolutionary tradition, all features that were exacerbated by its failure to create an independent working-class party. Yet these were *ad hoc* judgments, which did not constitute a sustained theory. And they were insufficient in themselves to account for what subsequently happened. The establishment of nationwide labour organisations and political parties throughout the countries of Europe led to the reproduction of reformist politics, not as a temporary expedient, but as a persistent tendency. That this was not just a British phenomenon seemed to be amply demonstrated at the end of the 1890s by the combination of the Bernstein controversy in Germany and Millerand's entry into a bourgeois government in France.

The aim of this essay is to provide a systematic review of the different explanations advanced for reformism in the decade or so around the turn of the century, when reformism came to be seen as a problem not only to be combated practically but requiring explanation at a theoretical level also.[1] All its opponents shared the assumption that reformism was antithetical to the permanent interests of the working class, and that it therefore did not constitute an autonomous mode of politics or form of consciousness for the class; its ultimate origins were to be found within the bourgeois society which it was the task of socialist politics to transform. All, that is to say, saw reformism as a mode of 'bourgeoisification' of proletarian politics. That term, however, hides markedly differing accounts of the *process* whereby the reformist tendency came to find its home within the organisations of the working class.

I shall distinguish three broadly different accounts of that process, which can be loosely termed institutional, social and economic respectively. The 'institutional' version argued that it was through the institutional structures of the labour movement, and in particular its elites, that reformism entered the working class. According to the 'social' version, the working class, being directly exposed to the influences of bourgeois society in its daily existence, generated of itself tendencies towards reformist politics, which were not simply the product of a 'deviant' leadership. The 'economic' version, finally, sought the origin of reformism in the relatively advantaged economic circumstances of the working class, whether of a particular country, or of a particular stratum, or at a particular conjuncture of the capitalist business cycle. Of these different explanations, the first two were mutually exclusive, and generated very different strategies for overcoming reformism in practice. The third, economic level of explanation offered a more particular and localised account, showing why reformism became established more firmly in some contexts than others. As such it could be used to elaborate one of the other more general explanations without contradiction, though in practice it was usually associated with the second.

What have these explanations for reformism to do with the educated middle classes? More than appears at first sight. One of the issues which the Bernstein and Millerand controversies brought to a head was the place of bourgeois intellectuals within the Social Democratic parties of Europe – what their role was, and whether they should be allowed in a proletarian movement at all. Their presence was widely held to be responsible for the reformist deviations. It was precisely in response to such assumptions that leading theoreticians of Social Democracy such as Kautsky found it necessary to insist on the essential role played by intellectuals in the party, in providing the socialist theory which enabled the working class to rise *above* reformism. So the two issues were inextricably linked, though sometimes in complex ways. Opponents of reformism were bound to take up a position on the place of bourgeois intellectuals in the labour movement, and the explanations they gave for the one depended on the position they took on the other, and vice versa.

The major part of this essay will be devoted to an examination of the three different explanations for reformism outlined above. Although they were first developed during the controversies around the turn of the century, they have been considerably elaborated since, and provide the theoretical basis for much of the historiography of the left. In the concluding section I shall turn to examine the basic assumption on which they are all founded: that 'reformism' comprises a single undifferentiated phenomenon, which constitutes a problem for explanation because it represents a deviation from what could have been expected. Finally, I shall ask what is left of the various explanations considered if this assumption is either modified or abandoned altogether.

REFORMISM AND THE POLITICAL ELITE OF THE LABOUR MOVEMENT

It has been a recurrent argument since the revisionist controversy at the turn of the century that the 'bourgeoisification' of working-class politics can be laid at the door of the leadership of the labour movement itself. A number of different variants of this argument can be distinguished in the period with which we are concerned. Most influential were the syndicalists, such as Arturo Labriola in Italy, and Edouard Berth, Hubert Lagardelle and, with some qualification, Georges Sorel in France.[2] They believed that the political party was the main site for the 'bourgeoisification' of working-class politics, and argued that only the trades unions, as exclusively proletarian organisations, could maintain the revolutionary class struggle against the existing order. A similar position was reached independently by Jan Machajski and his followers in Russia, in their critique of the leading role played by bourgeois intellectuals within Social Democracy.[3] Different from both was Robert Michels, who, though starting from a position sympathetic to syndicalism, developed a line of argument on the basis of German experience that was ultimately incompatible with it. 'Bourgeoisification', he contended, was not confined to the political party, or to the influence of bourgeois intellectuals, but arose out of the organisational structure and leadership roles of the movement as a whole, the trades unions as much as the party.[4] I shall concentrate on the syndicalist position below, and deal with the others in so far as they differed from it.

A central postulate of the syndicalists was the sharp distinction they drew between the economic sphere, in which the trades unions constituted an exclusively proletarian opposition to bourgeois society, and the political sphere, where the party, operating on bourgeois terrain, became an instrument for the bourgeoisification of the labour movement and the compromise of the revolutionary class struggle. A number of factors were seen to contribute to this process. One was that of electoral logic; in order to maximise its votes, the socialist party was bound to widen its appeal beyond the working class. Among those whom it particularly attracted were the new middle strata of white-collar workers, particularly those employed in the expanding state sector, who saw in the idea of state socialism a guarantee for their own position and prospects. This consideration was urged most forcefully by Labriola in relation to Italy, whose state employees flocked to join the PSI as the party most favourable to their own interests. Arguing that they also were 'workers', they demanded that the proletariat should continue to pay its taxes to keep them employed:

> But no one asks if it is compatible with the programme and interests of proletarian socialism to support the interests of bureaucratic parasitism. . . . It is perfectly evident that a party which depends upon state employees and seeks their support cannot represent any serious threat to the political order.[5]

Although the admixture of non-proletarian elements in the PSI was particularly striking, the syndicalists regarded it as a special case of a general problem: the political party as an electoral organisation could not be socially homogeneous; and heterogeneity meant dilution of the class struggle.

A second factor making for the 'bourgeoisification' of the political party was the fact that its characteristic sphere of operation lay in the bourgeois arena of parliament. Parliament, argued Labriola, was an institution run by the professional classes for securing compromises between the various factions of the bourgeoisie in the common defence of property. Its mode of operation as a forum for debate and the scrutiny of expenditure and legislation was antithetical to the idea of social transformation. 'It is difficult to imagine', he wrote, 'how a system so essentially bourgeois as Parliament could possibly become an instrument for the emancipation of the proletariat.'[6] Socialist party deputies tended to assimilate its style and procedures, especially when the system of representation divorced them from their working-class base. Even the party itself, argued Berth, assumed the character of a bourgeois democracy, and its congresses manifested all the trappings of a parliament, with the same 'sensational sessions, loud harangues and corridor intrigues'.[7]

The most decisive factor, however, in the degeneration of the socialist party, according to the syndicalists, was the occupation of its leading positions by bourgeois intellectuals. However apparently sincere their commitment to the cause of proletarian emancipation, their whole training, outlook and style of life were in fact inimical to it. Central to the idea of an intellectual was the hierarchical division of labour, in which the mental production of those with 'white hands' was both superior to and parasitic upon the activity of manual labour. 'Most intellectuals', wrote Lagardelle, 'scorn the manual worker; they readily imagine that they are omniscient and omnicompetent, and should therefore be omnipotent. "Work to the workers, power to the educated" is their slogan.'[8] They were particularly attracted by the idea of state socialism, in which they would replace the capitalists in control of production. In practice, however, their concern with obtaining public office for themselves made them reformist rather than revolutionary. 'The proletariat will have conquered power sufficiently', wrote Labriola, 'once it has nominated them to public office and given them the means to influence public opinion'. A socialist party with such a leadership, he concluded, could be defined as a 'suitable organisation of the moral and material interests of the professional stratum; from this stem its various degenerative features'.[9]

The figures quoted by Labriola of the proportion of PSI deputies with professional occupations (23 out of 33) gave added point to his argument.[10] But was the situation in Italy exceptional? Berth argued that the exact number was irrelevant; however few, the deputies of bourgeois origin would always be more at home in parliament, and come to dominate the socialist fraction:

In a socialist movement that is exclusively or largely electoral and Parliamentary, the bourgeois intellectuals will always predominate, qualitatively if not quantitatively. Parliamentarism is their natural vocation. An intellectual is in his element in Parliament; a worker, by contrast, is like a fish out of water.[11]

Parliament, he continued, is a kind of exchange, in which opinions and interests are advanced and evaluated, like goods in the market, and bargains are struck. And what is an intellectual? 'A dealer also, a merchant of intellectual values, a broker in the market place of ideas.' Who could be more suited to the parliamentary milieu?

But who exactly was to be included in the category of 'bourgeois intellectual'? According to Lagardelle, it was 'all those who made a living from the profession of thinking'. It was a commonplace to point out that such occupations had expanded enormously with the technical development of industry, the increase in state functions, the growth of a literate public and the expansion of education itself at all levels. In his article series 'Les intellectuels et le socialisme ouvrier' Lagardelle distinguished a number of different categories which had joined the socialist movement.[12] First were those involved in capitalist production in a technical capacity, engineers, chemists, etc., who most closely identified their lot with the proletariat. Second was the mass of the certificated yet unemployed, who, rejected by official society, found a ready source of employment in the socialist movement as journalists, officials, etc. Third were the established professionals who were attracted to socialism by the pull of fashion and by vague sentiments of sympathy for the downtrodden. Finally were the 'social pharmacists and fabricators of intellectual systems', who believed they alone had discovered the remedy for society's ills, and saw the socialist movement as a fertile ground for making converts. Of these groups, the second and third played the most significant part in the leadership of the movement, by virtue of the literary and organisational skills in which they were accomplished, and which had always equipped the intellectual for a political vocation. But what were they doing in the proletarian movement?

They represent, through the education they have received and the goal they pursue, the old parasitic, hierarchical society. They enter the labour movement as the bearers of traditional values, from whose influence it is precisely the mission of the proletariat to tear itself free. In conquering the state, in exalting the role of parties, they reinforce the hierarchical principle embodied in political and administrative institutions, which it should be the aim of the working class to eliminate or reabsorb within society itself.[13]

This last phrase points the way to the syndicalists' own strategy for overcoming the 'bourgeoisification' of the labour movement. If the socialist party had degenerated from a revolutionary organisation of the working class into an electoral organisation for sending bourgeois representatives to parliament, then the original revolutionary impetus had to be recreated within exclusively proletarian institutions, the trades unions. These were no mere associations for the achievement of piecemeal reforms, but prefigured the alternative non-hierarchical society of producers. Free from any bourgeois influence, they were ready to prosecute the class struggle to the point of overthrow of the old society, through the mass action of the general strike, unmediated by any representative process.[14]

Not everyone who accepted the syndicalists' analysis of reformism agreed with their strategy for overcoming it. But they articulated in a particularly forceful and cogent manner a widespread unease about the effects of bourgeois elements within the labour movement, particularly its leadership. Another who did the same was the Pole Jan Machajski, who reached broadly similar conclusions from his experience of Russian Social Democracy. He also developed a number of distinctive emphases of his own. One concerned the economic basis of the division between intellectual and manual labour. He argued that the differential salary commanded by the white-collared and professional strata constituted the return to a specific form of capital, intellectual capital, which depended upon the manual worker for its creation:

> The intellectual brings to market his knowledge which has been acquired thanks to the labour of the workers, just like the capitalist factory; while he studies at university . . . the workers sweat it out in the factory, producing the means for his education. . . . The diploma which he sells to the capitalist has been acquired from their exploitation.[15]

Like the syndicalists, Machajski saw these intellectual strata using the labour movement to consolidate a position for themselves within an expanded bourgeois state. But where the syndicalists claimed to be the true defenders of the Marxist tradition against the 'statist' distortions of Social Democracy, Machajski denounced

Marxism as itself the ideology of the new intellectual class. Its doctrine of the scientific inevitability of socialism, he argued, lulled the workers into passivity, and enabled their leaders to preach revolution while practising reform and supporting measures of state expansion. Even the Social Democratic revolutionaries in Russia, by postponing the socialist revolution to the distant future, and arguing that the bourgeois revolution must come first, had put themselves on the side of bourgeois constitutionalism.[16]

Machajski was not always clear about what sort of movement he would prefer in place of the Social Democracy he abhorred. Sometimes like the syndicalists he supported trades unions as the instruments of proletarian emancipation. At other times he eschewed all organisation, and advocated a general insurrection of workers, a 'worldwide general strike' by clandestine conspiracy.[17] What is clear, however, is that, like all proponents of a 'workerist' position, his starting-point was an assumption of the innately revolutionary character of the working class. The explanation for reformism was to be found in the defects or manipulations of the socialist elite, not in the working class itself, whose revolutionary spirit was made abundantly clear in the uprisings of 1905, which went far beyond the bounds within which the leaders of Russian Social Democracy sought to constrain them.

This elite perspective, the idea that the direction of the socialist movement was primarily determined by the character and outlook of its leadership, was central to the work of Robert Michels. His work is important because it is one of the few from the debates of the period that is still widely read. However, its context in these debates is usually overlooked. Michels's distinctive explanation for reformism developed from a critique of the syndicalist position, with which he had initially been in sympathy. Two criticisms in particular were important for the development of his ideas.

First, Michels argued that one could not conclude anything certain about the political tendencies of intellectuals in the socialist party simply from their bourgeois origin; they could as likely be revolutionary as reformist. Indeed, those for whom joining the party meant a sacrifice, and who had broken the bridges for any return to bourgeois society, were likely to keep their revolutionary idealism intact. He pointed to the obvious contradiction that the main spokesmen of revolutionary syndicalism were themselves members of the bourgeoisie. 'The anti-intellectualist current is in

no small measure itself the product of intellectuals . . . they address
the proletariat in the elevated language of the professoriat.'[18] It was
not so much here that the source of 'bourgeoisification' and deviation was to be found, he argued, but in a very different process:
that of the advancement of *workers* to full-time organisational and
representative positions within the party, which effectively deproletarianised them, and gave them a petty-bourgeois salary, life-
style and outlook.[19] It was particularly in Germany, where the
parliamentary representatives of the SPD were much more proletarian than in the PSI, that this process was visible. The SPD was
a vast *Klassenerhöhungsmaschine*, like the Catholic Church and the
Prussian bureaucracy, for the upward mobility of able and
ambitious members of the working class. Reformist policies were
the product of those whose own social revolution had already been
achieved, and their fear of doing anything which might endanger
their newly won positions.[20]

Michels's redefinition of the process of 'bourgeoisification' as the
advancement of workers into the ranks of the petty bourgeoisie via
the institutions of the labour movement, rather than the colonis-
ation of the movement by exiles or rejects from the bourgeoisie,
enabled him to sidestep the issue which the syndicalists had seen
as central. Bourgeois converts to socialism could be idealists or
careerists, but that was relatively unimportant. The issue tended to
obscure the much more significant question of what the institutions
of the labour movement were doing to the workers themselves.
The working class as a whole was essentially sound, he agreed with
the syndicalists, but only so long as they remained workers. Once
they became ex-workers, through being elevated to leading
positions within the movement, a process of degeneration in their
revolutionary idealism set in.

Michels's second criticism of the syndicalists followed from the
first. If 'bourgeoisification' was a process that applied to members
of the working class, then the trades unions could no more be
immune from it than the political party. Keeping the bourgeoisie
out was no solution. Again, Germany provided the crucial
evidence. The preference of German trades unions for bread-and-
butter questions and their opposition to any thought of a general
strike was, he argued, the product of a bureaucratised leadership
that was concerned only with the protection of its own position.
From the example of the trades unions Michels arrived at a general

conclusion; it was not the particular form of organisation, but the nature of organisation itself, that produced oligarchy and the degeneration of socialist ideals. In answer to Berth, Michels wrote: 'Instead of saying "the party engenders embourgeoisement", he should have said, "it is organisation which engenders embourgeoisement and deviation". But the principle of organisation includes the party and trade union equally.'[21] And in answer to Lagardelle's objection that the Germans were much more authoritarian than the French, Michels replied that differences of national temperament affected only the speed with which the process of organisation took effect, but not the process itself: 'of course the French will be more reluctant to submit to it than the Prussians . . . but they will submit all the same'.[22]

We can thus trace a process of evolution in the explanation of reformism from the syndicalist position to Michels's 'iron law of oligarchy'. Where the syndicalists defined 'bourgeoisification' as a problem of the bourgeoisie, Michels came to define it as a problem of deproletarianised workers. Where the syndicalists saw the political party as the main danger for socialism, Michels believed it lay in the nature of organisation itself, and its oligarchical tendencies. Where the syndicalists looked to the proletarian exclusiveness of the trades unions for a solution, Michels sought it, if at all, in the processes of democratic control. In fact, it is arguable whether Michels believed there was any solution to the problems he had identified; in the end he took refuge in the defeatism of 'unalterable scientific laws'.

For all these differences, however, there was one crucial premise which Michels shared with the syndicalists. This was that any explanation for the reformist deviation was to be sought in a degeneration in the leadership of the labour movement; the working class itself remained inherently socialist and essentially sound. It is precisely this assumption that was challenged in the second strand of explanation that I wish to examine.

REFORMISM AS A TENDENCY WITHIN THE WORKING CLASS

In the work of the major theorists of Social Democracy in this period is to be found an explanation for reformism which is exactly the reverse of that of the syndicalists. This was the view advanced by Kautsky that the working class on its own tended to become subject to a bourgeois outlook by virtue of the limited goals involved in purely trades-union activity. Trades unions, he argued, being associations for improving wages and conditions for particular sectors of workers, represented *Berufsinteressen* (occupational interests), not *Klassinteressen* (class interests). As such they became readily susceptible to bourgeois policies of 'divide and rule', and to a limitation of their perspective to the framework of bourgeois society. It required the Social Democratic party, representing the long-term interests of the class as a whole, and its intellectuals with their knowledge of the goal of the movement, to bring a socialist consciousness to the working class from outside. To simplify somewhat, for Kautsky the Social Democratic party and its intellectuals, far from being the cause of reformism as the syndicalists asserted, were necessary to enable the working class to transcend its limitations; any workerist exclusivism, such as the syndicalists advocated, would condemn the class to remain on the terrain of bourgeois society.[23]

As is well known, Lenin advanced the most sharply formulated exposition of this argument in *What Is to Be Done?*. The working class, he argued there, exclusively by its own efforts, was able to develop only trades-union consciousness; and this 'spontaneous development of the working-class movement, along the line of least resistance, leads to its subordination to bourgeois ideology'. Why should this be so? 'For the simple reason', he answered, 'that bourgeois ideology is far older in origin than socialist ideology, that it is more fully developed, and that it has at its disposal *immeasurably* more means of dissemination.' The theory of socialism, he argued, in contrast to trades-union consciousness, required a knowledge which went beyond the everyday experience of the working class: a knowledge of the conditions of all social classes, their interconnections, their relationships to the state, and so on. It also required a knowledge of the historical process as a whole, and its course of direction. Such a theory could be developed only by members of the bourgeois intelligentsia, and had therefore to be brought to the workers *from without*.[24]

It has often been pointed out that in these passages Lenin, far from making any radical innovation in Marxist thought, was simply restating Social Democratic orthodoxy, albeit in a typically accentu-

ated and polemical form. The lengthy quotation he gives from
Kautsky supports such a view.[25] However, Kautsky's position was
in fact more complex than this isolated quotation suggests. In the
first place, Kautsky's purpose in celebrating the role of the intellectual was primarily defensive. As I have already indicated, in the
aftermath of the revisionist controversy the place of intellectuals
within Social Democracy came under widespread attack, not just
among syndicalists. Local parties, such as those in Saxony, sought
to exclude university graduates from selection as deputies.[26] It was
not coincidental that at the Dresden party congress in 1903, which
passed the decisive vote against revisionism, the other main topic
of debate was the role of intellectuals in the party, and in particular
their 'freedom' to write about party matters in the bourgeois press.
Tumultuous applause greeted Bebel's warning that, while all
newcomers to the party should be examined carefully, 'graduates
and intellectuals should be scrutinised two and three times over'.
The masses, he added, knew better than the academics what the
proletarian class struggle was all about.[27]

It was thus in the context of a general suspicion among the
workers against the academically qualified that Kautsky made his
assertions about the indispensable role of bourgeois intellectuals
within the party. Socialism, he argued, required a knowledge of
the goal, the *Endziel*, of the historical process, and this was a
product of science. But since scientific knowledge was still a privilege of the propertied classes, it was from these strata alone that a
socialist theory could be developed:

> For this reason the proletariat is incapable of creating a vigorous
> socialism by itself; it has to be brought to it by thinkers who, armed
> with all the resources of bourgeois science, take up the standpoint of
> the proletariat, and from this perspective develop a new proletarian
> conception of history.[28]

It was no accident, he pointed out, that in England, the home of
reformism, of purely practical detailed work without *Endziel*, the
labour movement was exclusively proletarian. There 'the ideal of
the horny hand of labour' held most sway, and there was no place
for intellectuals. But without their help the class struggle of the
proletariat could 'never become a Social Democratic movement'.

Kautsky's response to the attack on intellectuals was thus to insist that they had not only a part to play in the Social Democratic movement, but an essential part. At the same time, however, he was unable to deny the main point of the attack, which was that bourgeois intellectuals had a marked propensity to support and strengthen the revisionist tendency within the party. How to explain this apparent contradiction? The elucidation of it is to be found in an earlier series of articles he wrote on 'Intellectuals and Social Democracy', which addressed the question of whether the rapidly expanding strata of intellectuals employed in industry, government and the professions could be won for socialism.[29]

In these articles Kautsky rejected the view that, because intellectuals had to sell their labour, they therefore counted as workers. Intellectual occupations had distinctive characteristics, he argued, which gave those who pursued them different interests and ideals from the proletariat. Among others was an individualist, competitive outlook, which stemmed from the fact that individuals were in constant competition with each other for career advancement. This was the antithesis of any ideal of collective solidarity. So too was the hierarchical conception of the superiority of mental over manual labour, and the belief that its privileged social position was the due reward for special intellectual endowment. Such a view was incompatible with the 'desire of the proletariat as the lowest class to abolish all privilege'. Above all, the interests of intellectuals in maintaining the market value of their qualifications led them in the direction of limiting, rather than expanding, access to further education, and hence restricting the educational opportunities of women and the working class. At this crucial point, 'the interests of the proletariat and those of the intelligentsia are diametrically opposed'.

Kautsky's conclusion was that the intellectuals could not be won *en masse* for Social Democracy, except possibly for the lowest strata of clerical workers, who had effectively been proletarianised by the creation of a 'reserve army' of the educated unemployed. For the rest, they could be won only as individuals, not as a group, by appealing to their convictions rather than their interests. But how were such convictions possible at all? For all that the interests of intellectuals diverged from those of the proletariat, Kautsky argued, they differed from those of capital also. Apart from those intellectuals who were themselves *rentiers*, or were employed as spokesmen for capital, they had no interest in capitalist exploitation. On the basic issues between capital and labour, therefore, they were able to be independent. In this they resembled the peasantry and petty bourgéoisie, though with one crucial difference; because of their intellectual training they were able to see beyond particular interests and local conflicts and grasp the nature of social development as a whole:

> The intelligentsia is that social stratum that can most easily succeed in raising itself above the narrow-mindedness of class and status position, that can take an idealist standpoint beyond immediate sectional interests, and has the vision to represent the permanent needs of the whole society.[30]

It was precisely this ability that led individual members of the intelligentsia to embrace the cause of the proletariat, and that enabled them to develop the socialist theory necessary to its future emancipation.

Kautsky's attitude to intellectuals and Social Democracy was thus more complex than can be captured by single passages from his writings. It was also inherently ambivalent. On the one hand intellectuals were necessary to develop socialist theory and combat bourgeois ideology, and their academic training gave them the breadth of view and the critical capacity to perform this task. On the other hand that same training made them members of a social stratum whose sectional interests and outlook were quite at variance with those of the proletariat. Kautsky along with others in the SPD tended to resolve this contradiction in practice by drawing a distinction between the 'sheep' and the 'goats': between those who embraced the socialist cause out of conviction in its ultimate victory, who identified with the proletariat in the class struggle and so came to 'change their character . . . losing the specific mentality of the intellectual';[31] and those, on the other hand, who joined the party out of fashion, sentiment or careerism, and in whom the basic instincts of the intellectual prevailed over any socialist commitment. Although these types could not always be distinguished in practice, there were a number of demands that could be made upon intellectuals to minimise their possible danger to the party. They should place themselves firmly on the side of the class struggle. They should sever their links with bourgeois society. They should submit to the discipline of the party. These were the demands made in the aftermath of the Dresden congress. And it was precisely their refusal to accept them that was seen to characterise the bourgeois intellectuals of the revisionist tendency.[32]

If we turn now to Lenin, we find that his writings of this period reveal the same ambivalence towards intellectuals as Kautsky's. This is hardly surprising, seeing that he followed Kautsky so closely.[33] For all his insistence on the necessity of intellectuals and their scientific knowledge to Social Democracy, Lenin was just as emphatic that, as a group, they shared characteristics which were damaging to the party. They brought bourgeois critiques of Marxism wholesale into the movement. They elevated freedom of individual opinion above class solidarity. They resisted attempts to create a disciplined central party organisation. And it was their extensive participation in the movement, he argued, that had 'promoted such a rapid spread of Bernsteinianism'.[34]

However, the intellectuals did not produce this effect on their own. Lenin's distinctive contribution to the explanation of reformism was to make explicit the link between the spontaneity of the workers or 'economism', on the one side, and the 'opportunism' of the bourgeois intelligentsia, on the other. It was the combination of the two that made reformism such an influential tendency. In like manner his strategies for combating each were also interconnected. Lenin's answer to 'economism' was the socialist theory developed by intellectuals. His answer to 'opportunism' was the collective discipline of proletarian organisation. It was the two together that constituted his theory of the Social Democratic party. It required the theory of socialism to make proletarian solidarity revolutionary. But it also required the proletarian discipline of the party to keep the socialist intellectual from backsliding.[35]

In conclusion, the theoreticians of Social Democracy, even while asserting the crucial role of the intellectuals, were forced to concede the criticisms made of them within the party, criticisms which the syndicalists were to make the centrepiece of their explanation for reformism. But this should not be allowed to obscure the fundamental difference between the two theories. The syndicalists advanced a highly simplified, almost deterministic account of the relation between class position and political ideas. In their view the proletariat alone could develop socialism, while members of the bourgeoisie remained imprisoned within an individualist perspective. 'Bourgeoisification' was for them a purely sociological category, and the bourgeoisification of the labour movement a purely institutional process, whereby the leading positions in the party came to be increasingly occupied by personnel from the bourgeoisie. What such an account manifestly could not explain was their own role as bourgeois spokesmen for the theory of proletarian exclusiveness. Nor could it explain the English trades unions, most workerist and yet reformist of all, without recourse to extraneous factors such as 'national character'.

The Social Democratic theoreticians, in contrast, operated with a more complex social explanation of ideas, whereby class position was no simple determinant of political outlook. The proletariat could itself become subject to the influence of bourgeois ideas, because these were pervasive within society at large. 'Bourgeoisification' for them was an ideological rather than a sociological category, in the sense that it was defined in terms of the content of ideas rather than the class position of the person holding them. And its roots lay in wider social processes than the political institutions or leadership of the labour movement itself. By the same token it was possible for individual members of the bourgeoisie, through a scientific understanding of society and the historical process, to transcend the viewpoint of their own class and embrace the theory of socialism. Whether this was merely special pleading on the part of Kautsky and Lenin, as the syndicalists maintained, depends ultimately on one's view of the validity of their socialist theory itself, and its claims to scientific status.

It is possible at this point to identify the most fundamental difference beetween the Social Democrats and the syndicalists in their explanation of reformism. This lay in their rival accounts of what a socialist consciousness and socialist theory entailed. For the theoreticians of Social Democracy, socialism was primarily a *science*, involving a scientific understanding of economy, social relations and historical process. As such it could be developed only by those with access to a scientific culture, the bourgeoisie, and brought by them to the proletariat via the medium of the party. For the theorists of syndicalism, on the other hand, socialism was primarily a *morality*, a producers' ethic of equality and solidarity, which stood in opposition to the whole of bourgeois culture. As such it could be developed only by the proletariat itself, from out of its own situation and experience, through the medium of the trades unions. 'The elaboration of socialism is the mission of the proletariat,' wrote Lagardelle; it 'creates institutions and an ideology which are its very own . . . and carries within itself the economic and moral values of the new society'.[36] Bourgeois intellectuals were therefore unnecessary to socialism, and their presence in the party could be made to carry all the weight of the explanation for reformist deviation.

Each of these competing positions claimed to be the true heir to the Marxist tradition. The syndicalists appealed to Marx's repreated insistence that the workers must be the agents of their own self-emancipation. They quoted lengthy denunciations by both Marx and Engels of those 'who wished to place the working masses under the tutelage of new categories of the professional intelligentsia'.[37] And they pointed to Marx's anti-statism in his writings on the Paris Commune, where he spoke of 'restoring to society all the powers till now absorbed by the state'.[38] The Social Democrats in turn quoted from the *Communist Manifesto*, according to which the working class was to 'win the battle of democracy' under the guidance of the Communists, who 'have the advantage of clearly understanding the line of march, the conditions and the ultimate general results of the proletarian movement'. They pointed to Marx's role as a bourgeois intellectual and man of science, and quoted Engels's glorification of the contribution of 'scientific socialism' to the proletarian class struggle.[39] What Bernstein had said in justification of his own revisionist argument – that 'it is Marx who carries the point against Marx himself'[40] – applied with particular force to the disagreements between revisionism's opponents.

THE ECONOMIC BASIS OF REFORMISM

It could be argued that the most characteristically 'Marxist' explanation advanced by the critics of reformism in this period was a directly economic one. Reformism became established as a political tendency, it was argued, because the working class, or a section of it, actually won an improvement in its material conditions through reform, however temporarily. This was an explanation that tended to be advanced by Social Democrats, who saw the roots of reformism in the working class itself, rather than by syndicalists, who located it in the character of its political elite. But even with the former we are presented at first sight with a contradiction. If the 'spontaneous development of the working-class movement', as Lenin maintained, led to its subordination to bourgeois ideology, what need was there of any further explanation in terms of particular economic circumstances? The answer, it seems, is that while reformism as a political tendency was present everywhere, it became a dominant tendency within the labour movement only at particular times and places. And these needed special explanation.

A further point of clarification is required at the outset. When writers linked reformism to the economic circumstances of workers, it was a quite different phenomenon from that described as 'embourgeoisement' by political sociologists during the 1950s and after. The latter debate concerned the supposed adoption of middle-class living and consumption patterns by affluent workers, on the basis of which they transferred their voting allegiance to conservative parties. No such process was in question in this earlier period. Here it was a matter of relative material improvement making policies of class compromise more plausible. 'Bourgeoisification' was thus again an ideological or political category, rather than a social one, though it had its material base. It was a question of the labour movement adopting a political stance acceptable to bourgeois opinion, rather than the working class itself adopting a bourgeois life-style, which was simply impossible, except for the few who rose out of the class altogether.

The logic of the explanation was relatively straightforward. At certain times and places, capitalists had room to meet demands for higher wages, shorter hours and improved working conditions, and also an incentive to do so. At such points the politics of social reform looked particularly attractive to the working class, or to sections of it. Two situations where capital had this room for manoeuvre were where it enjoyed a monopoly position, and in periods of boom. The classic exemplar of both was Britain in the middle of the nineteenth century.

It was widely accepted among the theoreticians of Social Democracy not only that Britain, or England as they called it, was the home of social reform, but that this was a consequence of its dominant position in the world market till the end of the 1880s. Engels had himself made this connection in correspondence with Marx, where he described the English proletariat as becoming 'more and more bourgeois', and 'merrily sharing the feast of England's monopoly of the world market'.[41] And in his 1885 introduction to the *Condition of the Working Class* he made explicit the political consequence. 'That is the reason', he wrote, 'why, since the dying out of Owenism, there has been no Socialism in England.'[42] It required only a short step for later Social Democrats to conclude that Bernstein was the spokesman of an alien tradition which he had imbibed during his sojourn in England.

This was the view advanced, for example, by Rosa Luxemburg in an article entitled 'Die englische Brille' ('English spectacles').[43] She began the article by challenging the view that the history of English trades unionism had always been pacific. Until the late 1840s, she argued, workers' attempts to improve their lot had been met with repression. But then the attitudes of employers underwent a change. The decisive factor was 'the achievement by English industry of undisputed supremacy on the world market'. This put the whole of the English employing classes in the position of an individual employer when business is in full swing; they would do anything to avoid a disruption of production. 'The golden era of industry', she wrote, 'made concessions to the workers both necessary in the interests of undisturbed business, and also materially painless.'[44]

Such concessions led the trades unions, in the wake of the Chartist defeat, to adopt a politics of everyday demands within the existing order: 'instead of the socialist class struggle, a bourgeois struggle for a bourgeois existence'. The employers fostered this approach by means of moral as well as material influences. English public opinion was sympathetic, but not to any labour movement, only to that which took its stand on the terrain of bourgeois society:

> The large-hearted bourgeois with his friendly disposition to the workers, and the blinkered proletarian with his narrow bourgeois perspective, presupposed one another, and were merely two sides of the same relationship, whose common basis lay in the unique economic position enjoyed by England from the middle of the century, viz., the stability and undisputed supremacy of its industry on the world market.[45]

Since the 1880s, however, she went on, this dominant position had been progressively undermined, and with it the room for English industrialists to make painless concessions to the workers. Arbitration procedures were progressively abandoned; the conflict between capital and labour increasingly took on the character of a class struggle; and the English trades unions began to resemble their militant and politicised counterparts on the Continent. So the older English model of a labour movement, she concluded, on which Bernstein set so much store, was not only inappropriate for Germany; it had ceased to be relevant for England either, now that the unique conditions had passed which made it possible.[46]

Kautsky gave a broadly similar account, but he superimposed upon it a more complex periodisation of the years 1837–90 in England, based upon his belief that the militancy of the labour movement followed closely the rise and fall of the business cycle.[47] As the latter oscillated between boom and slump, so the activity of the movement varied between periods of political stagnation, when its economic organisations advanced and social reform was on the agenda, and periods of political unrest, when it became clear that purely economic efforts were insufficient, and the struggle moved onto the political plane. The periods of economic advance, however, benefited only a section of the workers. Trades unions, he argued, tend to recruit only from an 'aristocracy of labour', and 'raise a stratum of privileged workers above the class as a whole'. The employers were willing to make concessions to these groups, because they knew they would have a divisive effect. But it was only because of England's special economic position that these tactics could have such a lasting effect in depoliticising the labour movement.[48]

Like Luxemburg, Kautsky concluded that the economic basis of social reform in England had been undermined by the loss of the country's world supremacy. Furthermore, he argued, the new monopolist stage of capitalist development made a reformist labour movement unsustainable anywhere. It was not just the intensity of international competition that allowed industrialists little room for concessions. The growth of trusts, cartels and employers' organisations across whole industries fundamentally altered the balance of power between capital and labour. The conditions for successful union advance were those where well-organised unions confronted individual capitalists in competition with each other. The concentration of industry altered all this, and forced the labour movement increasingly onto the terrain of the political struggle.[49]

The implications of this altered balance of industrial power between capital and labour were developed most systematically by Hilferding in *Finance Capital*.[50] He adduced other reasons also why the scope for trades-union activity was limited, and why the class struggle was forced onto the political terrain. Protective tariffs and cartels, he contended, meant a rise in the cost of living for the working class as a whole. Military and colonial policy increased the burden of taxation. Above all, the state's direct involvement in support of its national capital in competition with others politicised economic relations, and made the state manifestly the agent of dominant class interests. One condition for reformist trades-union politics had been the ease with which the state had hidden its class character behind the apparently neutral principles of *laissez-faire*. This was possible no longer:

> As long as the principles of *laissez-faire* were dominant, and state inter-vention in economic affairs, as well as the character of the state as an organisation of class domination, were concealed, it required a compara-tively mature level of understanding to appreciate the necessity for political struggle, and above all the necessity for the ultimate political goal, the conquest of state power. It is no accident, then, that in England, the classical country of non-intervention, the emergence of independent working-class political action was so difficult. But this is now changing. The capitalist class seizes possession of the state apparatus in a direct, undisguised and palpable way . . . and compels every proletarian to strive for the conquest of political power as the only means of putting an end to his own exploitation.[51]

In sum, we can see that the arguments advanced by Social Demo-cratic theoreticians to explain reformism in economic terms had a very specific purpose. This was to show that, while tendencies to class collaboration always existed within the labour movement, they could become the policy of the working class as a whole only in very special circumstances. These had existed in Britain in the past. They could not be repeated on the Continent in the present. The assumptions embodied in this contrast formed the bedrock of pre-war Social Democratic politics. They were of course shattered in August 1914. While a consideration of this moment takes us outside our period, it will be useful briefly to consider Lenin's explanation for it in the context of what has gone before. In effect, Lenin simply took the arguments that had become commonplace about nineteenth-century Britain, and transferred them to continental Social Democracy, thus showing that the contrast had never been valid in the first place. To do so, however, he had to develop a different theory of imperialism from that of Hilferding, a difference that is not always appreciated in the secondary literature.

Unlike Hilferding, Lenin argued that, despite the intensity of international competition, each national monopoly capital did have room to grant concessions to its working class, because of the super profits it enjoyed. In this the situation resembled that of England in the nineteenth century, though now there were several monopoly powers. He wrote:

> Formerly a 'bourgeois labour party' . . . could be formed only in one country, because it alone enjoyed a monopoly, and enjoyed it for a long period. Now the 'bourgeois labour party' is inevitable and typical for *all* the imperialist countries.

However, the comparison with England could not be pressed too far, or it would suggest that an unbroken era of class collaboration was in prospect. Here the differences became important. The facts of competition between the monopoly powers had not only led to imperialist war, but meant that only 'smaller strata of the "labour aristocracy"' could be bribed than had been possible in England. These strata were particularly represented in the Social Democratic parties. On the other hand the masses of the proletariat were more oppressed than ever, and more inclined to throw off the yoke of the bourgeoisie. 'The history of the labour movement', Lenin concluded prophetically, 'will from now on inevitably develop as the history of the struggle between these two tendencies: for the first tendency is not accidental, it is "founded" on economics.'[52]

The comparison between Social Democratic theories before and after 1914 illustrates the inherent difficulty of explanations for political events and processes couched in purely economic terms. The conditions of monopoly capital that Kautsky and Hilferding saw as the basis for optimism about the future revolutionary strength of Social Democracy provided Lenin with his explanation after the event of why it was 'inevitable' that it should have been a 'bourgeois labour party' all along. This is partly a difference of perspective between future and past. The future appears open, particularly to political activists; in retrospect it seems as if it was closed all the time. But there is also the difficulty that attends such explanatory notions as the 'labour aristocracy', of deducing political attitudes from economic interests alone. Is it short- or long-term interests, sectional or class interests, that are at issue? It was central to the theory of Social Democracy that the party itself could affect this question. Thus Kautsky was emphatic that the strata which constituted the 'labour aristocracy' of the reformist trades unions could also form the 'revolutionary vanguard' of Social Democracy.[53] It depended on the party which outcome occurred. But what if the party itself became reformist? It surely became circular to explain this in terms of the same 'labour aristocracy'. It is significant that Lenin adduced a further explanation for Social Democracy's betrayal; many of its leaders were themselves 'opportunists', a 'non-proletarian element hostile to the socialist revolution . . . officials of the labour unions, parliamentarians and other intellectuals'.[54] He fell back, that is to say, on an explanation with a distinctly syndicalist or Michelsian flavour.

There is a good reason why he should have done so. According to Marxist theory, economic interests are the product of objective determinants that are beyond conscious human control. Ideology and organisation, on the other hand, constitute a more 'subjective' domain that is amenable to human agency. A revolutionary has to believe that the objective constellation of economic relations at least allows for the possibility of revolution, and that any obstacles to it arise at the subjective level that is open to change. Marxist historians may explain the prevalence of reformism in terms of deep-seated economic interests. But Marxist revolutionaries must look to personal and organisational failings, i.e. the arena of human agency and responsibility. 'Leadership betrayal' forms a recurrent candidate for this role.

CONCLUSION

I have argued that the conjunction of two developments made the issue of bourgeois intellectuals in the continental labour movements more controversial in the period around the turn of the century than at any other time. One was the rapid growth of white-collar occupations, and the equally rapid expansion of further education to meet them. These provided recruits to the socialist parties who had the skills to obtain representative positions or full-time office within them. At the same time socialism became respectable for longer-established professional groups. 'It has donned evening dress,' wrote Engels, 'and lounges lazily on drawing-room *causeuses*.'[55] The other development was the manifestation of tendencies towards revisionism, social reform and class collaboration. It seemed obvious to many critics of the latter that the two developments were connected. Even those to whom it was not so obvious were forced to define their attitude towards bourgeois intellectuals in the movement. At best these represented an ambivalent and paradoxical phenomenon. On the one hand their skills were valuable. 'Brain-workers' could not plausibly be regarded as dispensable, whether in the realm of production or political organisation and propaganda. On the other hand, they were associated with a hierarchical division of labour and a social milieu whose assumptions were not readily conducive to the emancipation of the proletariat.

The debates aroused by this issue generated a number of characteristic explanations for reformism, which I have sought to distinguish. There was the view that it followed from the nature of the labour leaderships, and the inability of their supporters to control them. This implied a 'virtuous' mass and a 'deviant' elite. On the other hand was the view that the working class showed a tendency to sectionalism and class collaboration by itself, unless mobilised behind a Social Democratic party and its theory of revolutionary socialism. Finally there were explanations in terms of the space available to capital at particular times to make concessions, which placed the initiative in class collaboration with the bourgeoisie itself. As I have suggested, these different explanations carried very different implications for the strategy of revolutionary politics.

But what exactly was reformism, and in what sense could it be seen as a deviation? What I have termed 'reformism' in this essay went under a variety of different names, with rather different connotations: social reform, revisionism, economism, opportunism, etc. What they had in common was defined by exclusion; they were deviations from the revolutionary politics of the class struggle. And they were seen as 'bourgeois' deviations because they contributed to the maintenance of capitalist property relations, and thus represented a 'bourgeois' perspective within the labour movement. Such a characterisation was shared by all the main anti-revisionist thinkers, and can be traced back to Marx and Engels themselves. It must be questioned, however, whether a conceptual strategy is acceptable which rolls all working-class and socialist politics that are not revolutionary into one bundle, and treats them as equivalent, whatever their character – oppositional or acquiescent, aspirational or mundane. As with the proverbial cats that are all grey at night, it ignores distinctions and complexities that are important both for recovering the richness of a tradition and to political practice itself.

Reformism supposedly constituted a 'deviation' in a second sense, not just from revolution, but from the revolution that could have been expected. In historical perspective, of course, it is 'reformism' that has been the norm in capitalist societies, and revolution the exception. So there is much to be said for turning the question on its head: not, Why reformism? but, What exceptional combination of circumstances have produced revolutionary attempts? Important though this question is, to be preoccupied with it is to be mesmerised by the same antithesis between reform and revolution. A historian of socialism will be concerned as well with the less dramatic achievements of labour politics – and also with its less dramatic failures, failures to accomplish more radical change, more progressive structures, more effective defence of past achievements. Failures are by definition 'non-events', and as such are ruled out of court by strictly empiricist historians; but their consideration is inseparable from any critical interrogation of the past. To the extent that we are concerned with them, the explanations for socialist 'failure' reviewed in this essay will still have relevance for us.

NOTES

1 I have used the term 'reformism' because it captures most comprehensively the phenomena that were variously described as 'social reform', 'revisionism', 'economism', 'opportunism', etc. While these had rather different connotations, they were all contrasted to revolutionary socialism or Social Democracy.

2 The works I have used include: A. Labriola, *Riforme e rivoluzione sociale*, Milan, Società Editoriale Milanese, 1904; 'Le socialisme en Italie', *Le Mouvement socialiste* (hereafter *MS*), no. 136, 1904, pp. 1–15; 'L'erreur tactique du socialisme', *MS*, no. 157, 1905,

pp. 217–33; 'Syndicalisme et réformisme en Italie', *MS*, nos. 168–9, 1905, pp. 393–415; 'Syndicalisme et socialisme', *MS*, no. 170, 1906, pp. 44–64. E. Berth, *Les Méfaits des intellectuels*, Paris, Marcel Riviére, 1914; 'Socialisme ou étatisme', *MS*, no. 111, 1903, pp. 1–17; 'Politique et socialisme', *MS*, no. 132, 1904, pp. 5–27; 'Proletariat et bourgeoisie dans le mouvement socialiste italien', *MS*, no. 179, 1906, pp. 164–70; 'Marchands, intellectuels et politiciens', *MS*, nos. 188–92, 1907, pp. 1–12, 302–16, 384–96; H. Lagardelle, *Syndicalisme et socialisme*, Paris, Marcel Rivière, 1908; 'Le socialisme ouvrier', *MS*, no. 142, 1904, pp. 1–8; 'Les intellectuels et le socialisme ouvrier', *MS*, nos. 183–6, 1907, pp. 105–20, 217–32, 349–64, 409–20. My 'qualification' in respect of Sorel is that he is too idiosyncratic a thinker to be taken as representative of any political tendency. For a justification of this view see my 'Sorel and the left', *Government and Opposition*, vol. 4, no. 3, 1969, pp. 308–23.

3 For Machajski I have used the French collection of his works edited by A. Skirda, *Le Socialisme des intellectuels*, Paris, Le Seuil, 1979.

4 The main works in which Michels developed his views were: 'Proletariat und Bourgeoisie in der sozialistischen Bewegung Italiens', *Archiv für Socialwissenschaft und Sozialpolitik*, vol. 22, 1906, pp. 664–720; 'Die deutsche Sozialdemokratie', op. cit., vol. 23, 1906, pp. 471–556; 'Die oligarchischen Tendenzen der Gesellschaft', op. cit., vol. 27, 1908, pp. 73–135. For his critical reviews of the syndicalists, see *Neue Zeit*, vol. 22.2, 1903–4, pp. 59–61 (Labriola); *MS*, no. 184, 1907, pp. 278–88 (Berth); *MS*, nos. 247–8, 1913, pp. 90–6 (Lagardelle). For a fuller discussion of the development of Michels's views, see my 'Robert Michels: from Marxist revolutionary to political sociologist', *Political Studies*, vol. 25, no. 1, 1977, pp. 3–24.

5 *MS*, no. 136, 1904, pp. 8–9.

6 Labriola, op. cit. (note 2), p. 5.

7 *MS*, no. 179, 1906, p. 165.

8 *MS*, no. 183, 1907, p. 119.

9 *MS*, no. 136, 1904, p. 3; cf. Labriola, op. cit. (note 2), pp. 220–1.

10 Ibid.

11 *MS*, no. 179, 1906, p. 165.

12 *MS*, no. 184, 1907, pp. 217–18.

13 Ibid., p. 224.

14 One difference between Italian syndicalists like Labriola and their French counterparts was that the former still accepted a political function for the party, but only if purged of all its non-proletarian elements; Labriola, op. cit. (note 2), p. 253.

15 Skirda, op. cit. (note 3), p. 190.

16 Ibid., pp. 133, 138, 159, 172–5.

17 Ibid., pp. 134–5, 169.
18 *Archiv für Sozialwissenschaft und Sozialpolitik*, vol. 22, 1906, pp. 717–18.
19 Michels made this point as early as 1903 in his review of Labriola: 'The labour leaders who themselves stem from the working class are much sooner inclined to engage in compromises than the revolutionary ex-bourgeois', *Neue Zeit*, vol. 22.2. 1903–4, p. 61; cf. *Archiv für Sozialwissenschaft und Sozialpolitik*, vol. 27, 1908, p. 124: 'The much discussed bourgeoisification of the labour parties lies in a quite different direction. . . . They raise significant elements from the depths of the proletarian class and project them into the arms of the bourgeoisie.'
20 The argument is developed in detail in *Archiv für Sozialwissenschaft und Sozialpolitik*, vol. 23, 1906, pp. 526–53.
21 *NS*, no. 184, 1904, p. 282.
22 *MS*, nos. 247–8, 1913, p. 94.
23 For Kautsky's theory of the relation between the trades unions and the party, see e.g. 'Die Neutralisierung der Gewerkschaften', *Neue Zeit*, vol. 18.2, 1899–1900; 'Partei und Gewerkschaft', *Neue Zeit*, vol. 24.2, 1905–6. On intellectuals and the working class, see 'Akademiker und Proletarier', 'Die neue Bewegung in Russland', *Neue Zeit*, vol. 19.2, 1900–1; 'Das Programm der Sozialdemokratie in Österreich', *Neue Zeit*, vol. 20.1, 1901–2.
24 V. I. Lenin, *Selected Works*, 3 vols., Moscow, Co-operative Publishing Society of Foreign Workers in the USSR, 1934, Vol. 2, pp. 148–9, 156–8, 181–2, 190.
25 Ibid., p. 156. See M. Salvadori, *Karl Kautsky*, London, Verso, 1979, p. 76; N. Harding, *Lenin's Political Thought*, London, 1977, Macmillan, Vol. 1, pp. 168–9; M. Donald, 'Karl Kautsky and Russian Social Democracy, 1883–1917', unpublished MS, University of Leeds, 1985.
26 *Neue Zeit*, vol. 19.2, 1900–1, pp. 89, 123.
27 *Protokoll über die Verhandlungen des Parteitages der SPD 13–20 September 1903*, Berlin, Dietz Verlag, 1903, pp. 225, 255.
28 'Akademiker und Proletarier', *Neue Zeit*, vol. 19.2, 1900–1, pp. 90–1. Such statements were commonplace, e.g. F. Mehring: 'The intellectuals elucidate for the workers the social relationships which make their approaching victory a certainty', quoted in R. Michels, *Political Parties*, New York, Dover Publications, 1959, p. 327; E. Vandervelde, 'The intellectuals, who accept socialism for reasons other than their immediate interest . . . are the yeast in the working class that makes the dough rise', quoted in *MS*, no. 184, pp. 221–2; etc.
29 *Neue Zeit*, vol. 13.2, 1894–5, pp. 10–16, 43–9, 74–80.
30 Ibid., p. 76.

31 This was Kautsky's judgment on Liebknecht in yet another article on the relationship between the intellectuals and the proletariat, *Neue Zeit*, vol. 22.1, 1903–4, esp. pp. 101–3.

32 K. Kautsky, 'Wahlkreis und Partei', *Neue Zeit*, vol. 22.2, 1903–4.

33 Lenin, op. cit. (note 24), pp. 392–3, 457–60.

34 Ibid., p. 132. See the lengthy discussion on 'opportunism in questions of organisation', in 'One step forward, two steps back', ibid., pp. 440–66. There is no evidence that Lenin believed, any more than Kautsky, that the intellectuals should provide the main organising force of the revolutionary party, despite Salvadori's assertion to the contrary. See Salvadori, op. cit. (note 25), p. 76.

35 Ibid. For the conjunction of 'legal criticism' and 'economism', see p. 138.

36 *MS*, no. 184, 1907, pp. 218–19.

37 Ibid., p. 223; cf. pp. 219–20.

38 Ibid., pp. 224–5, n. 1.

39 Lenin, op. cit. (note 24), pp. 144–5.

40 E. Bernstein, *Evolutionary Socialism*, New York, Schocken Books, 1961, p. 27.

41 K. Marx and F. Engels, *Selected Correspondence*, Moscow, Foreign Languages Publishing House, n.d., pp. 132–3, 422–3.

42 F. Engels, *The Condition of the Working Class in England*, London, Allen & Unwin, 1892, preface.

43 R. Luxemburg, *Gesammelte Werke*, Berlin, Dietz Verlag, 1970, Vol. 1.1, pp. 471–82.

44 Ibid., p. 473.

45 Ibid., p. 478.

46 Ibid., p. 479–82.

47 K. Kautsky, *Bernstein und das Sozialdemokratische Programm*, Stuttgart, Dietz Verlag, 1899, pp. 163–4.

48 *Neue Zeit*, vol. 18.2, 1899–1900, pp. 388–90.

49 Ibid., pp. 492–5.

50 R. Hilferding, *Finance Capital*, London, Routledge & Kegan Paul, 1981, ch. 24, pp. 351–63.

51 Ibid., p. 368; cf. p. 366.

52 V. I. Lenin, 'Imperialism and the split in the socialist movement', in *British Labour and British Imperialism*, London, Lawrence & Wishart, 1969, pp. 146–7.

53 *Neue Zeit*, no. 24.2, 1905–6, p. 719.

54 Quoted in Harding, op. cit. (note 25), Vol. 2, p. 28.

55 Engels, op. cit. (note 42).

5

Education and Self-Education: Staffing the Early ILP

Carl Levy

INTRODUCTION

The Independent Labour Party was the first British socialist organisation which may be considered a mass party. There are a variety of analyses of the ILP's growth from its foundation in 1893 to the establishment of the Labour Representation Committee in 1900. But, curiously enough, historians as different as Edward Thompson and Henry Pelling have arrived at rather similar conclusions in seeking to explain the ILP's original appeal and chart its first decade of growth.

The ILP, for both historians, was the culmination of widespread industrial strife, leading to a growing awareness by increasingly numerous groups of British workers that direct political intervention through their own party was a necessity if their interests were to be properly served. Thompson expressed this notion in a stirring essay dedicated to one of the pioneers of the ILP, Tom Maguire:

> The ILP grew from the bottom up: its birthplaces were in those shadowy parts known as the provinces . . . when the two-party political system began to crack, a third party with a distinctively socialist character emerged, this event occurred neither in Westminster nor in the offices

of Champion's *Labour Elector* but amongst the mills, brickyards and gasworks of the West Riding.[1]

For Pelling, the results of the ILP's inaugural conference were a similar revolution in British working-class politics.

> For the first time working men were attempting on a national scale to take control of Parliament and thus fully to exploit the advantages given them by the franchise acts. For the first time, the trade-union democracy was extended to a political party, whose inspiration was to come from below rather than above.[2]

More recently, in which must be the definitive study of the early ILP, David Howell shows how the party gained support through a process of mediation between locally specific working-class political cultures and trade-union organisations, on the one hand, and the strength or weakness of popular Liberal or Tory traditions, on the other.[3]

Much of this essay addresses a rather different aspect of this process. The formation of the ILP's internal structure, its political ideas, its leadership and its organisers was, in fact, directly and substantially affected by the presence of middle-class socialists. This resulted, on one hand, from the structural constraints of politics and the lack of time or money available to working-class activists to allow them to pursue politics as a full-time vocation; and, on the other, from the subjective qualities which the education of the ILP leadership embodied. The professional politicians, the journalists and the professional lecturers became the predominant force in the party's national leadership. Their ability to remain connected to the rank and file, through journalistic skills and oratorial resonance, and their freedom to devote time to the committee structure that became the sinews of the national party, gave them enormous advantages over the self-educated trade-union activist. The literate, educated workers who early on thronged into the ILP from the northern labour clubs became dependent on their national leadership. Although small, this group forged the alliance between the ILP, the Radical Liberals and the TUC, and opened the way for the ILP's parliamentary breakthroughs of the early 1900s.

This essay will examine their effect upon the first decade of the

ILP's life. During the 1890s the party's national machinery began to displace the activities of local organisations. In a much admired essay Stephen Yeo examined the general grounds for the atrophy of local vitality in socialism, finding three main causes.[4]

With the creation of state agencies to handle poverty, local mutual aid was replaced by centralised forms of national welfare. The development of a mass leisure industry substituted for the intimate social atmosphere which the early socialist groups offered. Finally, a more hostile political and economic climate after 1900 made it harder for local groups to survive. Already by 1900 this meant that local initiative was on the way to being replaced by centralised, more durable forms of organisation.

All these factors were certainly important in explaining how a more centralised and specialised form of politics came about. But they are exogenous. What they exclude is the strong and persistent emphasis the movement placed on winning the middle classes to socialism, even in its pre-1900 'utopian' phase. A persistent theme running through the pamphlets and newspapers of this era was a call to the 'brain-workers' to unite with the self-educated manual workers within a common political organisation. Another important – and not unrelated – factor was the penetrative influence of business methods in running the organisations which directly affected the birth of the ILP.

ILP SOCIAL COMPOSITION: GENERAL OVERVIEW

Stanley Pierson's two studies of British socialism argue consistently that the ILP and other pioneer socialist groups drew their most active supporters from the lower middle class. 'Most often', Pierson writes in his latest work,

> the early Socialists came not from the working class but . . . from the lower levels of the middle class. They came from the 'salariat' or the 'professional proletariat'. Some were seeking careers in the civil service, journalism, teaching, or the literary world. Others were taking positions in the burgeoning world of business as commercial traders, clerks or shop assistants. . . . Each of the major socialist organisations – the Social Democratic Federation, the Fabian Society, and the Independent Labour

Party, drew their propagandists and organisers largely from this section of society.[5]

David Howell asserts that the ILP's working-class pioneers were largely frustrated entrants into this white-collar world.

> The activists of the early ILP were often the early products of compulsory education. Such an experience could generate aspirations which were often disappointed, with claims foundering on the reef of certificates. If individual hopes were blocked, then perhaps a collective solution should be sought.[6]

Nevertheless, empirical data demonstrating the actual numbers of middle-class members in the ILP are not readily available. Here I shall present what evidence is available for the party's social composition during the first two decades of its life.

The Socialist League was a typical stepping-stone for ILP activists.[7] William Morris's efforts welded together artisan, skilled-worker and a notable number of lower-middle-class members.[8] Impressionistic evidence reveals a high percentage of clerks as activists. Many of the League's correspondents described themselves in such terms, and in his diary William Morris wrote of the Glasgow branch 'a good deal made up clerks, designers and the like and rather under the thumb of their employers or they would be able to do more'.[9] Moreover many of these 'disciples' later became important within the ILP, such as Fred Pickles, a pioneer of the Bradford Socialist League and ILP, who described his social position to the Socialist League in London:

> I am what Mr Morris would term a 'slave of the Desk' for a firm of Machine Makers (bitterly opposed to Trade Unions) and I am certain that if they had any idea I sympathised with Socialism I should very soon . . . be unemployed. I am a lover of Art, Poetry and Nature, but the major portion of my days have been spent on a stool, writing 'To Goods', 'By Cash', without end. Outside the office window I can see nothing but smokey chimneys and ugliness almost unbearable and six yards from my seat is a horribly smelling stream literally blacker than the ink I am writing with.[10]

Besides the Socialist League, Secularist Societies and Nonconformist chapels provided additional early recruits to the ILP. While

Secularists were not prominent in the ILP, those who joined carried with them the particular traditions of the Secularist Society. Secularism had long been a meeting-place for the articulate skilled workers and the urban *nouvelle couche sociale*, and these professional, white-collar or commercial middle-class activists dominated its organisation.[11]

The Nonconformist chapel however was the greatest catchment area for middle-class recruits. The ethical socialism of the ILP found its deepest roots in Yorkshire where an older chapel culture was failing to maintain its grip on workers who were turning away from the paternalism of local mill-owners and the patronage of the Liberal Party. But if these older relationships were weakening, a shift to socialism, especially the 'religion of socialism', brought many professional and white-collar middle-class Methodists and Congregationalists over to the ILP. While many working-class lay preachers were active in the ILP, the chief spokesmen for the ILP's ethical socialism were educated middle-class individuals. The ILP merely 'bridged the gap between working class and middle class sensibilities more effectively than the older Socialist organisations'.[12]

If for the first period of ILP history (1893–1900) we do not possess a numerical breakdown of the social class of its membership, there are some interesting local accounts which illustrate the various routes through which the educated middle class exerted its influence on the party from its foundations.

In the early 1890s Bradford was one of the ILP's most important strongholds.[13] By 1894 the party had three thousand members enrolled in twenty local clubs, typically engineers, printers, cabinet-makers and dyers. The ILP's membership lived in the better-off working-class areas of small terraced housing. Through their control of local workers' clubs and trade unions they succeeded in gaining control of the trades and labour council, and gave the ILP a strong labourist flavour. Nevertheless, the middle class maintained a notable presence from the beginning through social networks invaluable for the mobilisation of organisational resources.

Although the ILP gathered a popular following when the local Liberal caucus refused to support worker candidates, the initial rapid growth of the ILP owed a great deal to institutions on the radical fringes of nonconformity and the Liberal Party itself. Some of those were public, such as the Horton Lane Congregational Church and the Sunday Society, which permitted socialists in the Socialist League and the ILP to address audiences they would never have been capable of mustering through their own efforts.[14] Others were informal discussion groups which permitted the exchange of ideas between middle- and skilled working-class socialists and Radical Liberals. Fred Jowett, Bradford's first ILP MP, a textile worker who graduated via night school to supervisory and designing posts, is emblematic of a social type whose political education was shaped in these public and private networks.[15] Indeed, his wife's prominent local Liberal family served as the location for one particularly interesting circle, among whom were included Hubert Llewellyn Smith, then a young lecturer, later a key figure in social reform and industrial relations.[16]

In Leeds middle-class influence was more direct due to the failure at mass recruitment in the early years. Although ILP popularity had been initially generated through New Unionist organisers active in the Gas Workers' and General Labourers' Union and the skilled worker activists of local labour clubs, unlike Bradford the ILP did not gain control of the trades council.[17] Not only did the ILP have to contend with a much stronger mainstream Liberal tradition at work within the skilled working class, but sharper social divisions present between skilled native workers and unskilled immigrants strengthened anti-socialist populism.[18] Since Leeds lacked Bradford's fairly numerous group of self-educated workers, most early ILP activists originated from the middle classes. A survey of Leeds's working-class history concludes: 'a white-collar leadership was influential in the ILP of the 1890s, a situation which highlighted the weak position of the manual working class and the failure to become actively involved, as a class, in socialist politics'.[19] If in Bradford one detects a mixture of skilled worker, supervisory personnel and self-made entrepreneur activists, Leeds is definitely less industrial, more professional or white collar.

Manchester, too, experienced sectarian and immigrant/host-community tensions which weakened working-class presence and undoubtedly increased the social and political weight of middle-class socialists. And as a national centre of labour journalism it attracted a particularly significant group of lower-middle-class journalists. Here Robert Blatchford's *Clarion* waged guerrilla war against centralising tendencies within the national ILP leadership.[20]

While the cultural appeal of *The Clarion*, as we shall see further on, was most definitely aimed at the lower middle class, the local ILP also attracted many progressive professionals, who placed their openly political commitments into a broader pattern of interests, such as the Garden City movement, Ruskin Hall and the Labour Church. The Pankhursts, for example, provided a link between the ILP and the progressivism of C. P. Scott's *Manchester Guardian*.[21] In fact, one particularly active articulate non-professional but white-collar activist went so far as to subdivide Mancunian middle-class socialism into aesthetic radicals, who equated socialism with a 'new joy of life', and the more prosaic workhorses, tending to be clerks and shop assistants, who actually developed the party's organisation.[22]

Leicester's ILP branch, too, remained weak until after the turn of the century. Here the leadership in the 1890s was drawn largely from nonconformist and socially-minded Anglican clergymen.[23] The local trades council and the important National Union of Boot and Shoe Operatives remained solidly Lib–Lab during this early period, but the recruitment of clergymen, lay preachers, Sunday-school teachers and Salvation Army leaders allowed the party to maintain a vocal and resonant presence within the community through meetings and rallies until working-class membership increased notably after the early 1900s.

This patchy survey of ILP branches in the 1890s has demonstrated how recruitment patterns of middle-class activists were as sensitive to locally specific political cultures and political economies as David Howell has shown for their working-class comrades. For a slightly later period (1904–10), we do have empirical data which suggests an active membership disproportionately recruited from the middle classes. Though the party attracted many skilled workers, it also drew a great deal of support from clerks and supervisory personnel.[24]

On the local level these two groups were particularly active. At the national level a considerable leavening of professional people were involved in party affairs. Some of these professionals were lawyers, accountants, architects, surveyors, clergymen and doctors, but the majority were teachers. Professionals were represented within the ranks of the party's activists seven times more strongly than their number in the population.[25]

While the unskilled and the semi-skilled were never in great abundance, there was a good representation of employers and proprietors within or sympathetic to the party. The soap manufacturer Joseph Fels, the chocolate manufacturer Cadbury and the Welsh coal-mine owner D. A. Thomas all contributed significant sums of money to its coffers during its first ten years of existence. On the local level employers sometimes influenced early branch development. In the Colne Valley, for example, the small mill-owner Frances Littlewood and the son of the valley's largest mill-owner, Ben Shaw, were pioneers. Littlewood helped the ILP financially throughout the 1890s; Shaw became Keir Hardie's deputy on the *Labour Leader*,[26] while in Bradford a mill-owner, William Leach, gave generously and later served as an ILP MP.[27]

Until the early 1900s the ILP had little success in parliamentary electoral campaigns. Locally, however, it did better, and by 1900 there were several hundred local government representatives.[28] The shift from local and voluntary enthusiasm to a more bureaucratic and centralised electoral strategy heightened the division between the centre and the periphery, and had the effect of beginning to dissipate the almost religious devotion which characterised branch life in the earlier period. In a sense, two ILPs developed. The original branches had grown in the particular conditions of a locality. But a large group of nationally oriented activists also arose as the party became more concerned with achieving parliamentary representation. Deian Hopkin identifies, in the early twentieth century, a group of nationally oriented activist and lower-middle-class ILP workers numbering around 1700 – approximately 10 per cent of the party's formal membership.[29] This group was very active, contributing a great deal to the party coffers, and it was crucial for the evolution of ILP strategy, being overwhelmingly of middle-class background, comprising particularly teachers, journalists and other professionals.

By this time, the ILP could be described as a 'cadre party', to use Maurice Duverger's definition – one with a small but active membership, whose main goal is electoral success, and which must thereby draw on the support of non-party members who sympathise with the aims of the party.[30] Much of the ILP's support was working class. But the active national membership which operated the electoral machine was largely middle class. This tendency for the machine to concentrate on skilled workers can also be related to its electoral strategy, since a good deal of the semi-skilled and casual working population was disenfranchised by residence requirements.[31]

The nationally active component among Duverger's 'cadres' was composed of three social groups. There were, firstly, lower-middle-class men who had started their working lives as minor civil servants, teachers, supervisory personnel and so on.[32] Secondly, there were middle-class women who had escaped the constraints of Victorian family life by finding employment in such expanding fields as teaching and social welfare – the archetypal 'new women'.[33] Finally, there were young trade-union officials who had won their spurs and developed their abilities organising unskilled and semi-skilled workers into the new general trade unions of the late 1880s and early 1890s. These were supplemented by a group of trade-union officials from older craft-based unions like the ASE, which felt threatened by an employer offensive.

Two activities in particular were important in the process of precipitating more professional politicians from the voluntary organisations and decentralised latitudinarian socialism of the 1880s and 1890s. Oratory was a traditional part of the equipment of an activist, and it remained important. If some activists were undistinguished speakers to begin with, many rapidly gained an impressive public speaking technique, often learning by example from their comrades. A more novel factor was the 'new journalism' that germinated in the 1880s and 1890s. Newspapers provided a new sort of 'transmission belt' to connect political leaders directly with their grass-roots support, and journalism acted as bridge-cum-training-ground through which the initial enthusiasm of activists was shaped towards a more professional political practice.

Our brief examinations of (a) the press and (b) oratory in the formation of the ILP will reveal much about the relations of social types within it.

THE 'NEW JOURNALISM'

Let me explain my principle. I would have the paper address itself to the quarter-educated; that is to say, the great new generation that is being turned out by the Board Schools, the young men and women who can just read, but are incapable of sustained attention. People of this kind want something to occupy them in trains and on buses and trams.

As a rule they care for no newspapers except the Sunday ones; what they want is the lightest and frothiest for chit-chatting information – bits of stories, bits of descriptions, bits of scandals, bits of jokes, bits of statistics, bits of foolery. . . . No article in the paper is to measure more than two inches in length, and every inch must be broken into at least two paragraphs.

George Gissing, *New Grub Street*, London, Nash & Crayon, 1927 edn,
p. 419

It might be maintained that there is a 'law' of the workers' press during Labour's 'Formative Years' – no significant institutional innovation is possible without the aid of periodicals; the editors as controllers of the periodicals see themselves as the fathers of these institutions, take a paternal responsibility for them which brings them into conflict with those whose responsibility is of a more direct and constitutional sort.

Royden Harrison, 'Introduction', in *Independent Collier*, Brighton,
Harvester, 1978, p. 10

The ILP depended to a great extent upon journalism to knit together its regional and local parts. The successful socialist journalist of the 1890s became associated directly or indirectly with the emerging ILP. A new regionally based popular form of journalism contributed greatly to the party's initial success and also acted as that training ground we have just mentioned.

The 'new journalism' consisted of applying both stylistic and printing innovations to these regionally based papers. Newspapers contained less commentary and more current news. The interview and the 'stop press', the human-interest story and the lurid scandal, imported from the United States, appealed to an expanding lower-middle- and middle-class readership. A more intimate style of writing identified the reporter in an informal manner. The successful writer became a celebrity who built up a devoted readership of tens of thousands.

The most important exemplars, the *Pall Mall Gazette* under the editorship of W. T. Stead, and *The Star* of the late 1880s and 1890s, had direct connections with the emerging London socialist movement, and with the New Unionists.[34] *The Star* was financed by a group of Radical Liberal industrialists who sought to influence the development of a London-based Progressive Party by harnessing the radical traditions of London's network of three hundred working men's clubs and the political mobilisation which accompanied the New Unionism in reviving the Liberal Party. The paper began in the aftermath of the unemployment riots of 1887, and made its name by exposing corruption in local government, and campaigning for the establishment of the London County Council. It gave lengthy sympathetic coverage to the Dock Strike of 1889. By the 1890s it was sponsoring progressive candidates for the LCC and (through its editor, H. W. Massingham) had established ties with John Burns and the Fabians.[35] At the same time, while it covered labour and progressive politics, it relied on sensationalism – such as a lurid series of articles on Jack the Ripper. Its founder, T. P. O'Connor, described its approach in its initial issue of January 1888:

> plenty of entirely unpolitical literature – sometimes humorous, sometimes pathetic; anecdotal, statistical, the craze of fashions and the arts of housekeeping – now and then a short, dramatic and picturesque tale. In our reporting columns we shall do away with the hackneyed style of obsolete journalism; and the men and women that figure in the forum or the pulpit of the law court shall be presented as they are – living, breathing, in blushes or in tears – and not merely by the dead words that they utter.[36]

The socialist press didn't really gain success until two northern ventures started: in 1891 the *Workman's Times* and in 1892 *The Clarion*. Both, in their own fashion, adopted the 'new journalism'. Before these breakthroughs, the socialist press was largely subsidised by wealthy patrons. The SDF's *Justice* was supported out of Hyndman's pocket and later through his printing company, the Twentieth Century Press.[37] The Socialist League's *Commonweal* survived through the munificence of William Morris.[38] Even if the organ of the Socialist League was not a financial success, its function foreshadowed the later attempts of socialist journalism – to link locally based groups to a national centre, serving as the main medium of communication with its variegated membership.[39] *Commonweal*'s writing, with major articles by Morris, Aveling and Belfort Bax, was often superb, but it was never successfully popular. Unlike the mass newspapers of the 1890s, it could never make up its mind whether it was to be a theoretical journal or disseminate socialist propaganda. Only a few exceptional workers wrote in it. Most contributions from the rank and file and provinces came from the young lower-middle-class men who made up the heart and soul of the League. Two of *Commonweal*'s more frequent provincial correspondents were Tom Maguire of Leeds and Bruce Glasier of Glasgow. Glasier was known as an orator, but also developed his nebulous religion of socialism through the columns of Morris's newspaper. Glasier, like many other lower-middle-class disciples of Morris, fancied himself a Pre-Raphaelite poet, and it took all of Morris's tact to get him to turn his attentions to the labour movement in Scotland instead. Glasier later wrote frequently for *The Clarion* and the ILP's semi-official *Labour Leader*.[40]

Another socialist newspaper of some significance but little financial success was H. H. Champion's *Labour Elector*. If *Commonweal* served as a nursery for the middle-class socialist journalists, Champion's paper allowed the most important New Unionists – Tom Mann, Ben Tillet and John Burns – to gain experience as journalists.[41] Between 1888 and 1890 the *Labour Elector* popularised the New Unionist demands of the eight-hour day and unions for the unskilled. Champion also used his newspaper as a network by which London New Unionists could establish contacts with Keir Hardie and other Scottish advocates of independent labour representation. Champion personally financed the *Labour Elector*. He was a shrewd politician who, like Hyndman, was a 'Tory socialist'. His association with the Tories eventually isolated him from the ILP, but he exercised a crucial influence on its prehistory.

If *Justice*, *Commonweal* and *Labour Elector* were dependent on subventions from individuals or private groups to survive, the *Workman's Times* and *Clarion* were highly popular newspapers. Their success was one of the main reasons for the emergence of the ILP.

The *Workman's Times*, like Champion's *Labour Elector*, relied on trade-union correspondents for its news, but it grew in the more fertile soil of the West Riding.[42] It, too, had commercial local prototypes. In 1889 John Andrews, owner of the *Cotton Factory Times* of Lancashire, decided to open the *Yorkshire Factory Times* in Bradford to expand his circulation to the other area of northern industry. Andrews's venture was purely commercial, but, as with the Lancashire paper, union organisers in localities were employed as his correspondents, not only to relay local news but to use their influence to push the sales of the paper. The formula was an enormous success. The new paper was used by organisers of the General Textile Workers' Union, such as Ben Turner, to widen unionisation, and it thus paved the road for the ILP. Turner recalled that 'the establishment of that paper made our union prosper'.[43]

The earlier career of its editor, Joseph Burgess, presents all the hallmarks of the new labour journalist. As a former Lancashire cotton spinner, Burgess was entirely self-taught. From the early 1880s he contributed articles to local northern newspapers. Then, in 1889, he edited the Oldham newspaper owned by a local lace industrialist.[44] Here he met John Burns during his campaign as the SDF's parliamentary candidate. In the late 1880s Burgess moved to London, and his earlier acquaintance with Burns served as an entrée into metropolitan radical politics. At the Democratic Club, a radical literary meeting-place near Fleet Street, Burns introduced him to a variegated group of foreign exiles and struggling journalists. The club's dinner table accommodated Liberal collectivists like Richard Haldane, the successful labour journalists Morrison Davidson and W. H. Thompson, feminists, radical Congregationalist ministers and New Unionists. The club served as a forum for socialist and Radical Liberal politics. In the early 1890s the Independent Labour Party's London supporters were largely drawn from its ranks, and it sponsored a series of resolutions and conferences which had led to the ILP's first Bradford congress. But it also served an equally important function as an informal labour exchange for, as Burgess recalled, the 'casual journalism of Fleet Street'.[45] Competition at the club was fierce, and provincial newcomers like Burgess survived only by selling 'scoops' to London dailies at abysmally low rates. Burgess, however, arrived in London at a fortuitous moment. In the wake of the 1886 unemployment riots labour journalism came of age. As Burgess recalled:

> Under ordinary circumstances it might have taken me a considerable time to receive a living wage connection, but it so happened that shortly after my arrival in London there was a considerable boom in Labour and Socialist journalism and of this I reaped the advantage.[46]

Burgess's reporting in the aftermath of the West End riots established his reputation 'with the Fleet Street sub-editors as a man with a good nose for exclusive Labour and Socialist news'.[47] In turn the Democratic Club's membership served as Burgess's 'unofficial source' for his London 'scoops'. He became the editor of the *Yorkshire Factory Times* in 1889, and two years later he was given the highly independent editorship of the newer and more ambitious *Workman's Times*. Two results came out of this venture; its correspondents became leading activists of the ILP, and Burgess used the resources and influence of the newspaper to organise the ILP founding congress. He later felt entitled to seek an almost proprietorial control of the new party.[48]

Like Burgess's and Champion's papers, Robert Blatchford's *Clarion* served as a personal platform. This was the paper which most successfully generated the mass appeal for the rapid expansion of socialism in the North during the 1890s and most fully incorporated the innovations of the 'new journalism'.

Although he remained close to the ILP, Blatchford was always critical of the central leadership. In 1898, when his own attempts at merging the ILP with the SDF were dashed by the National Administrative Council, he was to complain that

> the ILP is not managed on democratic lines. It is really controlled by a central committee who do as they please, subject only to the correction of an annual conference of delegates. Now, we all know how this system works and must work out. It means official rings and one-man leadership, all kinds of wirepulling, intriguing and official mystery, and the apathy of the general body, resulting in stagnation and green mouldiness.[49]

Blatchford was not so much opposed to 'one-man leadership' as to its location within a nascent party bureaucracy. For him the socialist movement was a movement of opinion, and *The Clarion* existed to mould this. In some ways his socialism was an offshoot of William Morris's – more authoritarian no doubt, but both men shared an essentially educational approach. Before social reform would be effective, they believed socialists had to be made. Both, therefore, adopted the stance of teacher and tribune.[50] In turn both developed circles of close followers, attracted to their personalities.

The Clarion carried on Morris's traditions but on a grander scale. If the Socialist League had attracted an active membership of lower-middle-class professionals, *The Clarion* not only catered to a similar readership but consciously sought to widen its appeal to the middle classes. At the peak of its success, in the late 1890s, probably between 35,000 and 50,000 copies were sold weekly. Its influence thus far exceeded the regular membership of the ILP.[51] It was an institution of the socialism of the 1890s and it prompted unreservedly the integration of middle and working classes in the socialist movement.

Logie Barrow, a student of its history, has claimed that *The Clarion*'s readership was composed mostly of clerks and shop assistants, while one of *The Clarion*'s own writers noted that its small adverts served as a major source of domestic labour in the North.[52] Blatchford always defined the 'productive classes' to include 'brain-workers'. (His brother Montague included lawyers and pressmen in the proletariat.)[53] In 1899 Blatchford was to plead for a 'mission to the middle classes':[54] 'if it were only practicable, a "Mission to the Middle Classes" would do more good in twelve months than twelve years of Van work among the ignorant'. *The Clarion* helped to spread its influence with alternative social attractions. The Clarion Clubs with their mixture of entertainment, culture and Bohemianism nurtured the 'intelligent reader' that Blatchford appealed to.[55] Traditional working-class culture was slighted. The existing working men's clubs were either ignored by Blatchford or, worse, criticised for their 'smelliness' and depressing locales. This tendency did not go unremarked. One worker wrote in 1899 to object to the evolution of a 'cultural, intellectual elite in socialism . . . withdrawing into select coteries where only subjects of philosophy and higher education are talked over'.[56] Blatchford and his group were little embarrassed.

The three newspapers which we have identified as shaping the early years of the ILP – *Labour Elector*, *Workman's Times* and *The Clarion* – had major similarities. All three were personal and political instruments of their editors. Instead of achieving popularity through its own party press, the ILP relied on the sympathetic if independent press. On the national level this allowed middle-class influence to be felt from the very beginning. If *The Clarion* was clearly middle class in accent, content and readership, Champion's more limited enterprise also displayed the elitist assumptions of *The Clarion*'s editorial group. In an article for *Nineteenth Century* written in 1890, he voiced similar sentiments, albeit more bluntly than Blatchford:

Given a great mass of uncultivated, ignorant, emotional human beings, stirred by unrest, discontent, and a sense of injustice, but without trained minds to reason back to causes or even to put other complaints into coherent form, you must have much confusion and discord. . . . Then the immensity and grandeur of the subject attracts fluent persons of a poetical temperament who scorn detailed argument and pipe a Paradise in which Kings, priests and policemen shall be no more seen, loudest and most enthusiastic of all are the constitutional mongers, each with a new Atlantis, who darken counsel by setting off on the wrong scent that large proportion of mankind, whose standard of intelligence is shown by the way they accept statements of a company prospectus, or a patent medicine advertisement, they either follow the few who know their own minds or act from unreasoning instinct.[57]

Burgess's case is slightly different. He was a self-made journalist who was apprenticed in the commercial working-class press. The success of the *Workman's Times* followed the formula which Andrews had devised. Its remarkable influence was due to shrewd commercial management that knew how to harness the mass enthusiasms of the labour unrest. In this sense not only were business operations present during the initial years of the ILP's history; it can be argued that they were crucial to the very birth of the ILP. The relationship between commercial methods and the ILP did not suddenly develop, but was born with the party itself.

Labour Leader and Keir Hardie's position

The one newspaper which we have so far not mentioned – *Labour Leader* – is commonly thought of as the ILP's official journal. In fact, until 1903 its management and ownership were completely in Keir Hardie's possession.[58] One thing which Hardie's ascent from miner to party leader illustrates is how journalism helped mould the ILP leadership. Hardie remained prominent in the party throughout its pre-war history. His *Labour Leader* served as one of the nurseries which helped shape the lower-middle-class leadership of the ILP's National Administrative Council. By 1900 the outstanding figures on the NAC were distinctly non-proletarian figures like J. Burce Glasier, a former designer, Phillip Snowden, once a minor civil servant, and Ramsay MacDonald, who started as a chemist's assistant and a clerk.[59] In all three cases their steps up the party ladder were via professional journalism and oratory or lecturing. Hardie succeeded, unlike the New Unionists, not only in becoming a professional journalist, but in graduating from industrial organising to a political career by his skilful use of the press. Hardie is therefore the odd man out. When the New Unionists faded from the party leadership at the turn of the century, he remained. Hardie's early life has all the hallmarks of the self-educated worker. He possessed an urge for self-improvement and self-education unusual amongst his fellow miners.[60] Even before he became a trade-union activist, he had attended night-school and learnt the rudiments of grammar and syntax. By the early 1880s he was acquainted with both Latin and French, and displayed an undisciplined passion for reading, mainly Burns and Scottish history, but biographies of prominent men attracted his attention as well.[61] The two theories which shaped his early self-education, the Victorian credo of self-help and the elitism of Carlyle, attracted him to edifying biographies. Here he could see the proof of Carlyle's precepts acted out again and again in history. As an evangelical Christian and a temperance advocate he further separated himself from the ordinary life of the miner. Through temperance and evangelicalism he established contacts at an early stage with the Liberal Party's local organisations. By 1880 he was elected to the prestigous post of miners' agent.[62]

His early trade-union career was jeopardised by his involvement in a strike which ended in fiasco and resulted in his unemployment. Forced to take other work, he found a position on the local radical newspaper, the *Adrossian and Saltcoats Herald*. It saved him from poverty and served as a major stepping-stone in his career. His clear, competent style kept him employed with this newspaper from 1882 to 1887.[63] In 1886, partly through the voice he acquired in his 'Labour Notes' for this newspaper, he was appointed secretary of the Ayrshire Miners' Union. His union official's salary of £75 per year was supplemented by journalism. In the following year he spread his growing reputation as a forthright labour leader. During his election campaign for the Mid-Lanark seat in the same year his relationship with Champion's *Labour Elector* helped him gain Tom Mann as his election agent. Until 1895 Hardie was connected to Champion in one form or another, and his financial assistance was invaluable. When Hardie was finally elected to his seat in Parliament in 1892, it was the assistance of London's progressive and socialist journalism which allowed him to gain widespread popularity in West Ham.[64] His entry into London politics had been through Champion's contacts, and journalism served as a springboard for Hardie's national political achievements.

Hardie's greatest ambition was to establish a London-based edition of the *Labour Leader*. In 1894 he succeeded in collecting enough share capital to allow it to open, although he was constantly in financial straits and to secure this money had to receive donations from middle-class Christian Socialists. One channel was his friend Frank Smith, a former Salvation Army member who had tried his hand at London journalism in the early 1890s. Smith became Hardie's closest friend. Both of them shared an interest in the occult and both were deeply influenced by the moralism of Nonconformity. It was partially because Hardie continued to enunciate his early self-help philosophy that he gained sympathetic support from Liberals and Christian Socialists.[65]

The London edition of the *Labour Leader* served as Hardie's 'megaphone' during the 1890s.[66] Before ILP annual congresses, for example, he regularly advised delegates from hostile branches to override their mandates and follow his political advice. Through his friendship with W. T. Stead he also tried to embody the 'new journalism' in the *Labour Leader*.[67] Like Blatchford he adopted a personal style and introduced his staff to his readers as if they were all members of one family. Hardie's control of the *Labour Leader* was highly paternalistic. He remained firmly in charge of all aspects of its management, writing not only the children's and women's columns but most of its chief editorials.[68] His staff were active members of the ILP. From Scotland, Robert Smillie, the miners' leader, cemented Hardie's relationship with his original power-base; Bruce Glasier wrote articles on the 'religion of socialism' for the benefit of the ethical socialists attracted to the ILP; Sam Hobson, a commercial traveller, and Fred Brocklehurst, a Cambridge graduate who sat on the NAC for most of the 1890s, kept the paper in touch with middle-class support.

While the *Labour Leader* was never as exciting as *The Clarion* and its readership was far less, the paper kept Hardie's name and image in the public's mind.[69] As the ILP's first paper, the *Labour Leader* maintained Hardie's popularity within party circles. It helped him remain the leadership's most popular figure. And when its financial problems became too acute it was a natural (though not smooth) development for it to become the ILP's official paper.

For many years previously, however, the press had been an integral part of the development of the ILP 'machine'.

In 1891 Eleanor Marx reported to the Brussels congress of the Second International that the British socialist movement possessed no organs which belonged to

> a definitely constituted working class party. Such papers as we have are either private property, run more or less as a speculation, or newspapers, giving very valuable information no doubt, but absolutely no theoretical teaching; or, as in the case of the Social Democratic Federation organ, *Justice*, they belong to sects, and do not reach the mass of workers.[70]

Eleanor Marx's account misunderstood the changing nature of the socialist press. Working-class journalism was moving away from the older Chartist tradition of supplying 'knowledge' to its readers. The more successful newspapers incorporated 'news' and entertainment in their columns. But veterans lamented the shift in emphasis.[71]

John H. Owen, a Manchester 'reform news vendor', wrote to the *Workman's Times* in 1893 recalling that 'our forefathers believed that the emancipation of enslaved men, would be a free press', but now, the dismayed Owenite continued, the great majority of workers supported the non-political sporting papers.[72] The demand for reform literature cut in the older Chartist style was out of fashion, and the 'reform news vendor' could only cry, 'shame upon the workman's clubs' which didn't bother to sell or report the movement's press.[73] Joe Waddington, another Mancunian socialist newsagent, was more sanguine. Writing a few months earlier to the same newspaper, he sought to explain 'Why Labour Papers Don't Pay'.[74] Successful labour journalism demanded enthusiasts and capital, reasoned Waddington, and therefore the sporting papers were not to be shunned; indeed they could serve as a model. Socialist journalism would have to change with the new times and employ less pedagogic and more sensationalist methods. He suggested that socialists read P. T. Barnum's biography and ask themselves how the Salvation Army had maintained its large circulation of literature. His own modest gains 'as a vendor of Labour literature owed much to the adoption of the system of Barnum and the Salvation lassies'.[75]

Socialist journalism during this period relied on 'self-made men', such as Joseph Burgess, Keir Hardie and Robert Blatchford, to widen circulation. All three of their newspaper enterprises had that touch of Barnum, which Waddington suggested was necessary. In one account, Hardie, for instance, reminded a dinner audience in 1893 that

> they must not forget that this was an age of feverish activity, an age, if they would, of advertisement. Whilst deploring the fact they must not forget its existence, but seek to turn it to the best account, and that was here he feared there was a weakness at the present in the Independent Labour movement.[76]

Hardie's, Blatchford's and Burgess's confidants were attracted to, and in fact part of, that 'age of advertisement'. In turn their journalism partook of a large dose of self-advertisement.

Besides these more celebrated labour journalists, the provinces boasted a similar mix of individuals quietly creating a network of lively local independent socialist newspapers. Clergymen, teachers and university graduates were prominent, and financial backers were found amongst local tradesmen and businessmen.[77] Active readership of these newspapers was located in the lower middle class and the skilled working class, but their journalists were more likely than not of the middle class.[78] Journalists, no matter of what social origin, formed the elite of the ILP.

PUBLIC SPEAKING

> It took me a long time to realise that Anderson and his colleagues were completely satisfied with preaching socialism. They had no real desire to accomplish any change, even though they thought they had. All they wanted was to gain artistic expression, to put into words the dreams that formed in their consciousness, to feel the joy of creation and of sharing that creation with an audience. For this they were prepared to endure hunger; to face hardship, provided always they could interpose between themselves and that hardship a barrier of beautiful words. For a long time I found compensation in exactly the same way. Day dreams in the workshop and night dreams on the Socialist platform masked the uglier realities of life.
>
> R. M. Fox, *Smokey Crusade*, London, L. & V. Woolf, 1937, p. 37

Another main path through which political enthusiasts were 'professionalised' was public speaking. The development of the ILP's public speakers produced a small group of spellbinders – Bruce Glaiser, Philip Snowden and certain 'new women' – who probably had as much to do with the popularisation of socialism as had Blatchford's *Clarion*. These were the 'stars' of a considerably larger body. For the working-class activist development as a speaker usually meant the first step away from manual labour, but for many middle-class men and women commitment to 'the circuit' was a daring leap in the dark. An examination of the practice of political speaking throws additional light on the social substances that were moulded into the early ILP machine.

At first, the itinerant speaker was a pioneer who tramped the countryside, and very often adopted a Bohemian or evangelical image, to fit his apostolic role. S. G. Hobson recalled that he never asked for a fee, only a meal and bed at the end of his day of lecturing.[79] But the itinerant speaker was in an ambiguous position. According to trade-union tradition lecturers should be paid. In the North this became standard practice, as Hobson recalls:

> The paid Liberal or Conservative speaker was not unknown but always discounted as a party hack. When the new type came to the scene it was another pair of shoes. These men, said the rank and file, 'are our people': they have nothing except their wages. If they give time and effort for our liberation, why shouldn't they be paid? It accorded with trade union practice: it was not even novel. But like the doctor or the lawyer with his practice they must establish a permanent and not ephemeral connection with their clients. It was really a new profession which, like the comedian's, depended upon continual popularity.[80]

Since the ILP did not develop a system of paid organisers until the turn of the century, the lecturer and orator served to link the rank and file and the party centre. Like the journalist, the speaker bound local movements together, and by the early 1890s a system of socialist lecturing had developed. The Fabians had pioneered it; in 1894 they had 107 regular speakers.[81] These were paid for their services, though few earned a living solely from this, and many ILP speakers doubled as Fabian lecturers. Though the Fabians' reputation was built on the sober presentation of facts, ILP lecturers did not alter their ethical emotive approach to suit them. Women who originated from the Christian Socialist movement regularly lectured for the Fabians and the lecture-sermons of Carolyn Martyn on the gospel of brotherhood, the sociology of the New Testament or the social teaching of Jesus Christ, for example, brought no complaints from London.[82]

The Webbs, in fact, sought to weld Fabian socialism to the ethical utterances of such 'new women'. Throughout the 1890s they lectured them on the need to spend less time on the aspirations of socialism and more on the facts of modern industry. They were invited to Fabian summer camps to become more fully acquainted with Fabian doctrine. In at least two cases – that of Enid Stacy and Carolyn Martyn – some progress was made (in Beatrice Webb's eyes) when they accepted subsidies from the Society to help them undertake formal academic study of economic and social problems.[83]

Besides the Fabian lecture circuit, a recognised system of payment and free hospitality did develop in the ILP. Top drawers like Enid Stacy and Philip Snowden received five shillings, free hospitality and their railway fares, paid by the local ILP branch.[84] Bruce Glasier received 7/6d, but had to pay all the fees incurred in organising the meeting. (If the audience did not materialise at the local labour club he refunded his fee.)[85]

Looking back on the 1890s the chief lecturers in 1901 agreed that lecturing was a precarious and highly exhausting occupation. Fred Brocklehurst thought that in 'the Labour Movement there [was] no demand for lectures of a character such as would guarantee them a respectable living. Even if Sidney Webb were to lecture for a living, stern necessity would compel him to abandon the project within twelve months.'[86] Overwork killed Carolyn Martyn and Tom Maguire by 1896. Fred Brocklehurst and Harry Snell suffered breakdowns, and on occasion Katherine Glasier and Enid Stacy were forced to cancel. Bruce Glasier was so terribly aged by the experience that, in his early thirties, he didn't expect to live out the decade.[87]

Since the ILP lacked funds, paid speakers were supplemented by volunteers. Commercial travellers figured largely among its speaker-activists in the 1890s. The *Workman's Times* noted: 'Commercial travellers are some of our most useful members, for they spread the light from place to place and do not cost anything for travelling expenses.'[88] Russell Smart explained that the commercial traveller was in an advantageous position to estimate the strength and weakness of provincial socialism. Instead of a 'flying visit from a popular Labour Leader', Smart claimed that the more mundane socialist commercial traveller could reach into the grass roots of the movement. 'My occupation as a commercial traveller', he informed the readers of the *Workman's Times*, 'takes me into every industrial circle in the country, and my services such as they are, are freely at the disposal of any society that cares to organise a lecture.'[89] Smart was joined by S. G. Hobson and the Social Democrat H. Alexander, who offered to lecture for the SDF and the ILP.[90]

This small band of socialist commercial travellers attempted to introduce the tools of their trade into the young ILP. Advertising and canvassing were two favourite subjects. Smart suggested that the ILP employ a small committee of five organisers to oversee the work of fifty canvassers/travellers, who would spread literature and gain party members on a commission system.[91]

Although working-class itinerant lecturers were present in the early days as well, most of the ILP's top speakers were from the middle classes. Snowden had been a civil servant, Glasier an architect; his wife Katherine had read classics at Newnham College and later became a schoolmistress. The other women fit the same pattern. Enid Stacy had been a pupil of Conway, while Carolyn Martyn had been a teacher in London. (Two others who became major speakers, Margaret McMillan and her sister Rachel, were respectively a teacher and a sanitary inspector.)[92]

In the middle 1890s Glasier met and married Katherine Conway, equally important as an ILP speaker. She had an attractive and magnetic presence. Her topics usually involved educational themes (which she embellished from her training in the classics) or themes from ethical socialism: the 'New Life', 'New Morality', and so on. Unlike many other speakers she was not dependent on her speaker's fee as a source of income. She was a well-educated middle-class woman – and she let her audience know it.

Speaking transformed the lives of Snowden, Glasier and the 'new women'. Margaret McMillan migrated from London to Bradford in the early 1890s. Here she found a popular movement in which she could exercise the oratorical talents she had first employed amongst London's foreign exile community:

The 'movement' was truly here. Our new comrades were alert and alive.

They offered a new platform, public office, every kind of opportunity even to the newest novice. Thus, for example, I began to lecture all over Lancashire and Yorkshire, and even visited Scotland, Wales and the southern counties.[93]

Glasier was freed from his job as a designer in a Glaswegian iron foundry through the dowry he received from his wife. In the 1890s he became one of the best known figures in the ILP. After mounting a free speech campaign in Manchester in 1896, he was elected to the National Administrative Council of the ILP.[94] Snowden joined him one year later. His ascent in the party was, perhaps, more traditional. Unlike Glasier, who had been a known figure on the left before his entry into the ILP, Snowden's conversion to socialism led him directly into the party. His progress through the party, like Glasier's, was also partly due to journalism. He developed a style which was concise and factual, contrasting with his presence as a speaker. Throughout the 1890s he contributed to the ILP circle of newspapers. His real chance came in 1898 when he became the editor of the *Keighley Labour Journal*[95] and changed the four-page to a major local newspaper. Within a short time its circulation was up to five thousand. He also collaborated on the London-based *Railway Review*, which allowed him to establish valuable contacts with the railway servants. When the ILP finally made its breakthrough in TUC circles it was through such contacts that much of its success originated.[96]

Hardie, Snowden and Glasier made up three of the four members of the NAC which shaped ILP policies at the turn of the century. Glasier employed the widespread knowledge of branch life gained from his peregrinations to act as the NAC's trouble-shooter after 1900. If branches were rebellious, or if local scandal threatened, he was on the scene with his soothing voice and personal touch.[97] In 1900 he replaced Hardie as ILP Chairman. Snowden was more plodding. He became a party leader through encyclopedic knowledge of local party conditions. His memory was renowned, and at annual party conferences he astounded delegates by recalling each one's name.[98]

RAMSAY MACDONALD AND THE ILP 'MACHINE'

If Glasier and Snowden served to bridge the gap between centre and periphery, and Hardie – parliamentarian, trade-union militant and journalist – became the embodiment of the ILP, J. Ramsay MacDonald was the individual who fashioned the machine through which they worked. MacDonald, Hardie and Glasier were all Scottish, and illegitimate. MacDonald and Hardie, unlike Glasier, had suffered great poverty in their youth. They came to be 'loners' in part because of their difficult childhoods. Both Hardie and MacDonald felt 'classless' – or at least they adopted an image which allowed them to mix with both workers and middle class. In a party based on working-class support, but where the active membership was largely from lower-middle- and middle-class backgrounds, this could be a powerful asset, allowing them to move between contrasting worlds. Hardie, for example, cultivated a persona that defied social definition. His eccentric behaviour in Parliament and his famous cloth cap owed less to working-class origins than to his own efforts to set himself off from the crowd. As K. O. Morgan states:[99] 'Even in the working class world he was an outsider; his dress, his cap and all, only confirmed the point. Mass movements were never congenial to him. He was instinctively attracted to minorities.'

MacDonald's political apprenticeship spanned the years 1885 to 1895, in the course of which decade he joined virtually every early socialist group in Britain. What is more, his livelihood was generally tied to his political involvements. Unlike Hardie, who had been a coalminer first and then a working-class politician, MacDonald's politics and employments were joined together. In many ways his political and cultural itinerary – the provincial intellectual arriving in London to seek his fortune in journalism and literature – placed him as a Fabian type. Like members of the Society – Bernard Shaw, for example – he had been drawn to London by dreams of literary success, only to have his aspirations thwarted by the tight literary world of the metropolis.[100] Two points, however, sharply differentiated him from many other London Fabians; he had a nose for power and he was a man who had made his own ascent into the educated middle class. Unlike Sidney Webb, for example, who came from a family of lower-middle-class Londoners, MacDonald had his roots in the Scottish working class. While both had made the rounds of university extension courses, ethical societies and free-thought lectures during their early adulthood, Webb had gone from an early training as a commercial clerk to a more rigorous one in the Civil Service. MacDonald's training was more superficial. He never approximated the theoretical work which Webb produced. But he had gained an excellent feel for the evolving methods of mass politics, and acquired a first-rate grounding in journalism and organising.

MacDonald's socialism was always tied to his quest for middle-class status and respectability. Respectability meant both education and moderation. In 1887, during his first year in London, the twenty-one-year-old MacDonald wrote to a friend in Scotland that

the spirit of Socialism is abroad [but that happily it was a movement dominated by the] better kind of Socialist . . . whose physical wants are all provided for and whose education and intellectual training preclude every idea of their being led away by any sentimental fad or impracticable scheme.[101]

MacDonald acquired skills, and a regard for social improvement, very early. As an illegitimate child he was taken under the wing of the dominie at his parish school, and in due course was appointed a pupil-teacher. This was crucial, since he enjoyed the undivided attention of his teacher.[102] (Snowden began his education similarly.) By the time MacDonald was a teenager, he had joined the local Mutual Improvement Society and participated in its debating club. After leaving school, he left for Bristol and worked as assistant to a local clergyman. In Scotland he had been introduced to radical politics through the Henry George Movement, and in Bristol he joined the local branch of the Bristol SDF.[103] During 1886 he was appointed the local SDF's librarian. Their little library, located above a coffee tavern, was kept in perfect order. He left the SDF soon afterwards, when the 'Tory gold' scandal broke. At this point he joined a small schismatic group of ex-Social Democrats.

Later that same year he arrived in London and tramped the streets for many weeks. Near starvation, he found a job as a clerk for the National Cyclists' Union. During his lunch hours he continued self-improvement, reading geology at the Guildhall

Library and taking night courses in the physical sciences at the Birkbeck Institute. He changed jobs and worked as an assistant for an analytical chemist while preparing himself for a science scholarship at the South Kensington Museum. After months of study he broke down and failed his examination. It was a great blow to his esteem, but he quickly found a promising opportunity as private secretary to Thomas Lough, a Radical MP.

He worked for Lough until 1891. The job was a turning-point in MacDonald's development. He made connections in the National Liberal Club and the editorial offices of the chief Liberal and Radical newspapers, and he received invaluable training in electioneering and canvassing. He also joined the 'St Pancras Parliament', 'where aspiring North London politicians cut their debating teeth and learned something of parliamentary procedure'.[104] Though he worked for a Liberal he remained in touch with the socialist world. He joined the Fabians in the late 1880s and was particularly drawn to the Fellowship of the New Life. The moral drive of the New Life uplifted his mundane office work. This too was an experience of crucial importance in the formation of his political style, for it allowed him to express his politics in the religious language of the ILP. David Marquand, his biographer, summarises its effects:[105] 'It was the MacDonald of Lough's committee rooms who was to create the Labour Party machine; it was MacDonald the New Lifer who was to capture the imagination and loyalty of ordinary party members.'

In 1891 MacDonald became a free-lance journalist. He lived in a communal house with other New Lifers – including Sydney Olivier – and became its secretary for the entire Fellowship. During his time in the communal house, he tried his hand at writing novels. One of these deals with young professional people and artists who are struggling to establish themselves as social reformers – a life seen as offering both social purpose and a career.[106] MacDonald did not, however, succeed as a novelist. He did better at journalism. In 1891 he started to write for *The Star* on the labour movement. A year later he was appointed a Fabian lecturer and began to gain knowledge of the labour movement at the grass roots.

The Fabians, like the Liberals, lacked the emotional dynamism he felt was necessary for a party of reform to get popular support. In 1894 he joined the ILP. His reasons are given in an article in *Seedtime*, the journal of the Fellowship of the New Life. The

ILP seemed to be evolving in a favourable direction. Its earlier voluntarism was being replaced by an efficient organisation which knew how to tap the enthusiasm of the grass roots:

> Paid secretaries, paid organisers, paid lecturers are at work in the North marshalling and encouraging the forces of Independent Labour. Beginning with the shallow optimistic man who could not see much difficulty in reconstructing English society tomorrow, the party is now having a substantial accession of clearer and more cautious heads, and still it has lost none of its 'go'. Nothing is too hard for the membership in their virgin enthusiasm to do. They run their little prints, they sell their stock of pamphlets, they drop their pennies into the collecting box, they buy their ILP tea and cocoa, etc. as though they were members of an idealist communist society.[107]

MacDonald had found his goal, and his new roots: a mass party which could retain its 'go' while developing an effective and regular internal organisation. Between 1894 and 1896 MacDonald worked mainly in the election campaigns of ILP parliamentary candidates. He was not received in ILP circles with great enthusiasm. During these years he engaged in a polemic with ILPers who were suspicious of his Liberal connections. He had supported a Liberal in a parliamentary contest in Southampton, and his ties with *The Star* led many activists to believe that he was working for the Liberal Party.

In time he succeeded in getting elected to the Fabian Society's executive. In 1895 a bitter dispute broke out between the Webbs and MacDonald as to how best to use the money bequeathed to the Society by Henry Hutchinson. The Webbs' proposal – the establishment of the London School of Economics – won out. MacDonald wanted to use the money to expand the Fabian lecturing system, but the Webbs feared that he wanted to use it to help set up provincial ILP branches. This was not too far-fetched, since many provincial Fabian Societies had joined the ILP since 1893.[108] The debate was one of strategy. Beatrice confided in her diary: 'Do we want to organise the unthinking person into Socialist Societies or to make the thinking persons socialistic? We believe in the latter process.'[109]

MacDonald was attuned to more immediate political realities, although, we have seen, his basic thrust was by no means very different from the Webbs'. What perhaps really separated them was sentiment. MacDonald had grasped his political chances inside the emerging socialist movement, while the Webbs felt at home in traditional political circles. MacDonald left the Fabians, but did not abandon their methods.

MacDonald had stood mid-way between two groups of Fabians. One group followed the Webbs' strategy faithfully; the other demanded a closer attachment to the working class. MacDonald's, with its undertones of ethical culture and evangelicalism, included Sydney Olivier and William Clarke and joined a new circle of intellectuals which paralleled the Fabians.[110] In 1896 MacDonald became the secretary of the Rainbow Club, which grappled with the problem of how to win the individualist professional middle class over to collectivist liberalism, with MacDonald editing its unsuccessful *Progressive Review*. Not only did he use the radical liberalism of its intellectuals to formulate his own political stance within the ILP; more importantly, the Rainbow Circle provided him a direct channel to Liberal anti-imperialists, which he so skilfully used when the ILP made its peace with the Liberal Party.[111]

In 1896 MacDonald was appointed to the NAC of the ILP, and from then on his political biography is intermeshed with the reorganisation of the party machinery. His experience in many organisations had equipped him with valuable skills. In this case the movement itself had really been his teacher. And when he finally escaped the necessities of earning an uncertain living as a political journalist through his marriage in 1899 to a middle-class socialist, Margaret Gladstone, he acquired a freedom from monetary concerns which was unusual in his generation of labour politicians.

The accession of the 'inner circle' – Hardie, Glasier, Snowden and MacDonald – to the national leadership of the ILP approximately coincided with the departure of many New Unionist leaders from the activities of the party. Before we turn to look at the changing nature of the NAC, we must sketch this group.

THE NEW UNIONISTS

The New Unions arose in the course of a series of massive strikes in 1889 and 1890. These strikes involved unorganised semi-skilled and unskilled workers who had been shunned by the craft unions and had so far proved impossible to organise. The basic theory behind the New Unionism was simple; the unionisation of the semi- and unskilled workers would strengthen the power of the labour movement generally. By creating New Unions which included all workers, the wages of the lowest paid would rise. The enormous problems of urban poverty would be alleviated and a source of blackleg labour eliminated.[112]

As a group the New Unionists were workers who possessed an education and general culture above the average of their class. The organiser of a New Union was typically a skilled mechanic, a textile worker or a printer. Their breadth of vision and wide-ranging interests set them apart from the average worker. They had travelled widely and had generally led adventurous lives.[113] They shared the common traits of the self-educated: a great love and reverence for books and a genuine interest in knowledge. The New Unionists were not part of the casual or semi-skilled working class, but were capable of organising their demands in an effective form. They represented the interest of the semi- and unskilled without necessarily being part of the culture of the urban poor. With their national prominence assured after the successful series of strikes sparked off by London's Great Dock Strike, the New Unionists were the perfect candidates for the ILP. They were articulate intelligent workers who knew how to command a crowd and win over adherents, and they represented a new assertiveness within the staid TUC. If the parliamentary campaigns of Tillet, Man and Curran failed to win the urban poor to the ILP during the 1890s, they did impart to the party a proletarian elan. Even so, by the end of the decade the role of the New Unionists had greatly diminished, as a white-collar professional national leadership assumed more and more influence within the national party machinery. The New Unionists as individuals either were absorbed in maintaining their own ailing trade unions or, as successful local politicians, were immersed in the tasks of social reform.

The New Unionists perfected their oratory to win over inarticulate men and women. But they also needed to be sharp-witted organisers able to co-ordinate strikes involving thousands of workers, with little or no previous organisational machinery available to carry on the struggle.[114] At the same time, they had to be expert at dealing with the press. The organisers of London's Great Dock Strike probably scored the greatest tactical victory during their strike when they gained sympathetic coverage from the practitioners of the 'new journalism'. Their ability at public relations had not been an overnight affair. Many New Unionists were practising journalists. In the North, Andrews's and Burgess's newspapers hired local worker correspondents, among the best of whom were J. F. Clynes and Ben Turner. In London, Champion's *Labour Elector* relied upon John Burns's, Tom Mann's and Ben Tillet's coverage of the labour movement to fill its columns in the last two years of organising which lead up to the Great Dock Strike of 1889.

Once the first, heroic strikes had been fought and won, the New Unionists were immediately confronted with the necessity of perfecting the machinery of the newly born organisations. The New Unions developed their administrative machinery in a shorter period than the older craft-based unions had done. Unlike the craft unions, the New Unions concentrated their funds on building up their membership and their national organisation.[115] Traditional expenditures on friendly societies were neglected for intensive recruitment campaigns. The original organisers soon secured permanent positions within the unions. They argued that only they possessed the practical experience and the organisational know-how to keep the unions viable. As the New Unions felt the combined pressures of an employer counter-attack and the ill winds of a downturn in the trade cycle in the late 1890s, the pressures to maintain a large membership to offset a policy of low dues forced them to import business modes of organisation into their unions. Craft exclusiveness became apparent as the vested interests of more skilled workers in previously unorganised trades surfaced.[116] In turn, organisational pressures helped professionalise the New Unionists. To a certain extent they had become labour experts and as such earned their place within the intelligentsia of socialism and social reform.

EDUCATION AND SELF-EDUCATION

The society in which the New Unionist official developed was rapidly undergoing great social and political change. The working class was changing in its composition and cultural habits. In the last half of the nineteenth century the artisanal culture, which had been at the bottom of worker radicalism in the 1830s and 1840s, was being swept aside by the mass culture of a heavily urbanised society. In the last decades of the century unskilled working-class culture became more self-contained and increasingly segregated from middle-class life. In terms of housing, recreation and consumption patterns the break with the middle classes was nearly complete. As organised sport and the music hall replaced the older artisanal values of pride in one's craft and independence, the radical heritage of the Chartist coffee house began to fade.[117] Recently compiled oral evidence would suggest that a good deal of the working class of the last two decades of the nineteenth century was largely apolitical, apathetic and resigned to a life which combined the constant dread of unemployment and poverty with fear of outside forces threatening traditional patterns of life.[118] At the same time, however, more and more workers were receiving some form of educational training. A growing stratum of highly literate workers appeared. They were shaped by the older institutions of the dying artisanal culture and by the educational networks maintained by the churches. But the self-educated worker seemed anomalous in a world of mass organisation. He or she could be considered 'queer' by colleagues and, in turn, might well nurse a grudge against others he or she thought illiterate bigots. Self-education allowed workers to articulate the demands of the confused and apathetic, but it also distanced them from much of ordinary working-class life.[119]

Secularism and Nonconformity provided the chapels and clubs in which the aspirant worker could learn to debate and organise. Many northern labour leaders were lay preachers, while Londoners like Burns and Mann had served their political apprenticeship in Secularism.[120] The educational traditions of the coffee house, the Owenite Hall of Science and the Chartist reading room still retained enough force in the 1870s and early 1880s to affect the education of many New Unionist officials. Before turning into commercial enterprises, London's network of working men's clubs were used by articulate workers to study and debate. The tradition of 'sharp practice' – the evening debate – served London radical workers in evolving into politicians.[121] In the North the Chartist tradition was carried down to a New Unionist like Ben Turner through survivors of the movement.[122]

If much of the radical content of the working-class educational institutions had been swept away in the 1850s and 1860s, even the middle-class virtue of self-improvement, and its embodiment in the mechanics institutes, might serve ambitious workers. Sunday schools have long been considered particularly important institutions of middle-class social control. But, as Thomas Lacquer has pointed out, the Sunday schools opened up the world of knowledge to the working-class child by instilling the discipline needed to continue studying once the child had entered into adult employment. The concept of 'rational pastimes' instilled in the young pupil caused future self-educated radicals to spend their spare time reading instead of gambling or drinking. Tom Mann and Ben Tillett, to name only two examples, started their self-education in Sunday school.[123]

In most cases the New Unionists, and other self-educated worker socialists, had attained only a basic level of numeracy and literacy when they started work. The expansion of their literary tastes was usually accomplished through a rather haphazard acquisition of books. Popular literature like Eugene Sué and Charles Dickens or the other radical standards, Cobbett and Paine, might serve as primers. Others might use the Bible, or secularist literature, to expand vocabularies and perfect their syntax.[124] John Burns seemed to have started with Mill and Adam Smith, while Tom Mann had Henry George's enormously popular tract *Progress and Poverty*. Ben Tillet studied Latin and Greek when he served in the Royal Navy, while Harry Quelch taught himself French so he could read the only readily available edition of *Capital*.[125]

Writing clear prose was as necessary as attaining literacy. J. R. Clynes started as a half-timer in an Oldham mill and taught himself enough grammar and syntax to become a successful journalist in the *Cotton Factory Times*. His command of language and profound knowledge of literature later impressed employers he met at the bargaining table. Ben Turner became a 'bookworm' after he attended Sunday school and the mechanics institute. He wrote labour notes for a radical newspaper in Huddersfield, and specialised in 'dialectic sketches' for the *Huddersfield Examiner*, before becoming a leading journalist in the *Cotton Factory Times* and *Yorkshire Factory Times*. By 1890 his journalism earned him 30 shillings a week. When he joined Burgess's *Workman's Times* in 1891 he combined his job as the organiser of the General Textile

Workers' Union with his journalism, by promoting the newspaper when he addressed trades councils in the North and Midlands.[126]

Literacy and a lucid prose style were prerequisites for most of the more successful labour organisers. Afterwards, the discovery of the power of one's voice seems to have been crucial. Clynes regularly recited in an abandoned quarry after working hours.[127] Harry Snell used to spend hours walking in London crowds to feel the sensation of being amongst a mass of persons, but yet utterly apart and alone. ('An extemporary speaker had to train himself to be alone in the midst of a crowd: he is in the throng but not of it. The multitude is about him; but he remains apart.') Every weekend he would speak in London parks. In the winter he would attend lectures given by the Webbs, Shaw or Stepniak at the South Place Institute, to improve his own style.[128]

Margaret Bonfield, organiser of the shop assistants' union and protégé of Margaret McMillan, arrived in London in 1894 and immediately joined a debating society called the Ideal Club. It was organised through connections in the Congregational Church and devoted to 'breaking down class barriers'. There she met Shaw and the Webbs. After joining the SDF, she became a member of the ILP and involved in the shop assistants' union.[129] At about this time she spoke at her first public meeting. She recalled in her memoirs that she experienced stage fright, but that her words tumbled out as in an automatic response. She brought the house down, and her satisfaction was complete: 'It was stimulating to discover that I could dominate a rowdy meeting, and reduce it to order, thanks to the gift of a good voice.'[130]

Ben Tillet described how he helped to start the Dockers' Union in 1887:

> At a stormy meeting at the 'Royal Oak' public house, I was driven along the cataract of passion and feeling until I found my frightened voice, but I knew we wanted direction, we wanted machinery; we wanted a base, a starting point; we wanted authority. It was agreed, before I could estimate that my sense of the obvious was what we had all been trying hitherto to express.[131]

The greatest speaker of them all was John Burns. At the age of sixteen Burns was arrested on Clapham Common in a free-speech fight.[132] He was acquitted, and by the middle 1880s had acquired such an impressive platform style that as a member of the early SDF he was cynically known as 'Hyndman's megaphone'. Even when he fell out with the SDF, Hyndman, who was never one to shower compliments on lapsed Social Democrats, admitted that he was the best orator he had ever known. A contemporary recalled Burns during the Dock Strike: 'For sheer oratory, the oratory that could be understood and relished by the multitudes, Burns at that time surpassed all his colleagues.'[133] During the first three days of the strike, he made thirty-six speeches in dockland, and it is not an exaggeration to say that his thunderous voice maintained morale during the four-week struggle.[134]

Tom Mann, the other major strike leader, was almost Burns's equal. 'On the platform', Joseph Burgess relates, 'he was all life and vigour. He accompanied a never-failing flow of words and ideas with abundant gesticulations, and invariably worked himself into an oratorial passion and his audience into enthusiastic cheers.'[135]

New Unionists, as Zigmunt Bauman has written, were self-educated crowd psychologists, who felt most at ease in a mass meeting where they could capture a crowd 'with eloquence and force of argument'.[136] They were aware that their persons had to represent the will of the inarticulate. During a court-room speech in 1887, Burns explained why he had engaged in his political activities: 'I have done my best as an artisan to educate my unskilled fellow workers.' But this statement could be turned around to mean 'not telling them how much power they have until they have become sufficiently educated to be worthy of it'.[137] During the Dock Strike his familiar face at the head of the dockers' procession through the City let middle-class opinion feel at ease; here was 'a man whose public position was a guarantee that the "mob" had a responsible leader'.[138]

Once the New Unionists had gained success as orators, their previous self-education provided them with sufficient momentum to be thrust into a full-time position as a labour organiser. Graduation to professional organising was a step beyond manual labour and everyday working-class drudgery. Even if some skilled workers suffered initial declines in income, a new and varied pattern of work, freedom to use initiative and imagination and the feeling of being one's own boss were liberating.

J. R. Clynes was a skilled textile worker when he was recruited as the organiser of Oldham's branch of the National Union of Gasworkers and General Labourers. His previous path through self-education had thrust him into a position of leadership:

> The Oldham men who wanted to form a local branch of this union were all of them older than I. But they needed a secretary who had 'education' and my peculiar fondness for books was well known. Also my 'piecer' letters [his journalism] and my platform talks had gained me a certain local fame.[139]

Will Thorne recruited him into the union, but warned that union work would be more demanding than his previous factory employment, and the pay would not be any higher. But for Clynes this was secondary; he had been freed from the mill:

> My new status meant a complete revolution in my life. In the first place I was able to say farewell to the mill. Passing out of the great grey building, with my discharge wages jingling in my pocket, I wondered a little uneasily how soon I would be back there again begging for a job.[140]

As an itinerant organiser for Thorne's union, his railroad fares were assembled from the 'tobacco money' of sympathetic workers. He slept in attics, and relied upon the meagre meals of sympathisers. But his new freedom far outweighed the loss of steady income from his skilled factory job.[141] On his first train journey to Plymouth, he escaped from the 'muck' of Lancashire. He thrilled at 'stretches of landscape in which the eye could not find a single factory chimney bellowing – this was sheer magic'.[142]

Ben Turner had already experienced a good deal of travel by the time he had become a professional organiser. For several years he had been a commercial traveller, and an insurance agent, but his shift to professional organising and labour journalism allowed him to mix in a more stimulating intellectual milieu. He joined the Leeds Socialist Party in 1890 and loved its 'intellectual debates'. He also frequented the Temperance Café, where 'Mayors and prospective mayors were regular habitués. Leeds, Bradford and Huddersfield had each their coffee house, where one was certain to meet thinking men and leading citizens.'[143]

Organising was Margaret Bondfield's entry into politics. She became an organiser of the shop assistants' union when she was working sixty-five hours a week for an annual salary of £25.[144] In the 1890s she gradually became acquainted with the chief personalities of the London left. ILP meetings and the Fabian lectures were not mere pastimes:

> I met William Morris at Kelmscott House, John Burns, Bruce and Katherine Glasier, Isabella Ford, George Lansbury, Ramsay MacDonald and Mrs Despard and other leaders of the ILP from all whom I absorbed knowledge of social trends. Truly a liberal education and a wonderful foundation for my work as a Trade Union Official.[145]

But the future had been uncertain until she was offered the post of assistant secretary of her union. Her speaking abilities had brought her prominence, and transformed her voluntary commitment into a professional career:[146] 'I discovered that I had the natural gift of a good speaking voice, which the movements I am proud to serve have used to its fullest extent.' Her new status liberated her from the long hours of shop work. As an assistant secretary to her union, she alternated stints of shop work with free-lance organising and social investigation. She experienced an exhilaration, a freedom from any fixed hours.[147]

The New Unionist organisers were enamoured of organisation. As self-educated workers who had spent their leisure time in voluntary organisations, they had deepened this inclination into an overriding passion by the time their careers as professional organisers commenced.

Tom Mann lived for organisation-building. Mann had joined the Labour Emancipation League after the anarchist engineer Sam Mainwaring had converted him to the cause of an industrially based socialism. But even before this he had been a member of Secularist Societies and Swedenborgian clubs. In the 1880s he travelled through a bewildering series of organisations. He was present at the foundation of the SDF, moved on to the SL, worked on Champion's *Labour Elector*, finally becoming secretary of the ILP in the middle 1890s.[148] He investigated every form of organisation which might provide useful recruits to socialism. He dabbled in the Labour Church movement. Even if he was a 'howling pagan' he briefly thought of becoming an Anglican minister – not because he subscribed to the thirty-nine articles, but because he thought of the Established Church as the best organisation in Britain:

What attracted me to the Established Church was the fact that it was about the most perfectly organised body in the country. I love organisation. I thought that instead of attacking the Church from outside, it might be possible to direct it from within.[149]

For Pete Curran the organisations of the New Unions possessed virtue in itself:

I am a strong believer in the power and influence of the New Unionist movement not only as a means of raising the general standard of living of the men and women but also as a means of good organisation and discipline.[150]

Ben Tillet's model of union organisation was definitely authoritarian. After the Southampton dockers lost a violent strike which he had opposed, Tillet lashed out at the rank and file:

The tail will not be allowed to wag the head. You must fall into your proper places, must await orders and be ready to fight when you are called upon – and not before. There must be generals and privates in every army, loyalty and obedience to order are necessary, and discipline must be maintained.[151]

The New Unionists were mass organisers and stressed the necessity to instil mass enthusiasm in their unions. Tom Mann believed that the trade union educated the workers 'in the benefits of organised action and in the real understanding of their industrial position'.[152] For Mann the trade-union organiser combined his specialised organising skills with what Ramsay MacDonald had identified as the necessity to maintain an organisation's 'go' – its momentum:[153] 'A new enthusiasm is required, a fervent zeal, that will result in the sending forth of trade union organisers as missionaries through the length and breadth of this country.'

The representatives of the New Unions who participated in the ILP's first ten years of existence did not sit very well amongst the group of national ILPers surrounding Ramsay MacDonald. While 'the labour specialist', such as the New Unionist ILPer, 'prized their sphere of work because it was their own, not shared with the management of the political movements, with men from outside whose superior training gave them an advantage', as ILP politicians they were incapable of devoting as much time to the party machinery as the lower-middle-class professionals.[154] An ILPer and unionist like George Barnes could be thrust into the position of secretary of the Amalgamated Society of Engineers after twenty-five years of manual work, not because he had clerical and administrative experience, but because of his extensive knowledge of industrial processes.[155] His time was spent learning how to administer his union, and only partly on ILP policy. J. R. Clynes had to assume the roles of an entire staff when he first became a full-time organiser:

> I had no office or staff and did all the work myself. I addressed meetings which I previously organised, distributed hand-bills at street corners, went all over the country speaking to builders, gas workers, umbrella stick makers and others. In every case I had to study their trade thoroughly before speaking, or they were very quick to detect the weakness of an orator who did not know the techniques of the trade whose members he was addressing.[156]

Ben Turner recalled the general situation of the pioneer New Unionist:

> In those days he had to be propagandist, clerk, errand boy, negotiator, general handy man, and be up-to-date with his own trade details. He was largely, if not solely, concerned with his own union, its work and nothing else.[157]

The pressing needs of the New Unions caused neglect of ILP business. In turn, Tom Mann, as the ILP's full-time secretary between 1894 and 1897, had to abandon his earlier nationwide oratorical barnstorming. He informed a South Shields trade unionist that he would have to decline a speaking invitation for the autumn of 1894, since all his Sundays were occupied by party work. He explained:

> you must remember that every atom of clerical work in connection with the Secretaryship of the ILP is done by me personally. I have no assistance of any kind, the organisation forming rapidly adds materially to my duties all of which is so much to be glad of only it handicaps me to some extent in touring as an agitator.[158]

THE PROFESSION OF POLITICS

In the 1890s and early 1900s local ILP branches deployed a liber-tarianism found universally throughout the British socialist move-ment. Firstly, local Social Democrats, ILPers and other unaffiliated socialists were broad-minded and tolerant; organisational divisions mattered little. Secondly, they practised what the Webbs termed 'primitive democracy' – direct democracy suspicious of represen-tation or permanent officials. Thirdly, there was a sensitivity to the problems of means and ends, as Stephen Yeo explains: 'agencies of socialism represented a pre-figuring of the society desired'.[159] Finally, a deep fear of leaders constantly surfaced during internal party controversies.

The emergence of a more professional ILP hierarchy reflected a conflict between two types of socialist: local enthusiasts demanding a policy of clean hands and pure democracy, and nationally oriented professionals intent on parliamentary success. It cannot be argued, however, that all educated middle-class socialists aligned perfectly with the national modernisers. Indeed, the *Clarion* group could prove the contrary. But the imagery, the language and techniques of professional politics and white-collar work were imported into the party by those members of whatever social background who sought to make the party more efficient and modern. Disillusioned ethical socialists looked back on their original religious commitment as charming folly; what was needed now was the practical skills which professional white-collar socialists promised to supply. The older strategies of 'making socialists' and 'spreading the gospel of socialism' were replaced by more insistent voices demanding prac-tical political results. The conflict between these two kinds of socialist was reflected in a series of controversies which engulfed the entire party on the eve of the Boer War. Would the ILP seek alliance with the radical collectivist wing of the Liberal Party or would it press for unification with the SDF? Would a limited parliamentary campaign be more realistic than running candidates in as many constituencies as there were viable ILP branches to maintain the expenses? If the new realism was accepted, would the rank and file allow for greater centralisation of party control through the NAC? How and where could the ILP find a steady source of financial support? As the New Unionist members of the NAC dropped from sight, the conflict shifted to the NAC and the veteran socialists of the labour unions, trades councils and labour clubs of provincial branches.

Here, of course, one can find local revolts against ILP leadership, what Stephen Yeo has identified as a distinctive 'working-classism', an aggressive, proud response to a leadership clique beginning to acquire its own interests: 'fee-hunters on the make', 'middle-class journalists' or 'literary blacklegs'.[160] Joseph Burgess defined it as socialist labourism: socialism in an imperfectly developed stage. Replying to Blatchford's call for a national socialist party to replace the 'overcentralised' ILP, Burgess explained that his type of labourism, rather than full-blown socialist ideology, would win trade unions over to openly declared socialist positions. Although the Lib–Labs, he wrote, had skilfully played upon the trade unions' widespread distaste for middle-class socialism, he knew of 'scores of trade unionist leaders', who, while believing the ILP and SDF were filled up with 'middle class adventurers', still claimed to be 'good Socialists' working for its attainment in their trade-union organisations.[161]

Such sentiments are difficult for the historian to chart. Their boundaries were ill-defined; their advocates included New Unionists, members of radical labour unions and even traditional trade unionists. During branch revolts, during the debate over electoral policy and party finances and in the activities of the NAC, 'working-classism' appears but then vanishes.[162] What can be said with certainty is that the NAC was seen on more than one occasion by provincial manual-worker activists as a foreign, colonising force with an overabundant complement of middle-class journalists.

This was partly accountable due to their process of 'socialist conversion'. Socialist societies and labour clubs carried with them into the ILP a distrust of political patrons. However, it is difficult to distinguish this aspect of 'working-classism' from Blatchfordite middle-class opposition to the 'ILP oligarchy'. Nor, for that matter, did 'working-classism' affect a more passive trade-union electorate. If this 'working-classism' merely socialised the Lib–Lab virtues of self-reliance, anti-statism and dislike or distrust of wealthy or highly educated patron reformers, the ILP's new professionalism was more attractive than its undemocratic drawbacks for both less or more recently politicised workers, because it promised greater national presence and political leverage in Parliament, and therefore afforded a greater chance to modify the class-biased legal system which had turned trade unionists towards the ILP.[163] It may therefore be argued that two strands existed within the ILP: meritocratic professionalism; and another, emphasising communal values, local self-government and rough-and-ready egalitarianism which in certain respects anticipated in the 1890s syndicalist arguments employed fifteen to twenty years later.[164]

By the late 1890s the NAC's powers had increased through newly acquired centralised prerogatives exercised in pursuit of expanding the ILP into virgin territory where it had no autonomous local tradition to contest. The inner circle of the ILP was assisted by a group of less prominent veterans who had been through the gamut of ILP, SDF, Labour Church and Fabian politics. They were generally white-collar workers or professional organisers with at least a decade of experience in socialist politics. Many, David Howell notes, 'had achieved some sort of niche in the late Victorian middle class'.[165] Moreover, besides the professionals of the NAC's 'inner circle', the party treasurer reinforced the ILP's new strategy. From its birth until well into the early twentieth century the party treasurer was a man of independent means who used his own financial resources to write off bad debts and subsidise electoral campaigners from his own pocket.[166]

Electoral policy

Nowhere is the shift in outlook and tactics more clearly revealed than in the changing electoral strategy proposed by the NAC. The major change occurred between 1897 and 1898, accelerating modifications of the ILP's internal structure and finances. Around this pivotal decision the NAC's policies towards the Lib–Labs, the Fabians, Radical Liberalism and socialist unity were transformed in a dramatic fashion. In July 1897 an NAC still influenced by the New Unionists outlined its electoral policy. The parliamentary subcommittee of the NAC outlined the ILP's two options. There was either 'one to concentrate on a small number of candidates so as to secure the return of a group to the House of Commons' or 'that of running as many candidates as there is legitimate demand for and these polling the largest vote possible for Socialism'.[167] The second choice was endorsed. It was thought of the utmost importance that a poll should bear some proportion to the relative strength of the movement in the country, 'and this is only made possible by running a large number of candidates'.[168] It was thought that where it was possible for a branch to raise the returning officer's fee and indications made it evident that a decent vote was possible, 'every encouragement to run a candidate should be given'.[169] Local men should be candidates, and local branches manage their election campaigns.

But the disastrous defeat of Pete Curran at Barnsley in 1897, and the already weak showing of Hardie at Bradford East one year earlier, opened the way for a new electoral strategy.[170] As David Howell has shown, this was facilitated by the changing membership of the NAC subcommittees and the growing power which they exercised in relation to party policy-making.

The subcommittees

At the centre of these complex changes were dramatic modifications of the ILP's national political apparatus. In fact, Ramsay MacDonald acquired power in the NAC through his tenacious work in its subcommittees. He excelled as a committee man, and after the middle 1890s important decisions were made within these officially powerless bodies.[171] If Hardie helped secure the NAC's financial independence from the ILP's branches, MacDonald's efforts at increasing executive power through the amplification of subcommittee prerogatives fashioned the efficient political instrument to carry out the 'radical alliance' strategy.

A committee system within the NAC did not appear until the ILP suffered serious defeats at the polls in 1895 and its forward thrust was blunted. In 1895 a parliamentary election fund subcommittee was created to raise funds for that year's disastrous election campaign. Its membership was a cross-section of an earlier less professionally political middle class. Such an unwieldy group did not last out the year. With MacDonald's election to the NAC one year later and the shaping of the 'inner circle' in the successive four years, a subcommittee system truly came into operation. The evolution of its membership charts the changing social composition of the NAC.

By 1898 New Unionist influence had completely disappeared from the subcommittees. Concurrently, the 'inner circle' came to dominate the most important subcommittees: publications, parliamentary and finance. Finally, MacDonald, although not as well known as Glasier and Hardie, became the major force in determining party policy by 1899 through his decisive influence in three subcommittees.

The evolution of the parliamentary subcommittee is the most significant aspect of this process. By 1898 it had become the linchpin in the new NAC's shift in electoral strategy. Its main tasks were by then to select areas where the ILP would apply funds and national figures to help parliamentary candidates. Once the ILP endorsed the NAC's limited parliamentary strategy, this meant that the parliamentary subcommittee made the most crucial decisions in party life.[172]

Finances

The shift in ILP financial policy also reflected these changes in its overall strategy. In the early days, when the party emphasised a merely propagandist role, or at most securing victory in local elections, the branches were encouraged to finance themselves. Even for the 1895 general election, the NAC encouraged local branches to raise funds for parliamentary contests.[173]

Fund-raising during the early period was focused on either building the local branch or maintaining the associated labour union. This was enough for even the most dynamic local movements. In 1894, the Bradford Central Independent Labour Club announced that it had to gain one new dues-paying member a day to remain financially viable.[174] The Bradford ILP relied on donations paid quarterly by ward labour clubs, and membership contributions were therefore directly dependent on the current economic situation.[175] In another example, the Glasgow branch had eighty-three members in its 'congregation' in 1893; it hadn't any member with an income over 30 or 35 shillings a week and therefore could not rely upon subscriptions from wealthy middle-class sympathisers.[176]

The early enthusiasm lasted at least to the 1895 elections, when finances were still raised partially from grass-roots efforts. It was a sign of independence that traditional parties and caucus politics had been left behind. But the number of paid-up members in that year represented a high point; the following year it had fallen dramatically.[177] With membership dues falling, Tom Mann persuaded the delegates at the 1895 conference to raise the annual contribution from threepence to one shilling. His request met with opposition, even from such pillars of the party as the Bradford Labour Union, which claimed that its members could not afford increased dues. Exasperated, Mann in a telling speech asked delegates,

> were they really going to finance their own democratic movement from their own membership? If democracy could not look after itself, it had to be cared for by outsiders, and it was this that had dampened the movement in earlier days. [178]

Earlier that year he had canvassed the branches to raise a £5 election levy from each. The response was less than encouraging and highlights the precarious financial situation at the grass-roots. F. J. Ellis, secretary of the Ipswich ILP, wrote that they could contribute only half the intended sum owing to a disastrous experiment in trading. The local tea business had been 'an utter failure'. [179] They had had to abandon their self-financing scheme and return to 'educational work', 'as we find it much easier to talk to some people than sell them goods'. Darlington could raise the levy only from outside subscriptions, [180] while Gateshead, with sixty members, was hard pressed; so many were unemployed that its financial membership 'would hardly total thirty'. [181] Macclesfield had run into serious financial difficulties by January 1895. 'We', its secretary pleaded to Mann, 'are seriously in debt to our Treasurer with the expense of formation, and other costs of fighting two bye-elections since our formation.' [182] And so it went. Branches were barely treading water, and some were on the point of going under.

Grumbling had been heard from national ILPers from the beginning. Conway had voiced the opinion at the 1895 conference that 'if they had less drinking, card-playing and lounging clubs' Mann's shilling levy would be easily raised. [183] Enid Stacy wanted all unspent local election funds to be transferred to the NAC. [184] By 1897 even nationwide levies were being belittled as unrealistic. [185] In 1899 the NAC announced it was 'sick of begging members to pay up their dues', and other avenues to finance the party were sought. [186]

In an oblique announcement in the summer of that year, the NAC stated that 'an effort is to be made to tap other possible sources of income'.[187] Of course these 'other sources' had always been present in ILP finances. Hardie's network was one example, while as early as July 1893 the party secretary was writing triumphantly to the treasurer that he was negotiating with a 'wealthy American' – no doubt Joseph Fels – for a several-hundred-pound 'advance' to the fledgling party.[188]

Freedom from monetary burdens came only when the new ILP policy of 'radical alliance' was put into action. By February 1898 the party was forced to secure an overdraft of £400, which was guaranteed by four wealthy ILP notables.[189] In the summer, when the ILP's new election policy was confirmed by the parliamentary subcommittee, a circular was sent out to the party's 'opulent members' to pay off this loan.[190] At the same time the NAC decided to approach friends of the party to make out subscriptions and pay them directly to headquarters, avoiding the vetting of annual conferences, and securing the NAC's financial independence from its own branches.[191] While ritual denunciations of lax branch dues payments surfaced at conferences and in the *ILP News*, the NAC's private subscription campaign gathered momentum with the opening of the Boer War. NAC members used their personal influence to get George Cadbury to raise a special fund for the party.[192] In September 1900 the *ILP News* boasted that the party was still 'sustained by weekly and monthly pennies of working men', but in a following issue it gladly acknowledged Cadbury's cheque for £500, delivered via the offices of the *Labour Leader*.[193] It was noted that smaller, if generous, contributions 'may be instanced as typical of numerous other subscriptions that betoken the sympathy in the literary and middle-class circles towards our movement'.[194]

The NAC instituted a special campaign fund in the autumn to assist in anti-war and reform work, stressing that funds did not necessarily go directly into the party's electoral efforts, but served to deepen the cause of radical alliance by supporting its broad aims. The ILP's 'task', the manifesto of the campaign read, was 'not only greatly extending the socialist agitation in the country, but promoting the active reform propaganda which the Liberal and Radical parties have relinquished'.[195]

The emergence of one of the typical characteristics of a 'cadre party' became evident in this manifesto. 'A national agitation for Socialism', the NAC wrote in its report presented at the Leicester conference of 1901, 'worthy of its aims and commensurate with the political opportunities of the time cannot be carried on by the present rate of subscription and system of branch meetings.' The real 'paying capacity of the socialist movement' was present in those thousands who could not join a 'political Socialist party', but only contribute at special appeals.[196] It was the task of the NAC to nurture its special independent relationship with this source.

Socialist Unity, Radical Alliance and the Fabians

Between 1896 and 1898 the ILP entered into a series of fruitless discussions concerning the possibilities of either fusing or federating with the SDF. Both organisations were facing hard times, and the idea was genuinely popular. Popular figures such as Tom Mann and Robert Blatchford were its champions, but, as David Howell shows, the new NAC consistently opposed either move and with its new found cohesion, based upon white-collar professional politicians, it would ride out a serious rank-and-file revolt.[197]

Soon after, in January 1899, an article appeared in *Nineteenth Century* arguing that British socialism would have to follow the model of the Jaurès socialists in France, who openly called for a 'radical alliance' against the reactionary threat of the anti-Dreyfusards. 'We can now afford', the article boldly stated,[198]

> to identify ourselves with those questions of immediate reform upon which Radicals and Socialists are alike agreed, with less fear of allowing our aim to be obscured and the party to be swallowed up in the ranks of the shiftless opportunists. We are in a better position than ever we have been to emphasise the fact that independence is not isolation, and in so far as co-operation with kindred sections is possible, while retaining our freedom there is no barrier to it in our methods or traditions. We recognise that a mere pulling down of the old, although an indispensable preliminary, will never build up the new.

The *ILP News* was quick to point to the importance of the manifesto.[199] Radical allies would allow the ILP to win a limited number of seats in Parliament, and at the same time not alienate those thousands of voters, be they 'the workers' or 'the middle and literary classes', who thought that socialist independence resulted in split votes and prevented reforms being carried out by 'any other party having the power to carry them'.[200] This policy of co-operation with Radical Liberals was cemented by the Boer War. As it appeared as if the Liberal Party was going to dissolve into anti- and pro-imperialist wings, the NAC's connections with the anti-imperialists allowed the limited parliamentary policy to find tactical and financial support outside the ranks of the ILP. The Boer War also discredited *The Clarion* opposition when Blatchford reverted to openly jingoist views; the NAC appeared in this case more enlightened than the chief opponent of its oligarchical tendencies.

But Hardie's and MacDonald's new policy had been long in the making. At West Ham in 1892, and at Bradford East four years later, Hardie had essentially run as a Radical candidate. He always wanted an ILP which would attract the flower of the working class and enlightened middle-class professionals. Radical alliance was a restatement of these aims.

MacDonald, as we have seen, never relinquished his connections with the Liberal Party. At Dover in 1896 and Southampton two years earlier, MacDonald also described himself as a Radical. MacDonald's Radicalism had also been shaped by his association with the Rainbow Circle and by his involvement in the Ethical Movement.[201] The Ethical Movement promised a broader and perhaps more popular ground on which MacDonald could both 'Fabianise' the ILP and lead it into a radical alliance. The movement in the late 1890s was heir apparent to Secularism. It found support amongst London's Radical workers, and its leadership was mostly drawn from the middle class. Through its publications the economic theories of J. A. Hobson, the educational reforms of Margaret McMillan and the town planning of Ebenezer Howard were discussed.[202] Unlike Fabianism it had a commitment not 'to cut' itself 'off from the working classes'. But it believed that its active membership could apply only to those 'whose mental training has been a little above the average of what obtains among our working class today'.[203]

Lib–Labism

While the New Unionist support of the first years was waning, in its stead ILP connections in the older, more established trade unions were beginning to bear fruit. An ILPer, George Barnes, was elected to lead the ASE; Hardie's friend and contributor to the

Labour Leader, Robert Smillie, helped steer the Scottish TUC towards independent labour representation, and Snowden's contacts within the railway servants' union were exerting a new pressure. A new momentum was developing within the TUC for independent labour representation. But such a sentiment did not mean that the trade unionists were openly in favour of severing all ties with Lib–Labism. The new NAC sensed this opportunity and began to work towards a change in TUC policy which led to the foundation of the Labour Representation Committee.

In 1900 the LRC was still largely a one-man affair. It had been established at the beginning of the year through a joint electoral association of the more advanced trade unions and the socialist societies. Until court decisions really threatened the trade-union movement, its funds were very limited. MacDonald, as its unpaid secretary, organised it from his flat in Lincoln's Inn Fields. It was his patient canvassing which won results.[204]

But the ILP's newly found support from the older trade unions did not lessen its middle-class orientation. The railway servants' proposal which had recommended the establishment of the LRC had rejected the suggestion that labour candidates be exclusively working class. This had elicited praise from MacDonald, who wrote that it was mistaken to believe that the

> Labour Movement is a movement of trades and not of opinions . . . no worship of labour, and no desire to be out-and-out democratic must ever obscure the fact that the Labour Movement is a movement of opinion first and last.[205]

MacDonald's views were published, appropriately enough, in the *Ethical World*.

Hardie also assumed a pivotal role in the dual shift towards radical alliance and Lib–Labism. He rallied the Scottish TUC to the cause of independent labour, while simultaneously attracting generous contributions from Cadbury, from his old friend W. T. Stead and from other wealthy sympathetic radicals who were attracted to the NAC's new position.

The first major breakthrough for the LRC came in 1906 when twenty-nine of its candidates were elected to Parliament. Twenty-six can be considered excellent examples of New Unionists and/ or Lib–Lab trade-union officials. They formed a group with an extensive knowledge and direct experience of industrial labour; they achieved self-education through working-class or religious institutions; their favourite and most formative books (even if the extent of the reading was exaggerated to impress the public) were typically Henry George, Carlyle, Ruskin, the Bible and poetical works; and they had been effective full-time trade-union officials.[206] Emblematic of this group was Arthur Henderson, who started his working life as an iron-moulder and graduated to journalism, Liberal politics and the Labour Party. Henderson, Ross McKibbin writes, would not have achieved his ascent 'without the division of labour within politics that was everywhere apparent at the end of the nineteenth century, and nowhere more so than in the great working-class parties of Western and Central Europe'.[207] Henderson was 'an example of the *homo novus* of politics, a man who, in Weber's words, has chosen politics as his "vocation"'.[208] He combined disciplined sober habits with administrative gifts which impressed his fellow Labourites and enemies alike.

The division is evident between his style of politics and that of the three other remaining members of the LRC, Ramsay MacDonald, Keir Hardie and Philip Snowden. They lacked his continued close intimacy with industrial life, and he abhorred the Bohemianism of Hardie. On the other hand, these three ILP socialists had created their own avenues of contact with Radical Liberals and professional and educated middle-class voters, who remained a pivotal voting block until the franchise reform in 1918.[209] They had more time to manage public opinion, while people such as Henderson were busy with trade-union and/or Labour Party internal affairs. But the importance of these differing attributes cannot be adequately evaluated without an examination of the history of the LRC and the Labour Party up to 1914.

CONCLUSION: THE POLITICAL AND THE SOCIAL

I have not attempted to argue that the political division of labour within the ILP caused its deradicalisation. If one defines reformism as an acceptance of the constitutional rules of the game, a reformist policy was accepted by most party members from all social groups. This process did nevertheless professionalise and nationalise politics. The ILP's self-made or certified white-collar socialists 'social-ised' an older tradition of professional reformism, and generally speaking socialist-inclined manual workers accepted this ideology. Politically, of course, socialism's white-collar class could be found on the right and left and at the centre of the ILP. What they may have shared was unspoken assumptions. To a certain extent their ethical socialism represented the distinctively modern life-styles of a new social group adept at practising professional national politics. But the difficulties of distinguishing altruistic motives associated with 'the religion of socialism' or 'socialism as service' from personal advancement are enormous. Indeed, it is a commonplace that the educated middle class's very ability to handle language magnified its influence throughout Western Europe far greater than numbers would suggest.

ILP pamphlets stressed the functional qualities which white collars possessed, but couched their message in an older Christian Socialist language. The repertoire of arguments, incorporating Utilitarian and Positivist themes – the need for experts and expertise within social movements – had been put forward by mid-Victorian professional reformers, except that (and this is a crucial difference) a small elite had been replaced by a numerous and growing coalition of white collars and trade-union officials.[210] The classes which therefore embodied technology, scientific advancement and a meritocratic society were on the side of the angels. The message was repeatedly broadcast through ILP pamphlets and leaflets in the early twentieth century. Looking back at the ILP's early history, Keir Hardie recognised their importance. He wrote that

> There are in the ranks of the ILP thousands of what, without offence, I may describe as the lower middle class and a fair sprinkling of the middle class itself. The majority of these are good comrades and their services to the party are invaluable. They very often bring into the movement a higher ideal of Socialism, and a much needed sense of business methods. The ILP would be much poorer today and much less efficient, without this element.[211]

Hardie's opinion was a confirmation of a long-established policy. The early ILP proclaimed the need to recruit from these classes in its 1896 *Statement of Principles*, where it is noted that the party 'refuses to confine the term [Labour] merely to manual workers, and includes in it all those who, whether by brain or hand, are doing social service'.[212]

The confessions of Percy Redfern, one of these 'efficient comrades' in the Manchester ILP, are precious evidence of the lower-middle-class socialist's subjective experiences. His activities in the co-operative movement, the ILP and labour journalism opened up a rich social life. As a shop assistant he had remained 'an ill-paid, black-coated littleness, neither knight squire nor good manual labourer'.[213] Redfern could totally identify with neither the New Unionists nor the more middle-class Morrisite socialists, but he found his niche as an ILP jack of all trades. He recalled:

> Steward at slum concerts, socialist writer, Labour Church worker, debater at the university settlement . . . amateur editor drawing on the ungrudged help of Walter Crane, H. G. Wells, Bernard Shaw . . . for an only issue of a *Shop Life Year Book* – like others of the time, I was all these – member of a stage army ever re-grouping. . . . I had little time for home.[214]

Redfern's type of lower-middle-class socialism was so widespread in the movement that the *Workman's Times* was moved to sketch its archetype, Mr Forest:

> Mr Forest was a man of wide and Catholic sympathies, he was equally at home in the SDF, Fabians, ILP, Labour Church, Pleasant Sunday afternoons and trade unionist platforms. He would go into a park single-handed, get on a chair and attract a crowd. He would take up a stand at a street corner and speak to the promiscuous passers by. His was an intensely missionary nature. With a substratum of belief in revealed religion he hated the artificiality of the churches and raised frequent protest at missionary meetings against the folly of attempting to convert the heathen abroad while the heathen at home was shamefully neglected. He hated intensely the commercial calling, for which he had to earn his livelihood, and more than once he had threatened to give it up and go into the world to work with his hands.[215]

Identification of this lower middle class was accompanied by attempts in the socialist press to discuss its specific needs. Katherine Conway wrote sympathetically in 1893 of 'innumerable clerks, advertising agents and managers, who do nothing but superintend the safety of their master's money'.[216] She thought there were recruits to be made here. H. R. Smart, one of the party's more articulate and prominent commercial travellers during the 1890s, justified his role in ILP politics by arguing that his professional life had equipped him with particular virtues needed in modern organisations. He was a man of balanced judgment who took a pragmatic view of mass politics.

Smart berated the long-winded didactic approach of many ILP lecturers. The language of commercial advertising should be imported into socialist propaganda, he believed, since politics had to be modernised to suit the modern mass man:

> We must have our mental pabulum, whether religious, educational, or recreational, served up to us in pithy paragraphs. The intense application which industrial development demands, exhausts our mentality and renders us incapable of lengthy concentration in matters outside our immediate business pursuits. The most successful newspapers are those that serve up their fare in severely condensed form, that can be assimilated in a few minutes and then forgotten. The five-act drama has had to give place to the musical, or rather music hall comedy, with its rapid succession of variety tunes, loosely hung upon a few threads of story, and the churches have also recognised the same necessity of adapting their sermons to the capacity and desire of their congregations.[217]

Propaganda managed by advertising experts was one example of this class's versatility. Smart opened up other employment opportunities for the commercial middle classes in managing the ILP's municipal socialist experiments. 'Municipalities', Smart noted in 1893,

> can carry out building operations at a less cost than the private contractor. Since the late reforms in the dockyard, government ships are built at a cheaper rate than in private yards. Enfield can turn out rifles at a lower rate than Birmingham. Municipal gas and water works do not compare unfavourably with those under private control. The keen commercial intelligence of the middle-classes that now dominates our local politics is quite capable of conducting municipal industries as private ones.[218]

Smart may have been one of the most openly consistent advocates of middle-class socialism in the ILP, but his approach surfaces in other pioneers of the 1890s. John Penny, a Preston organiser, rapidly made his ascent in the ILP hierarchy during this decade. Son of a coach builder, he became a pupil-teacher in a Wesleyan day-school and eventually found employment as headmaster of a local school. He helped found the local Fabian Society and ILP, and in 1896 he became the ILP's assistant secretary. Between 1898 and 1903 he served as its national secretary.[219]

Penny believed that the ILP's message was directed at 'the best type of working classes'.[220] But even these recruits were not properly prepared to assume full political responsibilities, and he suggested 'systematic training for working men before they could take a prominent part in public life'.[221] The majority of working men, Penny added, were not equipped for the part of legislator and administrator. 'It would be foolish', he felt, 'to expect such men to become Town Councillors or Members of Parliament, and cope with the cutest intellects of the district or nation. The genius might do it, but geniuses are few and far between.'[222]

Penny's involvement in the co-operative movement led him to believe that the labour movement could supply its own ascending ladder of administrative experience. At the bottom the active trade-union member became branch secretary or delegate to the local trades council. Local fame might result in election as town councillor or secretary of a national union. The final rung of the ladder was Parliament. 'Before he arrived at the last stage,' Penny concluded, 'he has become a speaker, a writer, a financier, an administrator, a travelled man, and a man of tact.'[223] All along, however, the trained expert helped supervise the worker politician's education. At the 1898 ILP conference Penny deprecated voluntary co-operative projects, revealing that he, for one, did not admire *ad hoc* organisations of amateurs. The ILP's trading department was the centre of party debate on this occasion. Penny believed that it had to be managed in a serious manner. 'While', he told the assembled delegates, 'it was necessary to provide for the welfare of men who were on public bodies and victimised members', a business, even one run by a socialist party, 'must have experts to conduct it, and not . . . unskilled workers and victimised members'.[224]

If, as Penny hoped, the working class could be gradually educated to assume political power, the lower middle classes remained not only important, but vitally necessary during the transition to socialism. Margaret Bondfield assured her fellow shop assistants that the socialist state would require a 'higher standard of intelligent service and a much deeper sense of civic honour than exists today'.[225] Socialism neither was social levelling nor entailed a sudden radical change. It, she continued, 'pre-supposes an educated people with highly developed mental faculties, and this, in turn, is your surety that you are not ushered to anything rash or revolutionary when you are urged to study Socialism'.[226]

Commercial travellers were assured by Norman Tiptaft of the commercial travellers' socialist society that under socialism the commercial traveller would not 'do dirty work'.[227] Abilities would be better employed; 'for instance, under Socialism, distribution of products will become a fine art'. 'Who', Tiptaft asked, 'will be more useful as inspectors of that distribution than the men who the moment they walk into a shop can tell whether the proprietor is using the most modern techniques or not?'[228] Competition would still exist under socialism; to fill administrative and supervisory jobs, 'only men who are fittest for the higher posts by expert knowledge and capabilities will get them'.[229]

The ideology of ILP socialism took comfort and strength in technical advance. The white-collar sector was therefore looked upon with respect and interest. Socialism was directly connected to science and technology.[230] Like other Second Internationalist parties, socialism for the ILP was equated with the automatic spread and natural development of industrial techniques. Social efficiency and scientific technocracy were, however, linked to its ethical socialism. If ILP socialism concentrated on 'social service', expertise and spiritual values, it was suspicious of class or economistic tendencies. Socialism, according to its advocates, ignored class and employed scientific methods to increase production and programme its more rational distribution, thereby reconciling these differences.

The ILP directed its proletarian propaganda towards the skilled working class. The ILP's chief spokesmen were naturally inclined to such a policy. The moralism which characterised ILP socialism had much in common with the nonconformist Liberal belief that the poor would have to change their personal habits if their social conditions were to be permanently improved. Keir Hardie constantly harped on the great differences between the 'deserving' and the 'undeserving' poor, and his voice was by no means unusual within the party press. Hardie stated general party policy when he wrote that 'It is the intelligent well-off artisan in Great Britain who responds to the Socialist appeal, and it is the slum vote which the Socialist candidate fears most.'[231] The literate, politicised worker, or lower-middle-class individual, was the natural material of the ILP's socialism.[232]

To what extent did 'respectability' and education permit white-collar socialists and manual workers to join hands? Did socialist workers assimilate white-collar values during their encounters at ILP branch meetings? Did their shared distrust of the 'undeserving' poor provide a common reference point?

First it is necessary to subdivide the politicised 'respectable' working class. The New Unionist organisers within the national machinery of the ILP, and the skilled artisans in the early branch organisations, were capable of political radicalism precisely because they possessed the intellectual equipment and free time to formulate autonomous political opinions. But their political clout was still dependent on the manual labour market. With increased unemployment and dual assaults by the state and employers' federations their attentions were directed from politics to defending their labour organisations. If some did graduate to white-collar work, it was employment very much dependent on the vagaries of the labour rather than the political market. On the other hand, politics did allow a smaller group of manual workers the opportunity to become white-collar officials. Some but not all of these individuals functioned quite well with another group. (Snowden and MacDonald are good examples, who although of working-class origins had been white-collar workers for their entire adult lives.) This lower-middle-class leadership, David Howell writes, liked to heighten the image of 'enthusiastic respectable, self-improving working men and women, ready to ally with other groups of progressives'.[233]

Recent studies reveal that this 'respectable' working class interpreted the aspirations of the whole manual working class in its communities. They were 'mediators' between professional labour leaders, political elites, voluntary working-class organisations and working-class subcultures. Mass socialist politics were based on this socially strategic group.[234]

But this first generation of working-class 'mediators' remained anchored to the world of physical toil and did not necessarily transmit middle-class values unproblematically to the working class as a whole. As Robert Gray explains:

The style of life created by the upper artisan strata may be seen, from one point of view, as a transmission of middle class values – certainly as an assertion of social superiority, a self-conscious cultural exclusion of less favoured working class groups. On the other hand, the very pursuit of 'respectability', especially in so far as it invoked claims to status recognition and participation in local institutions, was a source of social tension, a focal point in the growth of class identity.[235]

I would argue that those two types of respectability described by Gray, operating within British society generally, clashed at times within the ILP itself. Few working-class socialists achieved their respectability through successful political careers, but mobility was for certain workers a horizontal experience, a graduation from one manual job to another demanding greater skills.[236] Politically induced social mobility was distasteful; respectability was not achieved through clerking.

As I mentioned before, this assertion still needs a good deal of empirical research at the local level to define exactly how such a radical workers' respectability sustained itself. Concepts such as 'socialist labourism' and 'working-classism' need their social historians. Furthermore, how these mentalities differ from older forms of radical populism has still not been adequately explained. Indeed, some historian advocates of an immutable proletarian consciousness achieved at a fixed date in time have more recently modified their opinion.[237] It now seems clear that British socialism generally, and ILP ideology in particular, retained a distinctive 'middling-class consciousness' until 1914, if not beyond. Many of the ILP activists preferred the imagery of bucolic utopianism, rural redemption, which had little in common with 'workerism's' love of modern factories, ferro-concrete and scientific planning.[238]

Nevertheless, if shared vocabularies brought middle- and manual working-class ILP socialists together, daily life set them apart. Middle-class distrust of 'labourist' socialism accompanied an uneasiness of not being part of the manual working class. Announcing his intention to join the ILP as soon as he returned to England, the wealthy estate agent T. N. Benson wrote to Hardie questioning the name of the party. Benson felt uneasy with the word 'Labour'. Socialism and trade unionism were two distinct movements. Benson felt that 'people who are not working men joining the ILP lay themselves open to the charge of rallying under false colours, for objects of their own'.[239] He would not hesitate to take out his membership, but would rather join if the word 'socialist' were in the title.

Other middle-class socialists tried to solve this problem by threatening, and sometimes briefly attempting, to carry out Mr Forest's vow 'to go into the world and work with his hands'. Usually such manual labour was short term; their skills allowed them rapid ascent in the party to new white-collar positions in its hierarchy. D. B. Foster sold his business to be closer to 'useful work' and, as he explains in his autobiography,

> quickly looked around for a job, and finding nothing better I undertook travelling for a tea firm on commission. I was very dissatisfied and wished more than ever for an opportunity to work as a wage earning producer. Fortunately, this period of anxiety only lasted a few months, it being ended by an offer, which I accepted, to organise the Labour Party in the City of York.[240]

The 'new women' expressed similar yearnings. Advising them to go to the people, Margaret McMillan assured her audience that working men would not despise them, because the same 'electric current of new life flowed through the trade union and women's movement'. They had an important task to fulfil, and she pleaded for 'large-hearted, instructed women, for moral scientists, for thought-pioneers', for which 'the Labour movement is crying out today'.[241] But her real inspiration was when she 'comes first into contact with the living, breathing love of the working women of the movement'.[242] Conway could sense the spirit of William Morris moving amongst them.

The example of William Morris, or his 'spirit', repeatedly resurfaces in speeches and written propaganda of middle-class activists, not always in the most pleasant situations. Conway's working-class women were the backbone of the Colne Valley movement she described in this article for the *Workman's Times*. She wrote about 'women's work where the wages are joy of the heart in doing'. Conway noted the neat villages of the Colne Valley:

> First, there is the six or four roomed house with its shining stove to keep spotlessly clean and neat. Baking, washing, mending . . . get done as if by magic and snow-white clothes double the delight of delicious cakes and pies. The children have all that a healthy, practical love can

give them, and thrive mentally and morally under a little wholesome neglect. Husbands who come in and out at all hours under exigencies of night shifts and have their meals ready and more than one rejoices in wearing shirts and blouses royally embroidered.[243]

This socialist hostess to the 'various vagrant agitators' travelling through the valley handled unexpected guests with ease:

> Numbers seem of no kind of consideration. The meeting is over, and while the crowd disperses we find the wife has gone home . . . so . . . that all may be bright and ready for the campaigner's return. In they come, a small host, and fill every vacant corner of the room, but there is no sign of dismay in the hostess, no apparent recognition of the fact that all the washing-up and extra baking will fall to her already fully taxed energies.[244]

During such moments physical toil and 'brain-work' seemed like two entirely separate worlds which shared beliefs, hopes or prejudices could never completely join. At a speech opening Leek's William Morris Labour Church in 1897 Conway may have exposed the hopes of many like herself. 'Turning to human nature', the account of Conway's sermon relates,

> with the three-fold powers of hand, head and heart, it was shown how wholeness, harmony and the opportunity of fruition or gift were approaching extinction in the classes of extreme wealth and poverty but still survived to some extent in the middle classes the condition of which Socialism would universalise.[245]

While this socialism of the white collar became more noticeable as we approach 1914, by the beginning of the century the arguments were firmly in place. Although dependence on expertise and centralised control had been an argument favoured by the 'inner circle' of the ILP's NAC since 1896, now, however, it looked to a revolution in the social support on which the party machine would rest. In 1898 they sent a rather full and careful report to Australian and American socialists which diagnosed that

> Among the educated and professional classes also a great change is going on. School teachers and the younger clergy are very largely with us, and the next few years cannot fail to witness a revolutionary change in

the political thought of the nation. The movement is still distinctly a working class one, but the presence of an educated element with its business training is bound to be valuable. We are sometimes apt to overlook the fact that Socialism can never be realised until its main principles are accepted by the thinking portion of every section of the community. Human consciousness rather than class consciousness seems to us to be the great need of the age. This feeling of human solidarity need not be the prerogative of any class, and can only find its realisation through the application of Socialism. To deny this is to assert that no one other than the actual workers can become Socialist, which, of course, is absurd.[246]

NOTES

Abbreviations

FJC = Francis Johnson Correspondence
LL = *Labour Leader*
ET = *Workman's Times*

1 E. P. Thompson, 'Homage to Tom Maguire', in A. Briggs and J. Saville (eds), *Essays in Labour History*, London, Macmillan, 1967, p. 277.
2 H. Pelling, *Origins of the Labour Party*, Oxford University Press, 1965, p. 123.
3 D. Howell, *British Workers and the Independent Labour Party, 1888–1906*, Manchester University Press, 1983. See also J. Smith, 'Labour tradition in Glasgow and Liverpool', *History Workshop Journal*, no. 17 (Spring), 1984, pp. 32–56.
4 S. Yeo, 'A New Life: the religion of socialism in Britain 1883–1896', *History Workshop Journal*, no. 4 (Autumn), 1977, p. 46.
5 S. Pierson, *British Socialism: The Journey from Fantasy to Politics*, Cambridge, Mass., Harvard University Press, 1979, pp. 19–20. See also his earlier *Marxism and the Origins of British Socialism*, Ithaca, NY, Cornell University Press, 1973; also the remarks by Sheila Rowbotham in her 'Travellers in a strange country: working-class students, 1873–1910', *History Workshop Journal*, no. 12 (Autumn), 1981, pp. 63–95. Three recent accounts of the rise of Labour also reinforce Pierson; see E. D. Hunt, *British Labour History 1815–1914*, London, Weidenfeld & Nicolson, 1981, p. 370; K. D. Brown, *The English Labour Movement 1700–1914*, Dublin, Macmillan, 1982, pp. 181–91; J. Hinton, *Labour and Socialism: A History of the British Labour Movement 1867–1974*, Brighton, Harvester, 1983, p. 59.

6   Howell, op. cit. (note 3), p. 8.
7   S. Pierson, 1973, op. cit. (note 5), p. 88.
8   E. P. Thompson, *William Morris: Romantic to Revolutionary*,
    London, Merlin Press, 1977 edn, chapters 4, 5, 6.
9   Ibid., pp. 440–1. In Edinburgh students, clerks and other middle-
    class socialists were prominent in branch activity; see R. Q. Gray,
    The Labour Aristocracy in Victorian Edinburgh, Oxford,
    Clarendon Press, 1976, p. 177.
10 Thompson, 1977, op. cit. (note 8), p. 391.
11 E. Royle, *Radicals, Secularists and Republicans*, Manchester
    University Press, 1980, pp. 232–45.
12 Pierson, 1979, op. cit. (note 5), p. 37. See also H. Pelling, *Popular
    Politics and Society in Late Victorian Britain*, London, Macmillan,
    1968, pp. 195–7; K. D. Brown, 'Non-Conformity and the British
    labour movement: a case study', *Journal of Social History*, vol. 8,
    no. 2, 1974, pp. 113–20; D. W. Bebbington, *The Non-Conformist
    Conscience: Chapel and Politics 1870–1914*, London, Allen &
    Unwin, 1982.
13 On Bradford, see J. Reynolds and K. Laybourn, 'The emergence
    of the ILP in Bradford', *International Review of Social History*, vol.
    20, pt 3, 1975, pp. 313–46; T. Jowitt and R. Taylor, *Bradford
    1890–1914: The Cradle of the Independent Labour Party*,
    University of Leeds, Dept of Education and Extramural Studies,
    1980; Howell, op. cit. (note 3), pp. 181–3; K. Laybourn and J.
    Reynolds, *Liberalism and the Rise of Labour 1890–1918*, London,
    Croom Helm, 1984.
14 See the interesting remarks in F. Brockway, *Socialism over Sixty
    Years: The Life of Jowett of Bradford*, London, Allen & Unwin,
    1946, pp. 29–35.
15 Ibid., p. 33.
16 R. Davidson, 'Llewellyn Smith, the Labour Department and
    government growth 1886–1901', in G. Sutherland (ed.), *Studies in
    the Growth of Nineteenth Century Government*, London,
    Routledge & Kegan Paul, 1972, pp. 227–62; M. Langan,
    'Reorganising the labour market: unemployment, the state and the
    labour movement, 1880–1914', in M. Langan and B. Schwarz
    (eds), *Crises in the British State 1880–1930*, London, Hutchinson,
    1985, pp. 104–25.
17 T. Woodhouse, 'The working class', in D. Fraser (ed.), *A History
    of Modern Leeds*, Manchester University Press, 1981, p. 383.
18 Ibid., pp. 372–3.
19 This leadership included D. B. Foster, a clothing merchant;
    schoolteachers such as Isabella Ford, Adel Grange, Fenton
    Macpherson and the young O. R. Orage; L. A. Pease, Oxford
    graduate and brother of the Fabian Society's secretary; T. B.

Duncan, a shop assistant; and an Anglican Christian Socialist
clergyman and Fabian, Rev. H. A. Kennedy. See ibid., p. 383;
J. Clayton, *The Rise and Decline of British Socialism*, London,
Faber & Gwyer, 1926, p. 92.

20 J. Hill, 'The early ILP in Manchester and Salford', *International
Review of Social History*, vol. 26, pt 2, 1981, pp. 177–8, 184–5.

21 P. F. Clarke, *Lancashire and the New Liberalism*, Cambridge
University Press, 1971, p. 161; Hill, op. cit. (note 20), pp. 189–
90, 193–4.

22 P. Redfern, *Journey to Understanding*, London, Allen & Unwin,
1946, p. 48. Perhaps H. M. Reade, a clerk in one of the largest
warehouses in the city, and T. D. Benson, a suburban estate agent,
are representative of the 'workhorses'. Reade had been active in
radical politics since the 1870s and was elected secretary of the
Secularist Society in 1881. Converted to socialism after reading
George's *Progress and Poverty*, he joined the SDF and later helped
start the first ILP group. He contributed to the *Workman's Times*
and *Fabian News* and served as local secretary for the National
Clerks' Union. Benson became the ILP's chief financial adviser
by the turn of the century. For Reade, see *Labour Annual*, 1895,
pp. 184–5. For Benson, see 'How I became a socialist', *LL*, 20
June 1912, p. 397. By the turn of the century the ILP had six
members sitting on the local council. One was a manual worker;
the others were employed in clerical or professional occupations.
See G. S. Law, 'Manchester politics 1885–1906', Ph.D. thesis,
University of Pennsylvania, 1975, p. 26.

23 D. Cox, 'The Labour Party in Leicester: a study in branch
development', *International Review of Social History*, vol. 6, pt
2, 1961, pp. 198, 204. For the NUBSO, see Howell, op. cit. (note
3), p. 108.

24 D. Hopkin, 'The membership of the Independent Labour Party,
1904–1910: a spatial and occupational analysis', *International
Review of Social History*, vol. 20, pt 2, 1975, pp. 175–97; See also
T. G. Ashplant, 'The CIU and the ILP: working-class
organisation, politics and culture *c.* 1880–1914', D.Phil. thesis,
University of Sussex, 1983.

25 Ibid., p. 190.

26 Ibid., pp. 184–5; D. Clark, *Colne Valley, Radicalism to Socialism*,
London, Longman, 1981, pp. 26–7.

27 B. Barker, 'Anatomy of reformism: the social and political ideas
of the Labour leadership in Yorkshire', *International Review of
Social History*, vol. 28, pt 1, 1973, p. 3.

28 Pierson, 1973, op. cit. (note 5), p. 255. Indeed, almost one in every
thirty paid-up members held public office; see Hinton, op. cit.
(note 5), p. 61.

29 Hopkin, op. cit. (note 24), p. 184.

30 'M. Duverger, *Political Parties*, New York, Wiley, 1963, pp. 63–71, 110.

31 P. Thompson, *Socialists, Liberals and Labour*, London, Routledge & Kegan Paul, 1967, pp. 157–65; H. C. G. Mathew, R. I. McKibbin and J. H. Kay, 'The franchise factor in the rise of Labour Party', *English Historical Review*, vol. 41, no. 361, 1976, pp. 723–52; S. Meacham, *A Life Apart: The English Working Class*, London, Thames & Hudson, 1977, p. 204; Howell, op. cit. (note 3), p. 130.

32 On supervisory personnel, see J. H. Melling, 'Noncommissioned officers: British employers and their supervisory workers 1880–1920', *Social History*, vol. 5, no. 2, 1980, pp. 183–221. Very little systematic work has been carried out examining why certain white-collar groups are more heavily represented in the ILP and other British socialist groups while the majority probably constituted the backbone of popular Toryism. Geoffrey Crossick claims that certain 'socially trapped' employees in the more impersonal bureaucratic organisations turned towards socialism. Teachers may well have transmitted an older 'middling-class' radicalism to the new socialist groups. It is certainly true that many teachers were children of artisans and perhaps like railway clerks had less fears concerning trade unionism and political radicalism. While this may be so, it is also known that schoolteachers were decidedly over-educated for their immediate environment, sometimes earning themselves an unpleasantly snobbish reputation. Such a group could easily identify with the ruling elites for nationalistic reasons, but equally at times with ethical socialism. Its attractions lay firstly in an intensely moralistic outlook close to their daily behaviour in the classroom, and secondly in its emphasis on character formation and personal commitment, which could be very seductive to isolated educated individuals.

   For white-collar jingoism, see R. N. Price, *An Imperial War and the British Working Class: Attitudes and Reactions to the Boer War 1899–1902*, London, Routledge & Kegan Paul, 1972. For Crossick, see 'The emergence of the lower middle class in Britain: a discussion', in G. Crossick (ed.), *The Lower Middle Class in Britain, 1870–1914*, London, Croom Helm, 1977, pp. 30–1. See also Howell, op. cit. (note 3), pp. 8, 331; on p. 352 he describes the social type: 'The principal spokesmen for the party were citizens of the uncertain territory where respectable manual workers and aspiring white-collar merged.'

33 O. Banks, *Faces of Feminism*, Oxford, Martin Robertson, 1981, p. 123. See also M. Vicinus, *Independent Women. Work and Community for Single Women 1850–1920*, London, Virago, 1985.

34 The only general account of the ILP journalism is D. R. Hopkin, 'The newspapers of the Independent Labour Party', Ph.D. thesis, University College of Wales, 1981. For the 'new journalism', see A. J. Lee, *The Origins of the Popular Press in England*, London, Croom Helm, 1976; S. Koss, *The Rise and Fall of the Political Press in Britain*, London, Hamish Hamilton, 1981, Vol. 1, p. 343. For the connections between London's 'new journalism' and socialism, see P. Thompson, 1967, op. cit. (note 31), pp. 1, 46, 50, 105–7, 119; Howell, op. cit. (note 3), pp. 286–7.

35 A. F. Havighurst, *Radical Journalist: H. M. Massingham*, Cambridge University Press, 1974, pp. 18–53.

36 Ibid., pp. 18–19.

37 C. Tsuzuki, *H. M. Hyndman and British Socialism*, Oxford University Press, 1961, pp. 51, 68, 107–8.

38 Pelling, 1965, op. cit. (note 2), pp. 30, 45. In 1889 Morris claimed that he subsidised the Socialist League and *Commonweal* at £500 per annum; see P. Thompson, 1967, op. cit. (note 31), p. 521.

39 Ibid., p. 391.

40 Glasier was an architect's apprentice, Tom Maguire a photographer and newspaper vendor. Other who played important roles were James Leatham, a printer-journalist, and Joe Whittaker, a clerk. See Pierson, 1973, op. cit. (note 5), p. 88.

41 Howell, op. cit. (note 3).

42 Pierson, 1973, op. cit. (note 5), p. 178.

43 B. Turner, 'A short account of the rise and progress of the Heavy Woollen Branch, General Union of Textile Workers', *Yorkshire Factory Times*, Huddersfield, 1917, p. 66.

44 J. Burgess, *John Burns: The Rise and Progress of a Right Honourable*, Glasgow, Reformers' Bookstall, 1911, pp. 4–12, 30.

45 Ibid., op. cit. p. 41.

46 Ibid., p. 44.

47 Ibid., p. 42.

48 See Pelling on the role of the *Workman's Times*: 'It was a remarkable illustration of the power of the press in crystallising popular sentiment into widespread political activity' – Pelling, 1965, op. cit. (note 2), pp. 108–9. He also describes its editor as the 'loquacious and egotistical Burgess', ibid., p. 146. See also A. E. D. Duffy, 'Differing policies and personal rivalries in the origins of the Independent Labour Party', *Victorian Studies*, vol. 4, no. 1, 1962, p. 62.

49 *The Clarion*, 30 July 1898, quoted in L. Barrow, 'The socialism of Robert Blatchford and the *Clarion*, 1887–1918.', Ph.D. thesis, University of London, 1975, p. 319.

50 On the tradition of 'educationalism', see L. Barrow, 'Determinism and environmentalism in socialist thought', in R. Samuel and G.

Stedman Jones (eds), *Culture, Ideology and Politics*, London, Routledge & Kegan Paul, 1982, pp. 194–211.

51 Pierson, 1979, op. cit. (note 5), p. 71. Robert Blatchford himself came from a family of travelling players. Between the ages of fourteen and twenty he was apprenticed in a brush factory until he enlisted in the army. He spent the next six years, crucial for his self-education, in the service. He taught himself grammar and syntax. To improve his rudimentary shorthand he copied out a second-hand *Webster's Dictionary*. To improve his vocabulary he studied the Bible, and read Cobbett and Tom Paine to develop graceful style. Leaving the army in 1880, he became a journalist. Seven years later he was a highly paid writer for Manchester's *Sunday Chronicle*. At the height of his fame he was earning £1,000 a year.

The Clarion was founded in 1892 by Blatchford and a small group of journalists who left the *Sunday Chronicle*. It was funded by Blatchford and the others through their savings and through a loan; but later on, when the newspaper transferred to London, a Liverpool industrialist gave them a substantial donation. The heart of *The Clarion* consisted of a small group of journalists with decidedly Bohemian life-styles. This group established intimate connections to the lives of its readers. Besides Blatchford (who brought his *nom de plume*, Numquam, from the *Sunday Chronicle*) and his brother, who was a carpet designer and a journalist for *Punch* and the sporting papers, it was composed of two other journalists interested in literary criticism and the theatre.

For Blatchford's life, see L. Thompson, *Robert Blatchford: Portrait of an Englishman*, London, Gollancz, 1951. For the history of *The Clarion*, see Barrow, 1975, op. cit. (note 49); A. Thompson, *Here I Lie*, London, Routledge & Sons, 1937, pp. 67, 123–4. For the backgrounds of its editorial staff, see ibid., pp. 67, 82, 84.

52 Barrow, 1975, op. cit. (note 49), pp. 53, 56.

53 Ibid., pp. 249–50.

54 *The Clarion*, 23 December 1899, quoted in Barrow, 1975, op. cit. (note 49), p. 316.

55 H. McLeod, 'White-collar values and the role of religion', in Crossick, op. cit. (note 32), p. 78.

56 *The Clarion*, 2 August 1899, quoted in Barrow, 1975, op. cit. (note 49), p. 315.

57 H. H. Champion, 'Protection as Labour wants it', *Nineteenth Century*, vol. 31, June 1892, p. 97, quoted in Pierson, 1973, op. cit. (note 5), p. 180.

58 K. O. Morgan, *Keir Hardie*, London, Weidenfeld & Nicolson, 1975, pp. 138–41; F. Reid, 'Keir Hardie and the *Labour Leader*,

1893–1903', in J. Winter (ed.), *The Working Class in Modern British History*, Cambridge University Press, 1983, pp. 19–42.

59 Morgan, op. cit. (note 58), pp. 95–6.
60 F. Reid, 'Keir Hardie's conversion to socialism', in Briggs and Saville (eds), op. cit. (note 1), p. 21.
61 Morgan, op. cit. (note 58), pp. 6–7.
62 Ibid., pp. 8–10; Reid, 1971, op. cit. (note 60), p. 24.
63 Morgan, op. cit. (note 58), p. 12.
64 Ibid., p. 15.
65 For Frank Smith, see ibid., p. 146; V. Bailey, 'In darkest England and the way out. The Salvation Army, socialism and the labour movement, 1885–1900', *International Review of Social History*, vol. 34, pt 2, 1984, pp. 131–71. As Reid explains, Hardie attracted middle-class Christian Socialist support because he retained his Gladstonian mindset. See F. Reid, *Keir Hardie*, London, Croom Helm, 1978, p. 151: 'They would have not have contributed to a party which agitated on the principles of treating the poor and the unemployed as people with the same right and to the same living conditions as all members of society.'
66 Morgan, op. cit. (note 58), p. 67.
67 Reid, 1983, op. cit. (note 58), pp. 66–7.
68 Ibid., pp. 20–1; Morgan, op. cit. (note 58), pp. 66–7.
69 Loc. cit.
70 Y. Kapp, *Eleanor Marx*, London, Lawrence & Wishart, 1975, Vol. 2, p. 487.
71 Koss, op. cit. (note 34), p. 343.
72 *WT*, 22 July 1893.
73 Loc. cit.
74 *WT*, 13 May 1893.
75 Loc. cit.
76 *WT*, 24 June 1893.
77 Hopkin, 1981, op. cit. (note 34), pp. 86–7, 91–2; Howell, op. cit. (note 3), p. 330.
78 Hopkin, 1981, op. cit. (note 34), pp. 102, 302.
79 S. G. Hobson, *Pilgrim to the Left*, London, Edward Arnold, 1938, p. 36.
80 Ibid., p. 42.
81 Clayton, op. cit. (note 19), p. 85.
82 Pierson, 1973, op. cit. (note 5), p. 167.
83 Ibid., p. 168; N. and J. Mackenzie, *The First Fabians*, London, Weidenfeld & Nicolson, 1977, p. 185.
84 Clayton, op. cit. (note 19), p. 87.
85 L. Thompson, *The Enthusiasts*, London, Gollancz, 1971, p. 93.
86 FJC 1894 (1), 15 June 1894; *Young Oxford*, 2 January 1901, p. 150. Joseph Edwards believed there was room for 'but few lectures

and writers to earn a respectable living' (ibid. no. 17, p. 159).
Glasier 'would advise no young man to leave his present
occupation in the hope of founding even a meagre means of
livelihood as a lecturer in the Labour movement.' If, Glasier
continued, 'he has the spirit and call he will come, but he will risk
almost life itself in the venture' (ibid., p. 169). One reason the
numbers of labour lecturers had been halved since the middle 1890s
was 'the strain, the poverty and the uncertainty of their position'
(ibid., p. 161). Joe Clayton thought that those who had tried to
earn their livings as lecturers have in nearly every case been
compelled to give up the attempt after a precarious existence of a
year or two at work (ibid., no. 18, March 1901). Harry Snell,
one of the more prized Fabian lecturers, felt lecturing was a career
that young men and women would tire of, and they would have
to withstand almost endless disappointments (ibid., no. 20, May
1901, p. 273). Philip Snowden, the ILP's greatest orator in the
1890s, admitted the impossibility of earning 'a respectable living
merely as a lecturer, and for the ordinary platform men there is
nothing but failure before him, should he embark on the career of
a Labour lecturer' (ibid., p. 271).

Brocklehurst's 'respectable living' was not qualified. Enid Stacy
felt that since 'a lecturing specialist outside the movement would
consider £500 sufficient, a lecturer to Labour and Socialist Societies
in England would not get on an average more than £100 a year',
which for the solidly middle-class Stacy was not a respectable living
for any Socialist engaged in such arduous and responsible work
(ibid., p. 275). For H. R. Smart, commercial traveller and long-
term ILP free-lance lecturer, Stacy's standards were extravagant.
His idea of a living wage came 'nearer to 30s a week' (ibid., June
1901, p. 310). Both Harry Snell and Snowden agreed with Smart.
Snowden felt that it might be possible to earn the wage of an artisan
as a lecturer, nothing more (p. 271). But all the participants conceived
of lecturing as complementary to labour journalism, where a living
might be scraped together. Indeed, Brocklehurst claimed that he
knew of no lecturer for the labour movement who was not
'compelled to eke out his precarious income by writing for
newspapers unconnected with the movement'. (op. cit. p. 150).
And Joseph Burgess added that flexibility was the secret of success
for the labour lecturer-cum-journalist; he 'must cultivate an ability
to turn his hand to any subject' (ibid., no. 18, p. 195). Smart summed
up the social position of the labour lecturer. While middle-class
comfort may not have been obtainable, 'a man with special
knowledge on Labour questions should be able to get a fair amount
of journalistic work as well, and so be able to earn as much as he

could by weaving or getting coal. I could have done it myself and many others are doing it to-day' (ibid., no. 21, June 1901, p. 311).

87   Pierson, 1973, op. cit. (note 5), p. 247.
88   L. Thompson, 1971, op. cit. (note 85), p. 68.
89   *WT*, 30 September 1893.
90   *WT*, 10 June 1893.
91   *WT*, 27 May 1893.
92   Pierson, 1973, op. cit. (note 5), pp. 161–9; M. McMillan, *The Life of Rachel McMillan*, London, Dent, 1927, pp. 73–4.
93   L. Thompson, 1971, op. cit. (note 85), pp. 58–77; McMillan, op. cit. (note 92), p. 81.
94   L. Thompson, 1971, op. cit. (note 85), pp. 91, 99–101.
95   C. Cross, *Philip Snowden*, London, Barrie & Rockliff, 1966, p. 43.
96   Ibid., p. 41.
97   L. Thompson, 1971, op. cit. (note 85), pp. 114–15.
98   Cross, op. cit. (note 95), p. 41.
99   Morgan, op. cit. (note 58), p. 55. Also see Reid, 1978, op. cit. (note 65), p. 55.
100 W. Wolfe, *From Radicalism to Socialism*, New Haven, Conn., Yale University Press, 1975, p. 157.
101 D. Marquand, *Ramsay MacDonald*, London, Cape, 1977, p. 21.
102 On Snowden as pupil-teacher, see Cross, op. cit. (note 95), pp. 6–7.
103 The following biographical details are taken from Marquand, op. cit. (note 101), pp. 4–44.
104 Ibid., p. 23.
105 Ibid., p. 25.
106 Pierson, 1979, op. cit. (note 5), pp. 38–9.
107 Marquand, op. cit. (note 101), p. 35.
108 E. J. Hobsbawm, 'The Fabians reconsidered', in *Labouring Men*, London, Weidenfeld & Nicolson, 1964, pp. 252–5.
109 Quoted in Marquand, op. cit. (note 101), p. 42.
110 S. E. Conway, 'Theory and practice in the British labour movement, 1876–1893: a study of class ideology', Ph.D. thesis, University of Oregon, 1979, pp. 510–11.
111 Clarke, op. cit. (note 21), pp. 54, 61.
112 For accounts of the New Unionism, see Hobsbawm, 1964, op. cit. (note 108), chapters 9, 10; Hinton, op. cit. (note 5), pp. 40–63; E. J. Hobsbawm, *Worlds of Labour*, London, Weidenfeld & Nicolson, 1984, pp. 152–75.
113 Good biographical panoramas of the New Union organisers can be found in E. Grendi, *L' avvento del laburismo*, Milan, Feltrinelli, 1964, pp. 144, 165–77; Z. Bauman, *Between Class and Elite. The Evolution of the British Labour Movement: A Sociological Study*, Manchester University Press, 1972, pp. 146–98. But we still lack a

social history of the New Union organisers. Not all of them were self-educated. Will Thorne was virtually illiterate until Eleanor Marx taught him to read properly. But he had been in the Secularist Society and the SDF; see Kapp, op. cit. (note 70), pp. 323, 329–30, 334.

114 Hinton, op. cit. (note 5), p. 49.

115 B. Turner, *About Myself*, London, Toulmin, 1930, p. 102.

116 Hobsbawm, 1964, op. cit. (note 108), pp. 190–1.

117 G. Stedman Jones, 'Working-class culture and working-class politics in London 1870–1914: notes on the remaking of a working class', *Journal of Social History*, vol. 7, no. 4, 1974, pp. 460–508, now in Stedman Jones, *Languages of Class*, Cambridge University Press, 1983, pp. 179–238; D. Kynaston, *King Labour*, London, Allen & Unwin, 1976, pp. 101–9; K. Burgess, *The Challenge of Labour*, London, Croom Helm, 1980, p. 55.

118 Meacham, op. cit. (note 31), pp. 194–200.

119 R. Roberts, *The Classic Slum*, Harmondsworth, Pelican, 1973, p. 16; S. Macintyre, *A Proletarian Science*, Cambridge University Press, 1980, p. 38. A famous working-class novel illustrates this all too well: R. Tressell, *The Ragged Trousered Philanthrophists*, London, Granada, 1981; see J. D. Young, 'Militancy, English socialism and the Ragged Trousered Philanthropists', *Journal of Contemporary History*, vol. 20, no. 2, 1985, pp. 283–303.

120 Wolfe, op. cit. (note 100), pp. 302–3; Hobson, op. cit. (note 79), p. 104.

121 J. Taylor, *From Self-Help to Glamour: The Workingmen's Clubs, 1860–1972*, Oxford, Ruskin College, 1973; S. Shipley, *Club Life and Socialism in Mid-Victorian London*, Oxford, 1971, reprint London, Journeyman Press, 1983; Royle, op. cit. (note 11); T. G. Ashplant, 'London workingmen's clubs 1875–1914', in E. and S. Yeo (eds), *Popular Culture and Class Conflict*, Brighton, Harvester, 1983; I. MacKillop, *The British Ethical Societies*, Cambridge University Press, 1986; L. Barrow, *Independent Spirits: Spiritualism and English Plebeians 1850–1910*, London, Routledge & Kegan Paul, 1986.

122 E. P. Thompson, 1967, op. cit. (note 1), p. 288.

123 T. W. Lacquer, *Religion and Respectability*, New Haven, Conn., Yale University Press, 1975, pp. 221, 228, 237, 242.

124 R. Samuel, 'Sources of Marxist history', *New Left Review*, no. 120, 1980, p. 47: 'Research seems likely to show that many pre-1914 socialists came from Bible reading families.'

125 Bauman, op. cit. (note 113), p. 197.

126 J. R. Clynes, *Memoirs 1869–1924*, London, Hutchinson, 1937, pp. 33–5; Turner, op. cit. (note 115), pp. 48–9, 58, 78.

127 Clynes, op. cit. (note 125), pp. 40–1.

128 H. Snell, *Men, Movements and Myself*, London, Dent, 1937, pp. 120–1.

129 M. Bondfield, *A Life's Work*, London, Hutchinson, 1948, pp. 25–6.

130 Ibid., pp. 48–9.

131 Bauman, op. cit. (note 113), p. 159. In general, see J. Schneer, *Ben Tillet*, London, Croom Helm, 1982.

132 K. D. Brown, *John Burns*, London, Macmillan, 1977, p. 12.

133 Clayton, op. cit. (note 19), p. 61.

134 Brown, op. cit. (note 132), p. 46.

135 *WT*, 16 June 1894.

136 Bauman, op. cit. (note 113), p. 198.

137 R. A. Wood, *English Social Movements*, London, Scribners, 1891, p. 21.

138 H. H. Champion, *The Great Dock Strike in London*, London, Sonnenschein, 1889, p. 6.

139 Clynes, op. cit. (note 125), p. 62.

140 Ibid., p. 64.

141 Ibid., pp. 66–7.

142 Ibid., p. 65.

143 Turner, op. cit. (note 115), pp. 78–9.

144 Bondfield, op. cit. (note 129), p. 26.

145 Ibid., pp. 26–30.

146 Ibid., p. 48.

147 Ibid., pp. 48–9.

148 D. Torr, *Tom Mann and his Times*, London, Lawrence & Wishart, 1956.

149 Pierson, 1979, op. cit. (note 5), pp. 195–7.

150 L. Thompson, 1971, op. cit. (note 85), pp. 68–9.

151 J. Schneer, 'Ben Tillet's conversion to independent labour politics', *Radical History Review*, no. 24 (Fall), 1980, p. 53. See Tillet's remarkable speech during an unsuccessful parliamentary campaign in Bradford; he was addressing a working-class crowd: 'I have spent the best years of my life and the best energies I possess for the benefit of my class. . . . If I represent you, you will have to do your share of the work. . . . I believe in a division of labour, and if my part is working, speaking and travelling, it is your part to contribute the means for doing so' – quoted from *WT*, 28 August 1891.

152 D. Torr, 'Tom Mann and his times, 1890–1892', *Our History*, no. 5, 1964, pp. 26–7.

153 Ibid., p. 16.

154 V. Kiernan, 'Labour and the literate in nineteenth-century Britain', in D. E. Martin and D. Rubinstein (eds), *Ideology and the Labour Movement*, London, Croom Helm, 1979, p. 53.

155   G. Barnes, *From Workshop to War Cabinet*, London, H. K. Jenkins, 1923, p. 45.

156   Clynes, op. cit. (note 125), pp. 66–7.

157   Turner, op. cit. (note 115), p. 101.

158   FJC, 19 October 1894/ 196.

159   Yeo, op. cit. (note 4), pp. 249–50.

160   S. Yeo, 'Towards "making form of more movement than spirit": further thoughts on labour, socialism and the New Life from the late 1890s to the present', in Jowitt and Taylor, op. cit. (note 13), p. 84.

161   *WT*, 28 July 1894.

162   I have attempted to pursue this problem elsewhere. See C. Levy, 'The formation of a party oligarchy and the political culture of the ILP', unpublished MS, Open University, 1983.

163   On legal threats, see A. Fox, *History and Heritage: The Social Origins of the British Industrial Relations System*, London, Allen & Unwin, 1985, pp. 179–86. For more examples of 'socialist labourism', see B. Tillet, *Trades Unionism and Socialism*, Manchester, Labour Press Society, 1896; T. Mann, *The Independent Labour Party: Its History and Policy*, Manchester, Labour Press Society, 1896. On 'working-classism', see Yeo in this volume.

      Fear of London joined a distaste for candidates who appeared to have been parachuted into local parliamentary contests or were unpopular local middle-class candidates supported by the NAC. The Lib–Labs played on this resentment skilfully. In 1894 Frank Smith and Fred Brocklehurst were the target of 'workerist' attacks during their respective campaigns in Sheffield and Bolton. Accused of being London journalists seeking the support of gullible provincials, Burgess had to defend Smith in the *Workman's Times*, reminding his readers that he had been a cabinet-maker before he entered journalism. Brocklehurst mounted his own defence. He gave his would-be constituents a detailed account of his working-class background and claimed still to be in intimate contact with 'the lower strata'. See *WT*, 21 and 28 July 1894.

164   Levy, op. cit. (note 162).

165   Howell, op. cit. (note 3), p. 330; Pierson, 1973, op. cit. (note 5), pp. 192–206.

166   John Lister, squire of Shibden Hall, was the ILP's first treasurer. He was followed by mill-owner Frances Littlewood in 1896, who in turn was succeeded by the wealthy estate agent T. D. Benson in 1902.

167   NAC Parliamentary Subcommittee, 3 July 1897.

168   Loc. cit.

169   Loc. cit.

170   D. Rubinstein, 'The Independent Labour Party and the Yorkshire miners: the Barnsley by-election of 1897', *International Review of Social History*, vol. 23, pt 1, 1978, pp. 102–34; Howell, op. cit. (note 3), pp. 301–26.
171   Marquand, op. cit. (note 101), p. 59; Howell, op. cit. (note 3), pp. 312–18.
172   Decided at the NAC Parliamentary Subcommittee, 21 July 1898.

NAC Subcommittees (*'inner circle')

Oct. 1896

Publications:	H. R. Smart, J. R. MacDonald*, T. Mann
Parliamentary:	J. K. Hardie*, P. Curran, T. Mann
Finance:	J. K. Hardie*, F. Littlewood
Organising:	P. Curran, J. K. Hardie, T. Mann

Sept. 1897

Publications:	*J. R. MacDonald**, H. R. Smart, J. B. Glasier*
Parliamentary:	J. K. Hardie*, T. Mann, P. Curran, H. R. Smart, *J. R. MacDonald**
Organising:	J. K. Hardie*, J. B. Glasier*, Mrs Bell
Trading:	H. R. Smart, T. Shaw, Mrs Bell, T. Mann (ex officio)

April 1898

Publications:	H. R. Smart, J. B. Glasier*, Mrs Pankhurst
Parliamentary:	J. K. Hardie*, P. Curran (replaced by F. Brocklehurst), *J. R. MacDonald*
Organising:	F. Brocklehurst, J. K. Hardie*, J. B. Glasier*, Mrs Pankhurst
Trading:	H. R. Smart, F. Brocklehurst, J. Penny
Finance:	*J. R. MacDonald**, F. Littlewood

April 1899

Publications:	J. B. Glasier*, H. R. Smart, *J. R. MacDonald**
Parliamentary:	J. K. Hardie, H. R. Smart, *J. R. MacDonald**, F. Littlewood, P. Snowden*
Organising:	J. K. Hardie*, J. B. Glasier*, J. Burgess, J. Parker
Finance:	F. Littlewood, *J. R. MacDonald**

173   NAC, 3 December 1894.
174   Yeo, 1977, op. cit. (note 4), p. 43.
175   FJC 1893 (90), 18 July 1893.
176   FJC 1893 (30), 18 July 1893.

177 Pelling, 1965, op. cit. (note 2), pp. 163–4; Howell, op. cit. (note 3), p. 328.
178 *Third Annual Congress of the ILP*, Manchester, Labour Press Society, 1895, p. 24.
179 FJC 1895 (14), 21 January 1895.
180 FJC 1895 (13), 21 January 1895.
181 FJC 1895 (16), 20 January 1895.
182 Loc. cit.; Howell, op. cit. (note 3), p. 308.
183 *Third Annual Congress*, op. cit. (note 178), p. 25.
184 NAC, 2 January 1896.
185 *Fifth Annual Conference of the Independent Labour Party*, Manchester, Labour Press Society, p. 46.
186 *ILP News*, July 1899.
187 Loc. cit.
188 FJC 1893 (65), July 1893.
189 NAC, 26 February 1898.
190 NAC Parliamentary Subcommittee, 21 July 1898.
191 NAC, 1 and 2 July 1898.
192 NAC, 28 July 1898.
193 *ILP News*, September 1900, October 1900.
194 *ILP News* October 1900.
195 *Ninth Annual Conference of the Independent Labour Party*, London, ILP Office, 1901, p. 15.
196 Loc. cit.
197 Howell, op. cit. (note 3), p. 317.
198 Pelling, 1965, op. cit. (note 2), p. 190.
199 *ILP News*, January 1899.
200 A similar theme was expressed in a debate over Marxist 'revisionism'. In the autumn of 1899 Andreas Scheu, an Austrian socialist exile friend of William Morris, wrote a critical review of Bernstein's *Evolutionary Socialism*. Bernstein replied to his critic in the following issue, explaining that he was attempting only to modernise Marx. The ILP endorsed Bernstein's new emphasis on the middle class's role in socialism and saw his supporters in the SDP as 'an indication of the inevitable growth of an ILP spirit in the German Socialist Movement'. Radical alliance was therefore in tune with developments on the Continent. See *ILP News*, 31 October 1899, 30 November 1899.
201 Morgan, op. cit. (note 58), p. 93; Marquand, op. cit. (note 101), p. 63.
202 P. Thompson, 1967, op. cit. (note 31), p. 34; Mackillop, op. cit. (note 121).
203 *Ethical World*, 7 September 1898. A sociologist of religion describes 'ethical culture' as 'a middle-class Labour Church'. See S. Budd,

Varieties of Unbelief: Atheists and Agnostics, London, Heinemann, 1977, p. 188.

204 Pelling, 1965, op. cit. (note 2), pp. 192–206; Marquand, op. cit. (note 101), p. 72.

205 *Ethical World*, 10 March 1900.

206 D. E. Martin, '"The instruments of the people": the Parliamentary Labour Party in 1906', in Martin and Rubinstein, op. cit. (note 154), pp. 125–46.

207 R. I. McKibbin, 'Arthur Henderson as labour leader', *International Review of Social History*, vol. 23, pt 1, 1978, p. 94.

208 Ibid., pp. 94–5.

209 Mathew, McKibbin and Kay, op. cit. (note 31). Not only franchise restrictions affected recruitment patterns and electoral support for the ILP. Manual workers were unable to attend local council meetings during afternoons; for this very practical reason, the self-employed or professionals were chosen as candidates. See Howell, op. cit. (note 3), p. 332.

210 N. G. Annan, 'The intellectual aristocracy', in J. H. Plumb (ed.), *Studies in Social History*, London, Longmans, 1955; R. Harrison, 'The positivists: a study of Labour's intellectuals', in *Before the Socialists*, London, Routledge & Kegan Paul, 1965; H. Perkin, *The Origins of Modern English Society, 1780–1880*, London, Routledge & Kegan Paul, 1969, pp. 252–70; P. Hollis (ed.), *Pressure from Without*, London, Edward Arnold, 1974; C. Harvie, *Lights of Liberalism*, London, Allen Lane, 1976; C. Kent, *Brains and Numbers: Elitism, Comtism and Democracy in Mid-Victorian England*, Toronto University Press, 1978; R. N. Soffer, *Elites and Society in England*, Berkeley, University of California Press, 1978; Kiernan, op. cit. (note 154); S. Collini, *Liberalism and Sociology: L. T. Hobhouse and Political Argument in England 1880–1914*, Cambridge University Press, 1979, pp. 13–50; H. Perkin, 'Land reform and class conflict in Victorian Britain', in *The Structured Crowd*, Brighton, Harvester, 1981; N. Kirk, *The Growth of Working Class Reformism in Mid-Victorian England*, London, Croom Helm, 1983; P. Adelman, *Victorian Radicalism: The Middle-Class Experience 1830–1914*, London, Longman, 1984; L. Goldman, 'The Social Science Association, 1857–1886: a forum for mid-Victorian liberalism', *Economic History Review*, no. 398, January 1986, pp. 95–134; D. Powell, 'The New Liberalism and the rise of Labour, 1886–1906', *Historical Journal*, vol. 29, no. 2, 1986, pp. 369–93.

211 K. Hardie, *My Confession of Faith in the Labour Alliance*, London, ILP Publications Department, 1911, p. 7.

212 NAC, *The Independent Labour Party: Statement of Principles*, London, Labour Press Society, 1896, p. 3.

213 Redfern, op. cit. (note 22), p. 30.
214 Ibid., pp. 47–8.
215 *WT*, 14 July 1894.
216 *WT*, 30 September 1893.
217 H. R. Smart, *ILP News*, March 1899.
218 H. R. Smart, *The Independent Labour Party: Its Programme and Policy*, Manchester, Labour Press, 1893, pp. 8–9.
219 J. Bellamy and J. Saville, *The Dictionary of Labour Biography*, London, Macmillan, 1972, Vol. 1, p. 265.
220 J. Penny, *The Political Labour Movement*, London, Clarion Press, 1903, p. 7.
221 Loc. cit.
222 Loc. cit.
223 Loc. cit.
224 *Report of the Sixth Annual Conference of the Independent Labour Party*, Birmingham, Hudson & Son, 1898, p. 43.
225 M. Bondfield, *Socialism for Shop Assistants*, London, Clarion Press, 1910(?), pp. 14–15.
226 Loc. cit.
227 N. Tiptaft, *Socialism for Commercial Travellers*, London, Clarion Press, 1910(?), p. 10.
228 Loc. cit.
229 Ibid., p. 11.
230 Barker, op. cit. (note 27); Howell, op. cit. (note 3), pp. 354–8.
231 K. Hardie, *From Serfdom to Socialism*, London, ILP Publications Department, 1907, p. 26. See also Hinton, op. cit. (note 5), p. 38.
232 Roberts, op. cit. (note 119), p. 178: 'In factory and workshop they were very often the most skilled and knowledgeable hands, doing work to the highest standards, not to suit an employer but to satisfy their own integrity. They wanted nothing but what was earned: that they demanded and would fight for. Active in their "society" or "trades clubs" . . . member of choirs, cycling and walking groups, socialist Sunday Schools or Methodist Chapels, readers of Ruskin, Dickens, Kingsley, Carlyle and Scott, teetotalers, often, straitlaced, idealistic, naïve, they troubled and disturbed the Liberal voting artisan, made him feel that his preoccupation with mere pay issues of the day was pitifully inadequate when a whole new society waited to be born.'
233 Howell, op. cit. (note 3), p. 335.
234 A summary of these studies can be found in R. Q. Gray, *The Aristocracy of Labour in 19th Century Britain c. 1850–1914*, London, Macmillan, 1981; Hobsbawm, 1984, op. cit. (note 112), chapters 12, 13, 14. Recently the concept of the 'respectable' working class has been criticised; see A. Reid, 'Intelligent artisans and aristocrats of labour: the essays of Thomas Wright', in Winter,

op. cit. (note 58), pp. 171–86. Reid's evidence is largely literary. Besides, if respectability did not explain political behaviour for an entire social group, it seemed to be widespread amongst the workers recruited into socialist groups. See Hobsbawm, 1984, op. cit. (note 112), p. 222.

235 Gray, 1976, op. cit. (note 9), p. 142.

236 R. Price, 1986, *Labour in British Society*, London, Croom Helm, 1986, p. 116.

237 Stedman Jones, 1983, op. cit. (note 11).

238 Howell, op. cit. (note 3), p. 354.

239 FJC, T. N. Benson to J. K. Hardie, 1894/199, 19 October 1894.

240 Quoted in Yeo, 1977, op. cit. (note 4), p. 26.

241 M. McMillan, 'Woman in relation to the Labour movement', *Labour Annual*, 1893, p. 137.

242 *WT*, 3 June 1893.

243 Loc. cit.

244 Loc. cit.

245 *The Book of the Opening of the William Morris Labour Church at Leek*, Leek, William Morris Labour Church, 1897, p. 10.

246 NAC, Reports from Head Office, 1898–99, 21 February 1898, p. 108.

6

Socialism and the Educated Working Class

Jonathan Rée

The expansion of educational institutions and the extension of educational opportunity are standard socialist demands, along with health care and social security; and the desirability of something called education is common ground to all progressive thinkers. It seems to me, however, that the idea of being educated is much more ambiguous than we customarily notice; and I hope now to create some unease about it.

The main question is, what is an education, and by what criteria do we judge whether a person has been truly or successfully educated? Or indeed, by whose criteria? For the Middle Ages, a capacity to read Latin might be a reliable rule; and for Renaissance and post-Renaissance cultures, the ability to write it, too. But in the eighteenth century the question 'who is educated?' becomes an essentially contested issue. From now on, the criterion of Latin literacy is much too narrow; but one based on vernacular literacy would be much too broad. If we appealed to academic qualifications, we might have problems distinguishing the valid from the bogus; in any case, even the most liberal academic criterion would be far too restrictive. Almost no women would count as educated by that standard; and men like Mill, Dickens and Spencer would also be excluded. Even though these outsiders often treated formal educational qualifications with great respect, there were plenty of insiders (Mark Pattison, for instance) who denounced academic honours as an enemy of intellectual excellence.

Nor should we allow ourselves to be deceived by the ease with which the phrase 'educated middle class' trips off our sociologically trained tongues. The two terms do not necessarily lie peacefully together: one need look no further than Matthew Arnold's strictures on philistinism to see how education could be considered directly antagonistic to middleness of class. And then there are all those stories of lower-class self-educators – for example, little children making up for curtailments of schooling by reading with a candle when their parents think they are asleep; or young men forming mutual improvement societies, or exploiting the institutes, clubs, libraries and evening classes created for the benefit of working people – to remind us that an equally important, if equally paradoxical, category is that of the 'educated working class'.

There is a growing body of historical work in the 'sociology of education' which, in spite of methodological sophistication and empirical richness, is rather obtuse about the problem of defining who is really educated. I have in mind, for instance, the massive project on nineteenth-century Prussian secondary schools at the Ruhr University in Bochum; Fritz Ringer's impressive comparative study of *Education and Society in Modern Europe*; and various discussions of educated elites and the idea of a 'new class'.[1] What all these inquiries have in common is that they try to correlate facts about social class or status, on the one hand, with facts about educational experience and qualifications, on the other. In these circles the talk is not of 'education' but of 'educational systems', which are conceived as devices which pick up children from certain backgrounds, process and sort them, and then deposit them, some years later, in new social positions.

The empirical results of these inquiries are dispiriting; they indicate that the seemingly prodigious growth of 'educational systems' in the twentieth century has fulfilled almost none of the progressive hopes that were invested in it. The 'system' turns out to be as socially divisive today as ever it was in the past. The new opportunities have seldom given much benefit to children from working-class families; instead, they are seized by the children (and, since the First World War, most notably by the daughters) of educated men. This is at least as true in (nominally) socialist countries as under capitalist regimes.[2]

These findings are a sobering and salutary specific against false optimism, no doubt; but they can also be seriously misleading. It may even be that they are still too optimistic. They all tell a story of public educational institutions 'growing' from some small base established in the first half of the nineteenth century. The institutions were centralised by administrations associated more or less closely with various levels of the state; and these agencies produced statistical accounts of their activities. Since these statistics are the data on which today's historical sociologists of education base their conclusions, the result is a perpetual reconfirmation of a story about 'educational systems' expanding to fill a vacuum. But it is a tall story. The truth is that 'educational systems' stifled and obliterated unsystematic learning institutions – nurseries, apprenticeships, private tutors and private schools, self-help groups and clubs, evening classes, political and religious training and propaganda organisations, not to mention educational games and parental or grandparental conversation in the family circle. So whilst the statistical sources may display an expansion of the 'educational system', it may well be that so many uncentralised institutions were destroyed in the process that the net effect was a reduction in the quantity of education taking place.[3]

Another thing that often goes wrong when we think in terms of 'educational systems' is that the description of an education's intellectual content gets channelled into a disheartening and uninformative dualism. First there is the elegant brand of education, which claims to provide a graceful competence in classical humanities or in pure science – though we may knowingly suspect it to be nothing but a theme for snobbery, an instrument for intimidating the uncouth, a convenient filter for limiting the number of candidates for high office in industry, church or state and, for daughters, a secure and portable dowry which will enhance their value on the marriage market. Then there is, on the other hand, the inelegant and tediously useful 'modern' brand of education which is supposed to train for particular occupations: chemistry for industrialists, perhaps; law, social science, politics and modern history for politicians and bureaucrats; modern languages and literature for schoolteachers or the wives of professional men; and on down to the lowest-status training for poorly paid jobs.

The findings of historical sociology, organised in terms of this dualism between elite and utilitarian education, deliver yet another blow to optimistic educational progressivism, since they indicate that when the long arm of the educational 'system' reaches into the home of a poor family, it will be to force the children along the paths of ugly utility, excluding them as cruelly as ever from the privileges of high culture.

Once again, however, it is likely that the idea of an 'educational system' (in this case, of a divided one) is causing the data to delude us. Was the distinction between elite and utilitarian education as clear as the statistical record makes it seem? Who says that the 'modern' subjects are intrinsically dull? Who, indeed, says which subjects are 'modern'? To answer such questions, we would need to study not only the syllabuses and course objectives devised by teachers and officials, but also (more important by far, but less accessible) the effective knowledge actually acquired by learners: techniques and theories for handling the physical world; skills in holding down a job or holding off oppression; imagination to make unexpected choices or to fend off threats to personal cheer or survival; words and concepts for setting and contesting social goals and political programmes. Education provides people with more than ritualised etiquettes and empty symbols of social standing; it furnishes insights into the world, and powers over it; and it can inculcate aspirations quite at odds with the values of the social milieux in which it is located. For these reasons, I think we should revert to speaking of knowledge and learning, and discard the beguiling term 'educational system' altogether.

This sociological blindness to the content of education is particularly disabling when one is dealing with problems in the history of socialism, because it leads to neglect of some of the main ideas behind the socialist hopes of the past. One of these is that educational opportunity should be extended not as an indirect means of social levelling, but for knowledge's own dear sake; and that capitalism is to be hated not only for its economic injustice, but for the injuries it inflicts on working people's intellectual culture too. Another of these socialist ideas, vital once but hard to recover today, is that knowledge, provided it is not superficial or biased, is directly and automatically socialist, since socialism is, at bottom, the only reasonable arrangement of humanity. And a third idea, related to these, is that education makes socialists, because the inadequacy of all non-socialist social fabrics will be evident to any truly educated mind.

These ideas were embodied in the movement which I have tried to describe in my book, *Proletarian Philosophers*.[4] The story is that, in the first half of the nineteenth century, philosophy establishes itself as the supreme discipline of the European universities. It stands for the aspiration (it may be no more than that) towards an inclusive discipline within which all other pieces of knowledge will be accommodated as transcended, tributary sectors. And in this respect, to many minds, philosophy exactly matches socialism; for socialism, too, stands for a settlement in which all sectoral interests will be organised into a rational and harmonious whole. This kind of affinity between philosophy, the holy of holies of the university, and socialism, the outcast spectre which haunts civilised society, is of course perceived by Marx himself, in an epigram formulated soon after he gained his doctorate in philosophy. The statement (from the 'Contribution to the Critique of Hegel's *Philosophy of Right*') is quoted so often that its extraordinary audacity tends to pass unnoticed: 'Philosophy finds its material weapons in the Proletariat,' he wrote, 'just as the Proletariat finds its spiritual weapons in philosophy.'

The statement struck a chord in many members of the labour movement: militants who identified themselves not merely as representatives of unjustly impoverished workers, but as agents of philosophical enlightenment too. Consider Joseph Dietzgen, for example, the scantily educated tanner, born in the Rhineland in 1828, who died sixty years later in Chicago, having devoted all his spare time to Marxist socialist education, in Russia, Germany and America. He wrote extensively (and rather roughly, it must be admitted) on the history of philosophy, trying to show that its development led up to the possibility of the human mind understanding its own nature, but arguing that only the proletariat was equipped to carry out this historic philosophical mission. Or there is Tommy Jackson, born in London in 1879, who discovered philosophy (through G. H. Lewes's *Biographical History*) when he was a young apprentice, and was led by it, along a tortuous route, to Marxist socialism. He became an activist in the movement for independent, Marxist, working-class education, and then a founder-member of the British Communist Party, but courageously

denounced all those he suspected of treachery to philosophy –
including, eventually, those responsible for British 'Dietzgen-
worship'. 'For,' he said, 'as the thinking dies, the Communism dies
with it.'[5] For such worker-intellectuals as Jackson and Dietzgen,
therefore, the ideals of elite humanistic education were identical
with those of proletarian socialism; and we should not unthinkingly
approach the history of socialism with a conception of education
which makes this position not only over-optimistic (which perhaps
it was) but also crassly self-contradictory (which surely it was not).

Investigations of the history of socialism are sometimes governed
by an ideal which co-operates with the eye-sealing tendencies which
I am protesting against in histories of education. I am referring to
the ideal of proletarian purity – the line of reasoning according to
which the only thing preventing socialism springing up in the
proletariat has been the sirens of intellectual elitism which have
interfered with the proletarians' natural joy in 'proletarian culture'
and their natural hatred of bourgeois and aristocratic alternatives.
The Shoreditch Branch of the Social Democratic Federation showed
their contempt for this idea when they protested against the foundation of Ruskin Hall as a workers' college in Oxford in 1900.
They thought that working people ought to be admitted to the
university itself, not palmed off with some inferior college up the
road. 'Oxford and Cambridge,' they said, 'and other endowed seats
of learning, were the rightful inheritance of the people, and . . . to
attach themselves to any other educational institution would be to
give their acquiescence to this deprivation of their rights.'[6]
To evangelists of proletarian purity, however, this attitude will
itself appear anti-proletarian; and they will attempt to preserve their
idea of working-class culture by sweeping away all evidence of
contamination to detention centres at each wing of the proletariat –
on one side the 'lumpenproletariat', and on the other the 'petit
bourgeoisie' or 'lower middle class'. These categories could be given
definite descriptive and explanatory meanings, no doubt; but as a
rule, the only constant thing in them is the comminatory
Manichaean intention with which they are used. Listen, for
instance, to Christopher Caudwell's analysis of the 'petit
bourgeois':

Of all the products of capitalism, none is more unlovely than this class.

Whoever does not escape from it is certainly damned. It is necessarily
a class whose whole existence is based on a lie. . . . It identifies itself
with the bourgeois system. . . . It has only one value in life, that of
bettering itself. . . . It has only one horror, that of falling from respectability into the proletarian abyss. . . . It has no traditions of its own
and it does not adopt those of the workers, which it hates, but those of
the bourgeois, which are without virtue for it, since it did not help to
create them.[7]

And so, with thickening references to 'the petit-bourgeois hell',
Caudwell beat the bounds of what he took to be the true 'traditions'
of the workers. But he gave his readers no explanation of the
standards by which he (a petit-bourgeois intellectual himself) was
able to sort the true proletarian tradition from the false, and declare
any working person with other cultural ambitions to be a traitor;
and he neglected the possibility that there was a close alliance
between desires for education and aspirations to socialism.

I know of no more serious attempt to confront these problems
than Jacques Rancière's *La Nuit des Prolétaires*.[8] It deals with some
well-known events of the French 1830s and 1840s: the Utopias of
Fourier, Saint-Simon, Cabet and Enfantin; the 'free women'; the
socialist communities in the provinces, the journeys to Egypt and
the doomed colonies in America. These incidents are described in
the words of the proletarians involved; and the striking point about
these documents is that they express, not an enthusiastic convergence on some 'working-class' identity, but, on the contrary, a
yearning to escape to a better existence, envisaged mostly in
aesthetic terms as the life of painters, poets, philosophers and
musicians. 'They did not', says Rancière, 'lack an understanding
of exploitation; what they required was an understanding of themselves as beings destined for something other than exploitation: an
insight which they could attain only through the secret of others –
of middle-class intellectuals.' The scheme is perhaps a little too
neat; but at least it faces up to the fact that proletarian desires for
education and high culture have been vital to socialist movements,
and not merely, if at all, distractions from some wished-for (but
by whom?) pure proletarian socialism.

By the 1920s there were tens of thousands of people studying
philosophy in Britain, co-ordinated by the Marxist-inspired

National Council of Labour Colleges. In the winter of 1927 a young philosophy teacher, Dorothy Emmett, was taking University Extension evening classes for miners in South Wales. But when she tried to teach them philosophy, she ran into a problem. 'That's Dietzgen, isn't it?' they said; and she had to confess to never having heard of the writer whom they had taken to their hearts as 'the greatest philosopher who ever lived'.[9] No doubt they overestimated Dietzgen's talents; and no doubt her ignorance can be excused; but at any rate the incident should be borne in mind. For it shows that the questions 'what is real education?' and 'who is truly educated?' will keep rearing up in the historical record, even when political wishes and sociological proprieties are doing their best to keep them down.

NOTES

1 The Ruhr project, entitled 'Wissen und Gesellschaft im 19. Jahrhundert', is directed by Dr Detlef Muller, Ruhr-Universität Bochum; see also Fritz K. Ringer, *Education and Society in Modern Europe*, Bloomington, Indiana University Press, 1979; Alvin W. Gouldner, *The Future of Intellectuals and the Rise of the New Class*, London, Macmillan, 1979.

2 See George Konrád and Ivan Szelény, *The Intellectuals on the Road to Class Power*, Brighton, Harvester, 1979.

3 Cf. H. Silver, 'Aspects of neglect: the strange case of Victorian popular education', in Harold Silver, *Education as History*, London, Methuen, 1983.

4 Jonathan Rée, *Proletarian Philosophers: Problems in Socialist Culture in Britain, 1900–1940*, Oxford University Press, 1984. Some of the same ground is covered, from another point of view, in Stuart Macintyre, *A Proletarian Science: Marxism in Britain 1917–1933*, Cambridge University Press, 1980.

5 Jonathan Rée, op. cit., p. 122.

6 Ibid., p. 19.

7 Christopher Caudwell, *Studies in a Dying Culture*, London, John Lane, 1938, pp. 76–80.

8 Jacques Rancière, *La Nuit des Prolétaires*, Paris, Fayard, 1981; a short extract is translated in *Radical Philosophy*, vol. 31 (Summer), 1982.

9 Rée, op. cit., p. 23.

7

Notes on Three Socialisms – Collectivism, Statism and Associationism – Mainly in Late-Nineteenth- and Early-Twentieth-Century Britain

Stephen Yeo

For Andy Durr and Paddy Maguire

The world is going your way at present, Webb,
but it is not the right way in the end.
William Morris, talking to Sidney Webb in 1895, quoted in R. Page
Arnot, *William Morris: The Man and the Myth*, London, Lawrence &
Wishart, 1964

Revolution is not a thing you can let others do for you
Mau Kai Yey, talking to Jan Myrdal, *Report from a Chinese Village*,
Harmondsworth, Penguin, 1967

Stephen Yeo

A PROJECT AND ITS PROBLEMS

To use a distinction made by R. H. Tawney, the reach of these notes will exceed their grasp. Such excess, I comfort myself, is a necessary part of socialist construction.

The project is harder than it looks. It is to develop a class understanding of conflicts within and between socialisms. There is, of course, an international tradition of work on this, back, at least, to Bakunin. For Bakunin, Marxism in power would organise society 'under the direct command of state engineers who will constitute a new privileged scientific-political class'. This thesis had 'its most consistent and rigorous formulation' in the work of J. W. Machajski (1866–1926).[1]

In these notes, my base will mainly be Britain during the late nineteenth and early twentieth centuries, where thinkers like William Morris saw 'the creation of a new middle class to act as a buffer between the proletariat and their direct and obvious masters' (*Commonweal*, July 1885) as a likely development. Historical work on this period has forced me into a greater interest in theoretical differences between socialisms; I shall try here to define and to situate three of them: collectivism, statism and associationism.

By a *class* understanding, I mean one which relates conflicts within and between socialisms to materially available directions of development rather than just to ideas or to social groups. Class in its distinctive Marxist usage – though Marxists by no means always use it in this way – is a political concept. It is adapted for determining which groups have real, material futurity or capacity to remake a whole society in their own interest. Where, at any one moment, are the clusters of rival society-making potential?

To suggest that there might be such clusters within socialism is to excite suspicion among those who would prefer to keep no enemies to the left. In many quarters now, however, there is a sense that socialism has lost its guarantees.[2] It has to be made, rather than rising like the sun, and made now, not 'after the revolution'. 'Now, though, it seems to have become inescapably important to bring the real disagreements about how to make socialism which exist on the Left and the Labour movement out into the open in order to develop new understandings.'[3] 'Who makes it?', 'how?' and 'when?' are questions integral to what socialism will be.

From the inception of 'socialism' in Britain, within Owenism, there has been controversy about this. For George Jacob Holyoake (1817–1906) there were even 'two parties' within his own movement – working-class self-activity (co-ops) versus reform from above (Robert Owen):

> The device of self-government and the independent control of common means, and the reduction to practice of absolute equality on the one part, and the class control and class distinctions on the other were the respective badges of the differing parties. [1846]

During the late nineteenth century Holyoake watched the growth of state socialism with distaste. He fought over practices and names for practices: 'the co-operative scheme is no recent invention in opposition to the new socialism – for "new" socialism it is, since co-operation was known as "socialism" sixty years ago. . . . The policy of co-operation now was its policy then' (1890).[4] 'Which way?' as Leonard Hall asked in his pamphlet *Root Remedies and Free Socialism versus Collectivist Quackery and Glorified Pauperism*. Active in British socialist groupings, Hall announced in 1900 that the SDF the ILP and his old friend Blatchford shared a socialism in which the 'country was to be transformed into a vast bureaucracy'. But at about this time Hall also seemed to turn to 'the lower middle and professional classes', on the grounds that socialists had 'now drawn' from the 'labouring classes . . . the liveliest and most self-respecting . . . and have nothing more to hope from here'. 'There is not only more than one way *to* Socialism,' he wrote, 'but more than one way *of* it.'[5]

Quite so. Durkheim was clear in his book *Socialism* (1896):

> There are two movements under whose influence the doctrine of socialism is formed: one which comes from below and directs itself towards the higher regions of society, and the other which comes from the latter and follows the reverse direction . . . according to the place occupied by the theoretician, according to whether he is in closer contact with workers, or more attentive to the general interest of society, it will be one rather than the other. . . . The result is two different kinds of socialism: a workers' socialism or a state socialism.[6]

Like many thinkers in Britain at the same time, Durkheim wanted to encourage the latter, as an antidote to the former. Within the movement of would-be workers' socialism itself, there was fierce criticism of working people, descending to outright abuse. Ian Bullock's unpublished Sussex thesis on 'Socialists and democratic form in Britain, 1880–1914' is full of examples.[7]

'Socialism' in this period in Britain by no means necessarily identified with democracy or with working people. This is easy, if uncomfortable, for left-wing historians to notice in the past. It is harder to see when it involves looking in the mirror now. The obvious difficulty is that socialist writers and historians occupy positions rather different from those of the people they sometimes say they represent. They – and their ideas of socialism – are not immune from all the problems inherent in the 'mode of inheritance of cultural objects' in capitalism which so obsessed Walter Benjamin.[8] Social being has an awkward habit of intruding upon consciousness even at the highest, leftist levels thereof. I had plenty of occasion to watch this on my corridor in the School of Social Sciences in the University of Sussex during the early 1970s as hard-nosed, male, behaviouralist political scientists became Marxists. Attentive as university lecturers like to be to 'the general interest of society' and dependent as we are upon the state, particular structures of thought and feeling got uttered in our corridors and offices which called themselves 'socialist', but which did not feel much like 'workers' socialism'. The hard noses never softened.

Benjamin and Brecht were uncommonly sharp about such structures of feeling in their 1930s 'Conversations'.[9] The structures include: an overemphasis on 'policy' and on ideology and on affiliation to social- and other 'isms'; an underemphasis on *making*, here and now, or on production; a propensity for subtraction rather than addition (for 'either/or' ways of seeing rather than 'not only but also' ways) a propensity for saying that such-and-such a 'position' (a word meaning something in the head rather than some relation on the ground) is not socialist, or not some other kind of 'ist'; a penchant for seeing history in orderly stages, portered by class forces which act 'objectively' out there somewhere, and at some time or other, not here and now. In these structures of feeling, ideology acquires more salience than class, which becomes a Platonic concept, disregarding Benjamin's nice reminder that 'the mind which believes only in its own magic strength will disappear. For the revolutionary struggle is not fought between capitalism and mind. It is fought between capitalism and the proletariat.'[10] As socialists we still find it hard to see, because it is painful to see, our own 'positions' including our Histories and our Theories as constituting part of the problem from working people's points of view, as well as, maybe, contributing to a solution.

Notes like these and from this author are unlikely to be immune to such difficulties. To break up 'socialism' into different projects is one thing and, I would argue, necessary now. But then to name those projects clearly, as distinctive 'isms', is another and altogether harder thing. To go on to produce an accurate class geography and chronology of opposed socialisms, even in Britain in a limited period of time, would be another thing again. In spite of recent work, for instance that of Timothy Ashplant at Sussex, such a job will depend upon information not much of which is yet to hand.[11]

ENTER THE 'PMC'

For good reasons we have for some time now been adding labels like 'educated middle-', 'new', or 'professional-managerial' to older 'middle-' and 'working-' class ones. The 'PMC' or professional and managerial class is becoming a familiar shorthand. The facts seem to force them on us. Look at some British occupations 1841–1951, and the rise of the 'white-collar', 'public-administration' category (Figure 7.1).

The percentage of the economically active population in selected occupational categories in 1971 as compared to 1911 also give some idea (Table 7.1).

Whether or not this newish layer constitutes a class in the full political, Marxist sense, it has clearly been making new determinations within socialism. E. J. Hobsbawm studied these with reference to Fabianism.[12] Gender distribution is also worth noting, since it may help to explain developments I shall get to at the end of these notes. In the 'PMC' categories of increasing percentages, the increase is considerably greater for women than for men.

Two more observations can be made at this stage of the argument: first, that the phenomenon of the PMC as fact or as perceived problem for socialists is not new. The potential independence of

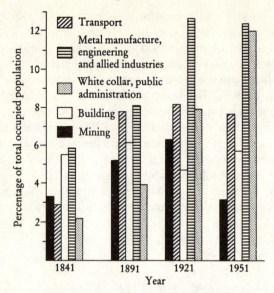

Source: E. J. Hobsbawm, *Industry and Empire*,
London, Weidenfeld & Nicholson, 1968, table 7

Figure 7.1
Source: E. J. Hobsbawm, *Industry and Empire*, London Weidenfeld &
Nicolson, 1968, table 7

Table 7.1

	1911 %		1971 %	
Categories increasing	*M*	*F*	*M*	*F*
Administrators and managers	3.9	2.3	9.9	3.3
Lower-grade salaried professionals and technicians	1.4	5.8	5.5	10.8
Inspectors, supervisors and foremen	1.8	0.2	4.5	1.2
Clerical workers	5.1	3.3	6.1	18.0
Categories decreasing (except for x below)				
Skilled manual workers (including self-employed artisans)	33.0	24.6	29.4	9.3
Semi-skilled manual workers	29.1	47.0	21.1	27.3
Unskilled manual workers	11.5	5.1	8.2	6.4x
Employers and proprietors	7.7	4.3	5.2	2.9

Source: A. H. Halsey, *Change in British Society*, Oxford University Press,
1978, p. 26

interest of groups other than workers in the same movement has long been recognised. To take a chain of examples: Hugh Gaitskell saw it in his friends as much as Beatrice Webb saw it in Hugh Gaitskell as much as contemporaries saw it in the Webbs. Crossman's *Diaries* report a remark of Gaitskell's:

> I am sometimes anxious about [Roy] and young Tony. We, as middle-class socialists, have got to have a profound humility. Though it is a funny way of putting it, we've got to know that we lead them because they can't do it without us, with our abilities, and yet we must feel humble to working people. Now that's all right for us upper middle class, but Tony and Roy are not upper, and I sometimes feel they don't have proper humility to working people.[13]

Moving back into Beatrice Webb's diaries for 1940, after a visit to her by Gaitskell and Eileen Power, she wrote:[14] 'What is wrong about this group of clever and well-meaning intellectuals [she was referring to Evan Durbin too] is the comfort and freedom of their own lives, they have everything to gain and nothing to lose by the peaceful continuance of capitalist civilisation.'

As early as 1901 Belfort Bax was clear, in his turn, about the likes of Beatrice Webb. 'Fabianism', he wrote, 'is the special movement of the government official, just as militarism is the special movement of the soldier and clericalism of the priest.'[15] Ministry of Labour weekly reports on 'the labour situation' in the period following the First World War were aware of such developments. They were watching the position of the professional classes in relation to the labour movement with great interest: the 'validity of [the] claim that there are three fundamental parties in industry, and not two, is a question of the first importance for the future'.[16] Connections between a 'new class' and socialism are, indeed, almost as old as the word 'socialism' itself (first used in English in 1837). Listen to Robert Owen in 1839:

> The working class never did DIRECT any permanent successful operations. . . . Now the middle class is the ONLY efficient DIRECTING class in Society, and will of necessity remain so, until our system shall create a NEW class of very superior DIRECTORS as well as OPERATORS, a class very superior to any men or women who have ever now yet lived.[17]

The second observation is that the problem cannot now be dealt with either by simple workerism or by hard scientificity, however tempting each might be. It is too late for either. Mike Hales's *Living Thinkwork* (1980) put it well:

> For the working class the Professional Managerial Class holds a threat; the systematic undermining of conditions of autonomous working-class practice; sabotage of working-class cultures, even identity. But equally, how socialism can be won in industrialised countries without the PMC and working class working at it together is hard to see.[18]

ENTER 'ENGLISH ASSOCIATIONS OF WORKING MEN'

Working-class consciousness of working-class activity and of its potential for replacing middle-class patrons was very strong in Britain during the last quarter of the nineteenth century. 'It is marvellous', Mr Horrocks wrote in the Amalgamated Society of Engineers' *Monthly Report* for December 1898, 'how many persons are desirous of controlling the affairs we ought to control ourselves.' Practical opposition to those persons was much stronger and got much further by the early twentieth century than historians have recognised. I have written about it before, and will do so again with special reference to the co-operative movement.[19] To cut a long history short, examples may be found across associations, from the clubs as much as from the co-op, from trade unions as much as from educational groupings, from friendly societies as much as from areas of life such as sport. Size, ambition, knowledge of what they were up against, detailed creativity, plus a sense of a future utterly different from where we are now in late-twentieth-century Britain, all need restoring to a culture (for this is what it was) which struck contemporaries, particularly foreigners, much more than it has struck modern scholars. The Webbs were the profoundest students of this culture, and their masterpiece, *Industrial Democracy* (1897), was used by thinkers as different from one another as Bernstein, Sorel and Lenin.

'Labourism' was reworked, by John Saville, as a label for some of this.[20] Because its dominant subtracting implications prevent close analysis (it is seen as not something else, not socialism) and because of confusion with the rather different forms of the twentieth-century Labour Party, I would prefer to look for another shorthand. At this point I want to enter an ugly word, 'associationism', as one of my three socialisms. I will return to it at the end of these notes. Was there a working-class practice or potential, in nineteenth- and twentieth-century Britain, which raised fundamental – even revolutionary – matters such as the nature of the state from a class point of view, but raised them in practice rather than in 'socialist' theory? Is this a more helpful way of seeing the nineteenth-century working-class culture of association than seeing it as *not* socialism, not Marxism, 'mere' liberalism, 'labourism', etc.?

Words to do with association were part of the cluster of terms from which the modern vocabulary of 'socialism' emerged during the late eighteenth and early nineteenth centuries.[21] It continued to have currency in nineteenth-century Britain, coming from Fourier through into co-operation, for example, via persons like Edward Vansittart Neale. An early Webb phrase for 'collective bargaining' was 'associated bargaining'. 'Association' was a keyword for the Christian Socialists, who were couriers for French ideas in England quite as much as the *New Left Review* a century later. Their journal in 1852 was *The Journal of Association*. But not only them: Marx used 'the associated mode of production' in *Capital*, Volume III. He wrote about associated labour replacing the 'hired labour' of capitalism just as the latter had replaced 'serf labour'. It continued to be a label for which worried inheritors of co-operative culture reached during the twentieth century. 'Is it not . . . true to say that whereas members of the Labour Party are collectivists, co-operators are associationists?' asked T. W. Mercer in 1920, in one of the many articles at this time which urged co-operators to bring co-operation into politics rather than politics into co-operation.[22]

Associations away from the state, 'states within the state', with the capacity to become another whole state, were certainly characteristic of the nineteenth century. J. M. Baernreither got excited about these in his *English Associations of Working Men* (1889). He saw England as a 'gigantic theatre of associated life', giving its culture a 'decisive stamp'. A Co-operative Wholesale Society official, Ben Jones, saw his project in this light, in his *Co-operative Production* (1894). To anticipate the detailed history, it might be possible to date a crisis in relations between working people and other classes in Britain during the mid-1890s. Keywords in this crisis were 'independence' and 'union', and it went beyond politics. A precise chronology would certainly help to pinpoint ensuing deformations and suppressions during the twentieth century. To fail to catch 'associationism' at its zenith is to fail to contest convenient capitalist myths about twentieth-century British history.

A final point at this stage: by no means always was this culture and practical consciousness seen by itself, or by socialists, as part of 'socialism'. Indeed, it was often articulated *against* socialists, who did not show and have not shown a lot of interest in it. Personal (class) feelings get very mixed up with political thoughts in this area, it being hard (but necessary), for example, to distinguish between an engineer like John Burns's feelings about socialists and his notions about desirable, possible futures. Just because he disliked some persons on the left does not mean he disliked all futures different from modern capitalism. We are still dealing with live class feelings in this whole territory, for which drama would often be a better medium than history. Messy social positions and experiences are involved, rather than neat, heady 'positions'.[23]

ASSOCIATIONS AND THE 'PMC' – SITES OF STRUGGLE: FABIANISM AND LIBERALISM

'Systematic undermining of conditions of autonomous working-class practice, sabotage of working-class cultures, even identity' (Mike Hales).

Fabianism

During the late 1880s and early 1890s it looked more like love. During the New Life moment there was extraordinary excitement among many professional persons about working-class practice.[24] Beatrice Webb's visit, in disguise, to her relations in Bacup in 1883 preceded this moment and her own 'socialism'. Her account of it in *My Apprenticeship* is a classic example of the impact working-class association could have on people 'of intellect and property' at this time. 'Were the manual workers', she asked, what I was accustomed to call civilised? What were their aspirations, what was their degree of education, what their capacity for self-government? How had this class, without administrative training or literary culture, managed to initiate and maintain the network of nonconformist chapels, the far-flung friendly societies, the much abused trade unions, and that queer type of shop, the co-operative store?[25]

She was impressed. People whose paths later diverged were, for a moment, concentrated in their fascination with associated, proletarian possibility. In the case of Edward Carpenter, it was physical, witness his poem 'As a Woman of a Man' in *Towards Democracy* (1883). But even in cooler cases like that of L. T. Hobhouse in Oxford at the end of the 1880s, it was highly strung.[26]

Life projects resulted, measured in key books. L. T. Hobhouse's *The Labour Movement* (1893) and the Webbs' *History of Trade Unionism* and *Industrial Democracy* (1894 and 1897) were the most theorised works from an intense period coming between the *Fabian Essays* (1889), innocent of working-class movements in any active sense, and the late 1890s. 'Projects' is the right word because, as happens in love, projection was strong. Allied to this was fear. 'One wonders where all the *feeling* will go, and all the capacity for *moral* self-government' (Beatrice Webb). She thought in terms of 'preventives':

> I can't help thinking . . . that one of the best preventives against the socialistic tendency of the coming democracy would lie in local government.

> I think the safeguard will be in a strong local government, with considerable power to check individual action . . . for the active regulation of their own and their neighbours' lives will be far less dangerous than theorising and talking about things of which they have no knowledge.[27]

The historian has to take care to avoid straight lines. It is important not to 'read' working-class association through the books of educated middle-class opinion about it. Theoretical autonomy must be allowed to working people, however much would-be 'scientists' resent them 'theorising and talking about things of which they have no knowledge'.

A good instance of unacknowledged conflict here is Beatrice Webb's next encounter, with J. T. W. Mitchell and the co-operative movement. Beatrice cut her intellectual teeth on *The Co-operative Movement in Great Britain* (1891) in the face of strong sexist advice from Alfred Marshall that she was not up to it. She got excited about how working-class co-operators in Britain were Jevonians without knowing it; but then she distorted them, through the lenses of her own class position. They had, she thought, hit on how 'it was in recognised "utility", or specific demand, that lay the dominating and determining factor of exchange value'. They had shown that co-operative production was an unscientific Shangri-La. But they remained irrationally committed to it when what they had proved, she thought, was that co-operators organising consumption could be one department in a neat industrial democracy. Co-operation, for the Webbs, was most valuable as moral training for citizenship elsewhere. In her book on *The Co-operative Movement*, Beatrice argued that the trade-union and co-operative movements, though bringing valuable 'moral reform', needed to be supplemented by socialist legislation.[28] This was her project, not theirs.

There was a personal dimension to all this as well. While she was working on co-operation Beatrice and Mitchell were teased about romance. This was never serious. There were, to say the least, problems of sensibility between them:

> Mitchell, chairman of the CWS, is one of the leading personalities of the Co-operative Movement . . . a sort of embodiment of the working-man customer. . . . As the representative of the Wholesale, he is inspired by one idea – the enlargement and increased power of the organisation of which he is head. . . . [He] eats copiously of heavy food and drinks freely of tea: no spirits and no tobacco. Corpulent, with a low bumptious pronunciation of long phrases, melting now and again into a boyish bonhomie . . . His Board of Directors are entirely subordinate to him: they are corpulent heavy eaters, but for the most part they are neither more nor less than simple tradesmen. . . . Three or four times I have dined with the Central Board. A higgledy-piggledy dinner; good materials served up coarsely, and shovelled down by the partakers in a way that is not appetising.

There is a continuing history of recoil by social reformers from the earthiness of practical co-operation. From the 1820s through to the 1970s idealists have been put off. Disgust with food and stomachs of a less fastidious kind than theirs has been common. 'Eating their way into the future', as a Co-operator put it in the 1870s, has never seemed quite the thing.

To do her justice, Beatrice Webb was genuinely impressed, as much as anyone outside the movement has ever been. She called Mitchell a 'business genius' and in *My Apprenticeship* gave space to his remarkable 1887 speech at the Carlisle Congress of the Co-operative Union:

> There was no higher form of co-operative production on the face of the earth than the Wholesale Society manifested in its co-operative works. . . . He would start productive works, when they would pay, in every centre in the United Kingdom; and would never be satisfied until the Wholesale manufactured everything that its members wore. . . . If co-operation was to be permanently successful, we should have to finally settle this question – To whom does profit and the increment of value belong? He held that, as it was created by the industrious classes, it belonged to them. Profit was made by the consumption of the people, and the consumers ought to have the profit. . . . He advised co-operators never to be satisfied until they got control of the entire producing, banking, shipping and every other interest in the country. The Wholesale had £100,000 in Consols, and in course of time co-operators might possess the whole of the National Debt of this country. If co-operators saved their money they might in time possess the railways and canals, besides finding employment for themselves.

In her enthusiasm, however, Beatrice and the Fabians added something rather large to this already large area of working-class association, namely the state. She regretted 'Mitchell's inability to perceive' that co-operation needed to be 'tempered by the intervention of the political State'.[29] 'Collectivism' was her label for this 'tempering'.

For Fabians, the state was no shy, neutral, hidden thing. It subsumed the 'community'. All private returns to ability, capital or land over and above those necessary to bring such factors of production into play (i.e. rents) were economically functionless. In so far as they were socially produced they were also unfair. The state should become their proprietor. 'In so far as the progress of public enterprise admits of indefinite extension, and at each step some fragment of Land or Capital pass to the Community',[30] there would be plenty of need for rent collectors and other scientific social managers. Advanced Liberals (e.g. Hobhouse) could accept all this, becoming advocates of 'those forms of Socialistic aspiration which may be included under the wider name Collectivism'.[31] The important thing to remember is that, however desirable such a project, it was not the same as J. T. W. Mitchell's.

The state was to be personned by collectivist experts, trained through institutions like the LSE. Its construction was to constitute a break, a new civilisation. Working-class associations were fine, even heroic. No one recorded them in more detail than the Webbs. But there was to be a next stage beyond them, in which the initiative would shift to 'social scientists'; these were not the Owenite and working-class critics of political economy who coined the phrase 'social science' earlier in the nineteenth century. They were to be a new cadre of professionals. Working-class associations would have their place, but many of their earlier practices would come to look 'primitive' from a professional point of view. For Mitchell and his ilk, working people doing it for themselves – the old 'who does what?' question of craft unionism – were all important. He was an egalitarian with gigantic ambition, but for his own association and all its federated forms, not for the state.

Reading Co-operative Congress proceedings during the late nineteenth century one can feel the friction between Mitchell and the Christian Socialists, quite beyond the specific subjects in dispute. One can hear the pride in 'our people' taking over in the early 1890s – just as one can sense Tom Mann's amazement at Mitchell's cool ambition in front of the Royal Commission on Labour in 1892. Initiatives were to come from the collective capacity for self-control and self-government of the kind of people who made up local co-operative societies or worked with the CWS. A face-to-face relation between organised consumers and organised producers was to be contrived. When working people employed themselves, they would be the same people anyway, all members of the same society. In so far as there was an abstract position on 'the state', it was that of its replacement by other modes, moving in from the outside. I am not confident that I have pieced this together properly yet, but it was a residual perspective which, at its best, threatened the emergent Labour Party directly. *The Producer, with which is incorporated 'The Consumer'*, the CWS magazine, in 1917 editorialised thus (there had just been a Labour Party conference in Manchester):

With all its teaching and agitation, its preaching and writing, its local and Parliamentary representation, the Labour Party does not yet seem to have realised that for the economic betterment of the common people collectively-owned fields, factories and workshops are better than speeches and resolutions; they could, in fact, be made more effective in the economic welfare of the workers than almost any kind of legislation. When we are treading the paths of national legislation we are upon very uncertain ground, that is apt to give way at any moment. But when we acquire fields and grow wheat, build factories and manufacture goods, erect warehouses and distribute the contents one to another, we know we are getting on solid ground.

The Labour Party does not proceed in this way. It calls for higher wages, and leaves those who supply the commodities of life to exploit the higher earnings by increased cost of living. . . . What is and always has been the failure of the Labour Party from a business point of view? It is that they have asked other people to do things for them rather than do things for themselves. . . . And when all has been said in favour of a high legal rate of pay, what does the term suggest? It suggests that the workers are still dependent upon other people for wages, as they are for the price of the means of life. They are between two oppressive stools – one to keep down wages, one to inflate prices. How can they disentangle themselves from the position? We presume some would say by State action; perhaps by forcing the Government to own and control industry and the distribution of food. But how full of doubt, uncertainty, and perhaps corruption such a course would be. Would it not be better, and as quickly done in the long run, for the people to get hold of the machinery of production by co-operative means? Once that process was anything like complete the workers could then determine by collective action their own rate of pay, their own price of food, clothing and shelter. And co-operators would then be so numerous that they could walk into the Houses of Parliament and take over the reins of government without any further palaver. This is not a dream. It is simply a business problem.[32]

When one does pick it up, the tone is unmistakable: 'without any further palaver'! Could another society have been built upon the 'Mitchell world' of temperance, Nonconformist chapel/Sunday School and labour movement? Was there an available class movement in the fullest political sense? The question haunts me and has, I think, at some level of unconsciousness, haunted many people in twentieth-century Britain.[33]

During the early twentieth century there were set-piece clashes between working-class associations and the state. The Fabians did not always like what was happening; in no way must the project of *Industrial Democracy* (1897) be confused with what has actually happened in twentieth-century Britain, any more than the project of the CWS. But there was a direction to the clashes, which was theirs. 'The world is going your way at present, Webb,' as William Morris told Sidney in 1895. Direct access to the rates, and an education system under the potential control of its 'elementary' end, was killed by the 1902 Education Act, a rare example of successful Fabian 'permeation'. Relations between trade unions and those outside, as well as relations within trade unions, were 'incorporated' through legislation. (Remember that Sidney Webb was in favour of the Taff Vale Judgment.) Friendly societies were made subordinate to their private capitalist competitors and the state through national insurance legislation, and so on. And what did *not* happen is as significant as what did.

A version of politics-for-labour which built upon existing working-class association did not grow up, although there was plenty of social 'reform' from above. The angle between popular practice and social change was altered, or rather the available space for narrowing it was occupied. A social democratic politics which held the ring, at the level of the state, for wider, more-than-political working-class forms to extend and grow in civil society never materialised. A working-class redefinition of politics never happened. We scarcely even know what such a sentence means any longer. We have been living with the consequences of our ignorance and failure of imagination on these questions on the left ever since. Comfort has been provided recently by historians. At least now the tragic consequences are being articulated directly by some of those who lived them.[34]

Liberalism

Fabians have found their place in the history of British socialism, even of the labour movement. But much of the relationship between the 'PMC' and working-class association went on within Liberalism and not within a discourse which would have thought of affiliating to the Second International. It went on in quarters hidden from socialism but with profound consequences for it.

Late-nineteenth-century Liberalism was inclusive, spilling over beyond dominant meanings of liberalism with a small 'l'. The party and the ideology were being stretched by problematics constructed outside them, but which they had to try to digest, in the interests of their own continuity. Much of the material, as it were, for Marxism went through liberalism in Britain, and made that liberalism different. It is a remarkable fact that it was the Liberal Hammonds, and no other historians, who came so near to E. P. Thompson's version of the early industrial period (the Industrial Revolution as civil war). And it was New Liberals and no other theorists who came so near to Gramsci's notion of hegemony, with their attempts to explain the subordination of the unorganised working class through mass culture and imperialism during the late 1890s and early 1900s.[35] It was the Liberal J. A. Hobson who came so near to Lenin's *Imperialism* (1917).

None of this is a problem if one takes the material relations which generate ideas, and hence in this case the working class and its associations, seriously enough.[36] If the alternative to late capitalism (other than barbarism) has anything (any relation) to do with what workers think and construct in struggles in and against the system, then strong, creative, continuous associations would indeed force everyone, L(l)iberals included, to shift position, and some to mount explicit counter-attacks.[37]

Liberalism did include distinctly illiberal folk at this time. J. T. W. Mitchell was one. L. T. Hobhouse was another, at least in some of his utterances which took on a brisk, authoritarian tone when threatened. Most people, if asked to characterise twentieth-century British Liberalism, would get to W. H. Beveridge fairly early on. His kindly face together with his famous welfare reports have become powerful symbols. But Jose Harris has recently reminded us how distinctly illiberal some of his pre-1914, 'collectivist liberal' positions were.[38] As for someone like Lord Rosebery, he is still something of a scandal, as he was to provincial Liberals when his horse Ladas won the Derby in 1894.[39] But if he could call for government by 'scientific methods' and urge the desirability of a 'dictator, a tyrant, a man of large mind and iron will who would see what had to be done and do it', so could others in his group of 'Limps' (like Asquith and Haldane). 'Take me to your leader' contributions also jump out of the pages of the ILP newspaper the *Labour Leader*, particularly under the by-line 'Marxian'.[40] It was a very complex time, when real class debates constantly crossed the lines of formal organisations and ideologies such as 'socialism' and 'liberalism'.

As soon as one thinks one has achieved any neatness of fit between ideology and organisation, the messiness reappears. Thus, so far in these notes I have leaned on Hobhouse the 'collectivist'. But from the late 1890s he recoiled, disgusted (and that is not too strong a word) by the Webb project – as much as H. G. Wells was in *The New Machiavelli* (1911).[41] Liberalism provided some of the best conduits for critique of bureaucratic collectivism and, for that matter, conduits for critique of Ramsay MacDonald's ugly pre-1914 Hegelian statism as well.

In a magnificent chapter of intellectual history, which replaces Helen Lynd's fine *England in the 1880s* (1945), Stefan Collini has recently shown how 'collectivist' became one pole in a field-of-force of argument between 1880 and 1914 – the other pole being 'individualist'. Differences were distinct enough for dinner tables to be arranged round them. But the field-of-force metaphor is appropriate because the structure of feeling informing 'individualism' also informed 'collectivism'.[42] So attractive were the poles in this field of force that the dominant antonym to 'socialism' at this time, in Collini's view, was not the expected 'capitalism' but 'individualism'.

The result was a complicated overlap between 'collectivism' and 'socialism'. The 1880s and 1890s were a time when the latter had become an attractive hold-all for hope, as a way out of darkest England and its culture of poverty. Socialism provided a banner, much used during the New Life moment, by working people.[43] But then there came a scramble for 'socialism' akin to the scramble for Africa and with comparable results for the natives. The word was up for grabs.[44] There was much bewilderment at its changes of meaning. There were forlorn attempts to keep it close to available forms of working-class association, particularly among writers close to large-scale English associations of working people and those with links with early-nineteenth-century Owenite socialism.[45] Unfortunately 'collectivists' got hold of large bits of it, just as twenty years later particular 'communists' were to get hold of *that* word and make difficult its continuance as a self-identifying label for popular projects in Britain.[46]

'Collectivism' was itself not simple.[47] But its loudest usages had more than semantic effects. All kinds of people could agree and, in their agreement, put on 'socialist' livery: people like the followers of T. H. Green (e.g. F. C. Montague, J. H. Muirhead and D. G. Ritchie) converging with Fabians (e.g. Graham Wallas, Sydney Olivier and William Clarke). In Collini's analysis, they

> shared an emotional as well as an intellectual aversion to Individualism, an insistence on the need for – at times, it seemed a craving for – a new ethical spirit in social relations, a stronger sense of community and of the duties of its members to each other. In the most general terms, they went on to argue that the state as the political expression of the community should embody this 'new moral world' in its legislation. On the substance of such legislation . . . they differed widely. . . . [But] such disagreement sent [them] back to the drawing room rather than the drawing board, for it was distinctively socialism for the middle classes – no mention of necessary antagonism between employers and employees, no celebration of the class solidarity so prized by the labour movement, little reference to the need for organisation, agitation or expropriation. Socialism was presented as a moral ideal which bound men together, not as a political programme which set them apart. But these declarations of moral intent were not merely decorative; like the insignia worn by medieval soldiers, they served to make one's allegiance easily identifiable. Those who wanted to reform the abuses of Individualism and particularly to see a new altruistic ethos replace the competitive spirit upon which the present system was alleged to rest, but who wanted at the same time to disassociate themselves from the merely 'mechanical' or even confiscatory schemes popularly associated with economic socialism, frequently felt obliged to display their moral colours in this way.[48]

Such convergence hindered emergent connections between working people and socialism. Charles Booth, Canon Barnett and even General Booth of the Salvation Army all looked for ways of approving of 'socialism' during this period. So where was that word being carried? Whose banner was it? As the SDF paper, *Justice*, complained in 1903:

> It is necessary that we should occasionally point out that . . . Fabianesque 'State Socialism' is far removed from genuine Democratic Socialism. The danger is that it may be used among the more unthinking portion of the workers as an argument against all forms of collective or common ownership.[49]

Fine spiritual autobiographies characterise this period. Among the best is Percy Redfern's *Journey to Understanding* (1946). Having described the New Life days, he got to the turn of the century:

> And now, in 1900, after six socialist years, I was becoming conscious of a still more determining force, a fixed state of mind. I was beginning to find it impossible to think of any social good to be done except through state or municipal or other authoritative large-scale organisations and their friends. The capacity to see a more social world began to appear only in terms of establishment and regulation by law. . . . Everything which I loved personally called to me as a free person; but on another side I was being moulded in spirit to a complete dependence on collectivist aims and plans, especially as to be authorised by the state.[50]

Redfern went into the Co-operative Wholesale Society, becoming its official historian. He himself adopted the word 'collectivist' later.[51] But it is interesting how few workers used that word to label themselves during the 1880–1910 period. There were exceptions, including John Burns and Londoners around the LCC, Progressives during the 1890s. But even those like the CWS/J. T. W. Mitchell strand in the fierce debates in the co-operative movement from the 1870s onwards, who had antagonists who were identified as 'individualists', preferred labels like 'federalist' for themselves or even, on occasion, 'communist'.

A NOTE ON 'ISMS'

By now the 'isms' in these notes will have become irritations. They were at the time, too, particularly to co-operators who had a better class understanding of them than most:

> Among all these contending -isms clamouring for support, the ordinary working man may well be perplexed, wondering which of them is the most likely to fulfil the promises of its advocates, and in many cases he may refuse to discuss or adopt any of the systems offered him. . . . Cooperation is not an -ism.[52]

But 'isms' accumulated, and have gone on doing so since, to a degree which is itself significant. It is as though, once more, there is a problematic (again, it is an active working-class presence) beyond the control of the labellers, who stick on more and more, in case naming the parts might bring them together again, neat and under control.[53] By finding an 'ist', one somehow re-establishes one's own sense of knowing better, the security of having a 'position' over against those people who 'stress the problematic and contradictory nature of individual experience' and insist on conveying class 'experience as a constellation of still unresolved disputes and tensions'.[54] It *is* irritating; but irritation is not enough in one of those semantic situations where, as Raymond Williams says in his introduction to *Keywords*, 'the problem of meanings seems . . . inextricably bound up with the problems [they are] being used to discuss'.

In the next two sections of these notes I am going to make it worse, in order, as the doctor said to the patient, to make it better. I shall come back to late-nineteenth- and early-twentieth-century Britain. In order to try to come back better equipped, however, and in order to return, at the end, to 'associationism', I am going to try to give ahistorical, ideal-typical definitions of my two other socialisms, first 'collectivism' and then 'statism'. By removing myself further from history, I want to try to clarify different types of socialist project, even different types of existing state.

COLLECTIVISM

In 1970s socialist discourse 'collectivism' was given a pointed meaning.[55] It was used to refer to a project or to a society where the factory relations of large-scale industry have been extended to giant, society-wide, transnational systems; where scientific knowledge has become a pre-condition and supervisor of production, subordinating hands to heads; where (many of the items in this list are different ways of saying similar things) the minutest divisions of labour are celebrated rather than problematised, and find expression in political as well as in economic 'machinery'; and where, finally, a social group (class?) commands the heights of knowledge and is in a position, from within its site in material production, not to cling to private ownership, but to compose a new society through limited competition and the market, as well as through state planning. Collectivists seek to transform the state, but not (at least not directly) in the working-class interest.

Within 'collectivism', as project or as society, there is no private ownership, as we generally understand it, of the means of production. There is, however, individual ownership of know-how which is – to use economic language – 'accumulated' through education. Expertise is an important force – and hence relation – of production. 'Profit', to go on with the same language, is realised through individual sale of monopolised skill on the labour market. Individual wage payments, ownership of skill and restricted higher education are all features of collectivism, in this definition. The surplus product is appropriated, in part, by the collective technical class, via unequal wages plus privileges and perks determined directly sometimes at enterprise level, sometimes politically. Basic to this whole characterisation of 'collectivism' is the importance of science/knowledge (what Mike Hales has called 'pre-conceptualisation') to production, together with the possibility of a thrust towards control over it by a social group (class?) which is neither simple 'labour' nor simple 'employer'.

It is hard to distinguish between capitalist managers who are 'collectivists', in the industrial changes occurring in the USA and Europe at the beginning of the twentieth century, and socialists who deserve the same label. As a project or tendency 'collectivism' is deeply rooted in large-scale industry and in the divisions of labour which accompany it, regardless of the label used to describe the surrounding system as a whole. Doubtful about whether to welcome it as a 'stage' in history or whether to fight it directly, associationists have only just begun to identify collectivism clearly for what – and whose – it is.[56]

STATISM

Here we are on more familiar ground, with my definition corresponding more closely to established, though still contested, usages.

'Statism', in this context, refers to a project or to a society in which the political and economic claws of private capital have been clipped but where – as in most actual socialist revolutions in our time – the conditions for collectivism listed above do not obtain.

In other words 'state power' has in some sense been captured (or its capture proposed) but in a situation where large-scale industry, large-scale politics, large-scale culture and society have yet to be constructed. 'Modernisation', to use the bland modern euphemism, thus becomes the task (or the opponent) of socialist construction rather than its parent. 'Revolution', or even electoral victories, never wait till the 'objective conditions' for socialism, whatever these may be, are ripe. And if we cannot, as socialists, deal with that, we cannot deal with electoral victories, let alone revolution. In the conditions of the twentieth century, long periods of (seemingly stable) 'communist' statism have been as characteristic as shorter periods of the 'social democratic' variety.

To cut a long story short, in statism a group (precisely not a class in the full Marxist sense), without a direct base in material production, seeks to exercise control. It concentrates, perforce, on circulation/distribution, rather than production. The material base of this group is often within its own movement, party or apparatus, which itself becomes a considerable employer. The group gropes, rather blindly because it *is* blind – blind to labour processes and to the state as sites for class struggle and therefore preoccupied with formal, external 'control' over them. Statists have a problem: politics and economics remain separate. This separation, the great bourgeois achievement, remains in place.[57] Reaching out from the top of one to control the other (from its top), through projects of 'nationalisation' (even 'collectivisation'), etc., does not bring it to heel.

How can the political group of 'office holders', having formed an 'administration' (nice phrases because they include more than 'bureaucrats' now does), reproduce itself? Our collectivist technocrats have less of a problem, since their site, at base, is in how things (and thus relations) are made at 'the points of production'. And they are usually strengthening such a base, back at the ranch, as a consequence of statist 'administrations' being 'in power'. 'Office holders' often, of course, fail to reproduce themselves. They lose an election through the political market, or get invaded or destabilised from inside or from without. They have to seek to achieve centralised control of politics and keep it. This means preventing the independent association or solidarity of those classes (skilled or deskilled, collectivist technocrats or petit-bourgeois proprietors or wage labourers) based in production.

In twentieth-century Britain there has been plenty of evidence in Labour Party history of how statists have as much trouble with their own party, and even more so with unions, as do ruling parties or juntas in other contexts. They do not much care for independent associations of working people. Statists tend to be very 'public' people, ignoring or suppressing their own and other people's 'private' labour in civil society. In fact historically in Britain – and until the 1970s women's movement challenged them – they have held their hands over the private. They have let capitalism rule it, with disastrous long-term political and psychological consequences even for themselves. No wonder Labour is no longer, if ever it was, a fish swimming in a sea of wide social assent, with its very narrow view of politics. 'I get impatient', wrote Hugh Gaitskell in 1955,

> with those who think that everybody must continually be taking an active part in politics or community affairs. The vast majority find their happiness in the family or personal relations, and why on earth shouldn't they? There will always be a minority who are genuinely interested in social activity and social work. They can get on with the job.[58]

'There will always be a minority': precisely, and with that kind of thinking their power will either have to be authoritarian or as tenuous as that of Labour in twentieth-century Britain.

In statism, the ruling group tries to determine the division of labour *between* different units of production through state planning. The division of labour *within* units of production is better understood by collectivists. Indeed it is the basis of their power and potential. The statist ruling group also tries to determine the allocation of surplus product, for example, by statutory incomes policies, state enterprise boards, taxation and the sticks and carrots of planning. But the task is difficult. As Peter Shore so sadly wrote in a piece called 'Insoluble Equations' (*Observer*, 29 July 1979):

> There are . . . major lessons to be learned from . . . economic management in 1974/9: and the most important by far is the weakness of the contemporary State. The British people overwhelmingly will the ends of economic revival, industrial growth, full employment, and more stable prices. Yet the Government they elect is palpably unable to exercise sufficient persuasion or control over the institutions concerned to make these ends achievable. And the State power is increasingly

hobbled and fettered by external authorities. . . . Until these trends can be changed, the economy will continue to weaken and so too will confidence in political democracy itself.

This can stand as a classically statist diagnosis of statist failure – and just at a time when many working people had turned in another political direction altogether, because of their perception of the intrusive *strength* of 'the contemporary state'!

COLLECTIVISM AND STATISM: SITES OF CONFLICT

Mainly theoretical

At this stage I am capable only of leaving my definitions as rather fixed ideal types. In the next sections of these notes I will add to them by closer juxtaposition, and then illustrate them from examples in late-nineteenth- and early-twentieth-century Britain. I shall hope to bring out new aspects of that place and period, as well as greater clarity of definition.

Collectivism in the sense that I am trying to characterise it here is altogether more 'theoretical' than statism. Collectivists are not afraid to articulate their project with a theorised sense of the 'general good'. Collectivists are confident in their own actions, and not just in the movement of history in a providential sense. They analyse trends and tendencies – 'social movements' being existing developments with which they identify (e.g. the Post Office or the income tax) rather than voluntary associations.[59] What they want is difficult to separate from what they analyse as already happening; to separate the two would, after all, be sentimental or utopian, less than 'scientific'.

Modern social science, such as sociology or political science, may perhaps be seen as collectivists' emergent ideology, as well as providing them with jobs (professions). They are very 'modern' people, and very 'public' too; and they know what is not so, disliking archaic hole-in-corner practices not open to licensing and inspection. They are full of new brooms and dead wood and of what one can do to the other. They know what 'the state' is, for them; and their project realised would enlarge and transform it, with them moving in and out of its apparatus – to use a Blake image – like caterpillars. They have no love for private capital, with its waste and irrationality. If Max Weber's 'rationality' was the enduring spirit of capitalism, they would find it perfectly acceptable. Many of them do. Indeed they are the heirs, in modern conditions, of precisely that spirit. As such, on behalf of a specific social layer, they have a theory and a practice which threaten older notions of the state and of private capital, particularly in places like Britain.[60]

By contrast, statism is wilfully unclear, militantly so. In one sense 'l'état c'est moi' was a quintessentially statist remark. Statism's theory is more in the nature of presupposition. It therefore has to be reconstructed by the historian, rather than easily quoted. 'It is sometimes charged against the ILP', wrote Keir Hardie in 1908, 'that it has never formulated its theory of socialism. That is true and therein lies its strength.'[61] 'The state' for statists is not theorised; it is left as it is. It is very often seen as 'the government', to be changed through the normal political channels. New governments will drive the same machine, but in different directions.

'Social democracy' has often been the term, within Marxist discourse, for statism. It has been well understood since 1848 in Marx, for example, but also in William Morris, Leon Trotsky and many others. Trotsky was especially sharp about it, in ways which still point directly to contemporary practices on the British Labour left.[62]

The continuing tendency to anthropomorphise the state can be well illustrated from British social democracy. In 1912 the ILP paper the *Labour Leader* wanted to distance itself from Fred Jowett's pressure for socialist changes in parliamentary forms:

> We feel, for our part, whilst recognising the disinterested advocacy of Mr Jowett, that changes of Parliamentary procedure are not the supremely important matter for our movement. . . . As Mr Snowden said, *our central grievance is that we ourselves are not the Cabinet.* With the rise of Labour to power many of the Parliamentary difficulties would tend to adjust themselves [emphasis added].[63]

By 1946 the central grievance had been met. Union leaders were pleased that they would now be negotiating with friends. At the annual conference of trades councils in that year, H. W. Harrison said: 'We are no longer petitioning for a place in the counsels of the State, we are the State.'[64] Louis XIV could scarcely have done better.

In statism, therefore, the key late-nineteenth-century problem of the nature of 'representation' is carried no further. It is mystified. Indeed, it is carried less far as a problem than it had been in Gladstonian Liberalism,[65] much less far than it had been in works like *Industrial Democracy* (1897), and very much less far than it had been in the predominantly delegatory culture of English associations of working people. This is a tragic case of arrested development.

Mainly examples

In contrasting two kinds of socialism, I have been reaching for definitions, at some distance from fully articulated history. But Fabian–Webbism has kept intruding into definitions of 'collectivism', and the best of British social democracy – the ILP and the Labour Party – into statism. This is appropriate, provided the definitions and the movements are not collapsed into one another. Better articulation of one must continue to depend upon better articulation of the other.

There *was* a partial fit between Fabians and collectivism, not only in their use of the term but also in their whole structure of feeling. Fabians did like 'system' and 'complete solutions'; they did wish to train a new class of expert or professional; they were unembarrassed about relegating other practices as 'primitive' or 'sentimental' when they involved masses of working people. Having bases away from the state, they did, at least to begin with, keep their distance from narrow politics, and 'permeate' instead; and they welcomed the division of labour characteristic of large-scale industry and large-scale politics. They were unashamed elitists; the elite was themselves, not in person but as social types. If these notes do nothing else, I hope they make clear what a distinctive 'socialism' theirs was. In February 1906 the 'Special Committee' of the Fabian Society, 'appointed to consider measures for increasing the scope, income and activity of the Society', reported thus:

Democracy is a word with a double meaning. To the bulk of trade unionists and labourers it means an intense jealousy and mistrust of all authority, and a resolute reduction of both representatives and officials to the position of mere delegates, mouthpieces and agents of the majority. From this point, Democracy would find its consummation in a House of Commons where, without any discussion, divisions were taken by counting postcards received from the entire population on questions submitted to the people by referendum and initiative.

Because the Fabians have given no countenance to this attitude they have been freely denounced as undemocratic and even Tory. Fabian democracy is in fact strongly opposed to it and certain to come into conflict with it at almost every step in the practical development of socialism. We have always accepted government by a representative deliberating body controlling an expert bureaucracy as the appropriate public organisation for Socialism. When asked where government by the people comes in, we reply that government has to be carried out by division of labour and specialisation as much as railway management has; and what Democracy really means is government by the consent of the people. . . .

Between these two conceptions of the elected person as representative doing the best he can according to his own judgement after full discussion with other representatives of all shades of opinion, and as a mere delegate carrying out previous instructions from the majority of his constituents, there is a gulf which will sooner or later become a party boundary, and this gulf unfortunately cuts the Labour Movement right down the middle.[66]

They could not be much clearer than that, although the Webbs became so later, when they represented the darkest years of Soviet history as a 'new civilisation'.

And there *was* a fit between 'social democrats' around the ILP and statism. The most explicit example of this is Ramsey MacDonald, in his pre-1914 books of socialist theory.[67] For MacDonald his own 'following' was always a problem, as it constantly threatened to lead itself away from his 'careful, not to say circuitous course, between the perils of isolation and parliamentary impotence and the . . . still graver perils of old fashioned "Liberal–Labourism".'[68] 'Democracy' for MacDonald was an existing national fact, not a current class struggle. Under the promising heading in one of his books 'Socialist Construction', the problem turns out to be narrowly 'political'.[69] Duty to, rather than rights against, a state was emphasised, and the state was seen as an organic being with a life of its own. Four of the subheadings in the chapter in *The Socialist Movement* (1911) entitled 'What

Socialism Is Not' were: Anarchism and Communism, The Abolition of Private Property, Equality, and Class War – 'the idea of the State being essential to Socialism'. The flavour is unmistakable, not of 'stark collectivism' as David Marquand calls it (his biography is inadequate on MacDonald's writings), but of mystified, Hegelian Comtean statism:

> The State does not concern itself primarily with man as a possessor of rights, but with man as the doer of duties. A right is the opportunity of fulfilling a duty, and it should be recognised only in so far as it is necessary to the performance of duty. . . . Nor should the State grant the 'right' to the franchise unless by doing so it is promoting its own ends . . . as man approaches the fullness of liberty which he can enjoy only when he is perfect, his rights become more ample. . . . The State regards the man as a carrier of human life between the Past and the Future, and assigns to him the work of realising the Future from the Past. It shows him the path.[70]

If this was 'socialism', no wonder there was a pause in its popular growth after the mid-1890s. But of course it was not, or not entirely. Movements are not defined by their leaders' utterances, any more than histories proceed through the interaction of abstracted 'isms'. The Webbs knew this well. Their historical work is deeply determined by forces quite other than their favoured 'collectivism'. They allowed it to be so, which is why they left us with such usable stuff. 'Where we expected to find an economic thread for a treatise,' they tell us at the beginning of the 1894 edition of their *History of Trade Unionism*, 'we found a spider's web; and from that moment we recognised that what we had first to write was not a treatise, but a history.'[71]

RE-ENTER ASSOCIATIONISM

> The amount of talent there is locked up within the working class is enormous. If we had socialism, you'd see all that talent come out, it would be a most wonderful awakening. You don't see it under capitalism. You can hardly imagine it. The Labour Party has always talked about what it will do for you; never what you can do for yourself, and that's where it has made its mistake.[72]

Marx spoke often of how the working class demonstrated future social

247

forms in their current organisations of struggle – he saw the Paris Commune as a vindication of this, particularly with regard to precisely the question of the State. It is curious that nobody has made any attempt to found (historically and theoretically) a programme of (revolutionary) politics in Britain upon these insights.[73]

Pushing into the stories of Fabianism, Liberalism, ILP socialism or almost any other form of continuous association which purports to relate to the working class in Britain, one finds elements of another practice, other possibilities. These may be either residual or emergent, but are never dominant.

Such elements are by no means always political, in either intention or immediate consequence. In my work on the social history of late-nineteenth- and early-twentieth-century Reading, I found them present as much in the stories of the Reading Football Club or the Royal Berkshire Hospital as in the Reading branch of, for instance, the Social Democratic Federation. There was strong local evidence of working-class practical critique of bourgeois democracy, pushing against the 'vice-presidents' in voluntary associations, and more evident outside political forms than within them.[74]

This other practice was, and is, hard to name, from the inside or by outside analysts. It will be difficult – impossible – to deal with satisfactorily in these notes. It is only partly a matter of empirical observation: what the Webbs called 'that persistent sentiment of solidarity which has distinguished the working class'.[75] It is also a matter of theoretical imagination. 'Let us imagine for a change . . .' as Marx began one of his sentences about the associated mode.[76] It is a matter of using *class* to indicate future, material possibility as well as present, or past, reality. The difficulty is great for reasons which are, literally, systematic. If it had been any easier to name and to put together, the modern history of Britain would have been rather different. At this point, therefore, these 'notes' become even more note-like.

Writing the history of some things (some relations) which do not exist, in the hope that they may come into being, is a hazardous enterprise for anyone, let alone a professional historian. My subject becomes a cause looking for self-definition, looking for connection, looking for a name. I enter 'associationism' again here, having earlier established some historical presence for it in Britain, *faute de mieux*. Alternatives can emerge only through practice.

'All theory makers', wrote John Berger in *A Fortunate Man* (1976), 'have cast at least one eye on the seat of power.' Since associationism would be about the dissolution or generalisation of power itself, rather than about grabbing its seat, its 'theory' is bound to be hard to articulate. We have lost the habit earlier English radicals had of contesting power itself: 'it was the duty of a people to stand up and curb power wherever it existed'.[77] We have names ready now for people who think like that, institutions to put them in.

Locating workable prefigurative examples is obviously difficult. Even at the level of aspiration, there are bits of Rudolf Bahro's *The Alternative* (1977) which make one gasp, just like *News from Nowhere* (1890) still does. When the division of labour itself is contested, rather than particular historical forms thereof, or when it is seriously proposed – to paraphrase Samuel Smiles – that all people could become what some people are, the modern socialist lapses into 'realistic' sighs, saying 'this really *is* nowhere' or 'things can never be like that'.[78] It need not all be speculation, all difficulty. There were of course voices in Britain during the nineteenth century pressing similar distinctions within socialism. William Morris's thought is the pre-eminent example, though the sharpness of his analyses is still not widely appreciated. 'Making socialists' is a well-known key phrase in Morris's politics, as well as being fundamental in giving the New Life period its characteristic unity. But in my own essay on New Life socialism in *History Workshop Journal* in 1977 I interpreted it too thinly. I discussed it too much in terms of what one socialist in that period called 'opinions hung around'.[79] There was insufficient emphasis on socialist construction in what I wrote, and Morris's remarkable critique of parliamentary reform – 'The Policy of Abstention', published in 1887 – can provide the best corrective. The essays and lectures, of which he wrote and delivered many in that year, were themselves an example: 'direct and rhythmic in cadence, they reflect the intense simplicity which Morris considered appropriate for dignified popular art'. And they did not always go down as badly at the time as Morris thought.[80]

He expected too much of them, as well as too much of himself in the variety of his output. 'Making socialists' was an urgent pre-condition of anything else for Morris, because without them there could be no articulation of need or desire, based upon that 'consciousness of oppression' which was 'the token of the gradual formation of a new order of things underneath the decaying order'.[81] The task was formidable: to construct an embryonic new order within the constraints of the old, independent and yet capable of frontal assault at the right time, and through the right channels. Meanwhile, 'my hope is that what we shall do will show us to be Socialists in essence and in spirit even now when we cannot be Socialists economically'.[82]

Change was going to occur. And it would, Morris rightly thought, take the shape of social reform. The state was going to assume responsibilities for deprivations and injustices, hitherto neglected. Property was going to pay a ransom. How that fact was perceived from the left was going to be crucial. Legislative enactment might have improving effects but it would be 'damaging to the cause *if put forward by socialists as part of socialism*'. 'We should be clear *that they are not our measures.*'[83] The danger of pursuing the Policy of Parliamentary Action (as opposed to the Policy of Abstention) was that necessary concessions would, if made 'with the expressed agreement of Socialist representatives in Parliament', 'be looked upon as a victory'. This would be confusing to emergent hopes for another kind of society. A fundamentally different society could be constructed only through workers producing it themselves.

For Morris, there had to be a base for socialist construction away from the state in order, ultimately, to come at it with another kind of formation 'when society shall be what its name means'.[84] The base had to be in labour or production, certainly; but in a different layer of the labour process from the collectivists. Their practical drive for efficiency in the division of labour would only replace one set of private masters for another set of public ones, managers instead of owners.

In Sidney Webb the language of the professional-managerial class was explicit. It was a language of hope. 'Along with your engineers and chemists in the dominant class of the future', he wrote to H. G. Wells in 1901,

will be the trained administrator, the expert in organising men – equipped with an Economics or a Sociology which will be as scientific and as respected by his colleagues of other professions as Chemistry or Mechanics. You seem to ignore this class.[85]

Morris made it clear to a correspondent in *Commonweal* in 1885 that he understood the phenomenon, in class terms too. But his language was one of dread:

> I should like our friend to understand whither the whole system of palliation tends – namely, towards the creation of a new middle class to act as a buffer between the proletariat and their direct and obvious masters; the only hope of the bourgeois for retarding the advance of socialism lies in this device.[86]

The problem, for Morris, was to dispense with masters altogether. 'Take this for the last word of my dream of what is to be – the test of our being fools no longer will be that we shall no longer have masters.'[87] Even in the long period 'while the national systems cannot . . . be directly attacked with success as to their more fundamental elements', a process of 'starving out' or 'sapping' could go on. More and more responsibility could be taken by local associations, as constructive instruments, and by working-class unions (limbs of a future socialist commonwealth) who, through federation, should already be dealing with the 'details of change'. During the period in which the old political nations were 'weakening into dissolution',

> The form which the decentralisation or Federation will take is bound to be a matter of experiment and growth; what the unit of administration is to be, what the groups of Federation are to be, whether or not there will be cross-Federation, as e.g. Craftsguilds and Co-operative Societies going side by side with the geographical division of wards, communes and the like, all this is a matter for speculation and I don't pretend to prophesy about it.[88]

Although in a certain sense they never met, Morris's way of putting the problem would have been congenial to many in the English associations of working people mentioned earlier in these notes. Doing without masters was what so much of their project was about, even the 'unpolitical' club men who liked their clubs because they had masters all day at work and could do without them in the evenings. Morris's audiences in the Radical clubs, whose styles of sociability he rather disliked, were not a million miles away from his own project. But because of his own class position and conversion – crossing his 'river of fire' – Morris probably went on about socialism as ideology too much, although the details of a 'practice of transformation' were all there in his repertoire. He was an original producer who could make tables as well as theories, someone who could challenge fundamental divisions of labour with his being as well as with his consciousness. But, of course, he was not a magician. He could not conjure away class differences. And these were strong within the Socialist League as well as without.[89]

For Morris one base was in association, in the movement itself, in politics with a small 'p', away from the licensed forms of the big 'P' so fascinating to statists. 'The Policy of Abstention' argued that a great 'Labour Combination' had to be created powerful enough to boycott or abstain from Politics. It would need a material life of its own:

> Its aim would be to act directly, whatever was done in it would be done by the people themselves; there would consequently be no possibility of compromise, of the association becoming anything else than it was intended to be; nothing could take its place: before all its members would be put but one alternative to complete success, complete failure.

The means towards *communist* revolution – for this was Morris's favoured label – were, as part of the very definition of that change as communist rather than something else, prefigurations and early intimations of its ends.

The alternative outcome Morris often labelled 'socialist'. 'Socialism' *would* happen, was beginning to happen under his very eyes. Of that he was sure. And it *did* constitute a great change. At times he thought it a necessary change, transitional to communism. But he always saw the means to one as sharply distinct from the means to the other. The change would have benefits, and particular beneficiaries:

> It has two faces to it. One of which says to the working man, 'This is Socialism or the beginning of it' (which it is not) and the other says to the capitalist, 'This is sham Socialism; if you can get the workers, or part of them, to accept this, it will create a new lower middle-class a buffer to push in between Privilege and Socialism'.[90]

Morris was interested in those 'who occupy a middle position between the producers and the non-producers', like 'artists and literary men, doctors, school-masters etc.':

> They are doing useful service, and ought to be doing it for the community at large, but practically they are only working for a class, and in their present position are little better than hangers-on of the non-producing class, from whom they receive a share of their privilege, together with a kind of contemptuous recognition of their position as gentlemen – heaven save the mark.[91]

He feared

> the danger of the community falling into bureaucracy, the multiplication of boards and offices, and all the paraphernalia of official authority, which is, after all, a burden, even when it is exercised by the delegation of the whole people and in accordance with their wishes.[92]

There were whole categories of occupation 'which would have no place in a reasonable condition of society as e.g. lawyers, judges, jailers and soldiers of the highest grades, and most Government officials'. 'Directors of labour' and 'men of genius' had to be watched. Masterdom based on property in intellect was as much masterdom as that based on any other kind of property:

> A decent life, a share in the common life of all, is the only 'reward' that any man can honestly take for his work, whatever it is; if he asks for more, that means that he intends to play the master over somebody.[93]

Morris never identified 'official authority' as he surely would have had to do a century later, as a particular carrier of 'socialism'. But he did identify 'the revolution of State Socialism' as leaving the state ('that is society organised for the production and distribution of wealth') and the nation ('a body of people kept together for purposes of rivalry and war with other similar bodies') enlarged but not transformed.[94] And he dreaded 'the revolution of State Socialism' as likely to 'lead us back again into a new form of class society' where

> those who developed the greatest share of certain qualities not necessarily the most useful to the community, would gain a superior position from which they would be able to force the less gifted to serve them. And in

fact those who limit the revolution of Socialism to the abolition of private property in the means of production do contemplate a society in which production shall be in tutelage to the state; in which the centralised state would draw arbitrarily the line where public property ends and private property begins, would interfere with inheritance and with the accumulation of wealth, and in many ways would act as a master, and take the place of the old masters.[95]

It was against this that Morris set the commune, federation, combination, association, co-operation, 'that true society of loved and lover, parent and child, friend and friend, the society of well-wishers, of reasonable people conscious of the aspirations of humanity and of the duties we owe to it through one another'.[96]

It is impossible, in my view, to overemphasise the difference between the 'socialist' project as defined by Morris and that of statists and collectivists as characterised in these notes. The projects need different names. The difference is much more than one of sensibility or of emphasis. The Fabian 1906 Special Committee Report was right to suggest that schisms were involved – between opposed projects. One was not likely to emerge from the other without conflict; Morris knew this, but sometimes hoped otherwise. Rival interests, rival clusters of social potential, rival class trajectories, rival languages, rival objects were at stake.

Much later on, in the 1980s, it has again become possible and necessary to say this clearly. So polluted has the language of socialism and communism been by happenings since the 1920s, and so far away from either have most working people in metropolitan capitalisms moved (probably in actually existing socialisms too), that the search for 'another name' to accompany another practice, may make some sense. Morris's beautiful saying (in *A Dream of John Ball*) about struggle, defeat and 'another name' gets richer in meaning as the history goes on:

Men fight and lose the battle, and the thing that they fought for comes about in spite of their defeat, and when it comes turns out not to be what they meant, and other men have to fight for what they meant under another name.[97]

Fortunately it is not a matter of beginning all over again. The practice of what I have called 'associationism' is, as it were, historically available – perhaps particularly so in England. There are obvious echoes of early-nineteenth-century English radicalism and socialism in 'The Policy of Abstention'. These echoes are altogether more frequent in the late-nineteenth-century labour movement, and in the socialism of the same period, than historians have yet pointed out.

Historical links, through time, can be made. It is the material links, through class, that are more difficult. They are difficult even at the simple level of description, let alone employing fuller usages of class. If Fabianism, as Belfort Bax proposed, is the movement of the government official as clericalism is of the priest – whose movement has statism been? Whose material interests does it serve? What has been the sociology of 'social democracy', at leadership levels, but also at the level of entire movements? In whose interest has it been? Obviously in the interests of working people, for necessary welfare reforms. But they have not been in the driving seat. Who has?

What has been, could be or is now a material basis or carrier for associationism? Just as statism neglects private labour, so associationism neglects the existing state; how can a socialism which thinks and constructs through both come into being? How can complex rather than simple co-operation be realised? Again, we do not know. All we know is that something like associationism is still being practised, here, much more widely than it is named as having anything to do with 'socialism' or 'politics'. Whenever a major strike takes place in Britain, such as the miners' strike of 1984–5 or the lorry drivers' strike of 1979, practices of community sustenance and survival are noticed which can look like potential for another kind of society:

'What do you want to carry? Where from and to? How many loads? Who will suffer if it doesn't go through? Using your own vehicle? Paid-up union driver? . . .'
The emergence of these committees as the unpaid administrators of supplies may be the most disciplined extension of direct union power for years. . . .
If the public has been surprised by the spectacle of the Transport and General Workers' Union organising not only labour but the nation's lifelines, these committee men on the first floor of Transport House, West Bromwich, were not. Yet there was no sense here of a Soviet that had found it could break the system and might remake it; just a comfortable feeling that the men in the cabs had shown their strength.

John Chew, one of the picket committee said: '. . . This has shown that when we need to stick together, we do. . . . I think they've woken a sleeping giant. This co-operation will go on. These action committees will be keeping in touch'.[98]

That 'voluntary action' need not have the stigma of patronage or social work attached to it is now being realised, all over again, by socialists who had looked forward to its demise.[99] As the 1984–5 miners' defeat gets represented in history, examples of its extraordinary community activity, especially by women, will come to resemble partial, preliminary victory. As John Foster wrote of the other famous miners' strike, in 1926:

> Concretely and locally, in towns and villages, working people had started to organise themselves as an alternative power to the capitalist state. They only started. And they were defeated. . . . Yet sooner or later . . . this basic experience will have to be drawn on again.[100]

To what extent were there any links between the culture of associations of working people and socialist culture between, say, 1884 and 1948? How strong were those links in different places, and how were they severed? We do not know.

We do know, particularly among the contemporary *nouvelle couche*, that there are interesting things happening in the 1980s. That social group which has had an elective affinity with Fabianism (widely defined) *and* with Marxism (narrowly defined) seems now to be scattering in all kinds of creative directions, with or without the support of working people. Feminism, peace activity (e.g. Greenham), community initiatives, transformations in the practice of local government (e.g. the Greater London Economic Policy Group, and Enterprise Board), new ways of seeing and living trade unionism (e.g. Lucas Aerospace), socialist self-consciousness about 'think-work' . . . and much else besides, are all coming from that key social layer. It has also largely taken over the Labour Party in many wards, with consequences which have not yet become fully visible.[101]

A feminist reader of these notes noticed the gendered weighting of the 1911–71 occupational statistics quoted from A. H. Halsey on p. 224 above (Table 7.1). She suggested that the relative position of women *within* the *nouvelle couche*, in lower-paid, more front-line jobs and so 'in closer contact with the workers' (Durkheim quote, p. 221 above), might be, in part, responsible for the leaven they have provided in many of these developments. Their particular public and private positions may fuel their demonstrations in action, of how hierarchy and power structures block solutions which are possible and more human.[102]

'How socialism can be won in industrialised countries without the PMC and working class working at it together is hard to see' (Mike Hales). Maybe socialisation on capital's terms has now gone so far that to think in terms of a single, detachable social group being the carrier of a future social order is anachronistic. Maybe 'humanity' or 'the people' or 'the community' have again become the operative categories to use against a common enemy, rather than 'the working class'. Maybe socialism is 'objectively' no longer a class project but in some real – rather than mystified – sense a human one. 'How are we to explain', Raymond Williams recently asked (in a very different context), 'the possibility of liberating responses to a system that do not seem to have in any obvious way been prepared by social conditions?'[103]

We can, perhaps, take comfort in Britain from the complicated overlapping, and hence unpredictable nature, of some responses. Thus it was the authoritarian-collectivist, then free-market Hayekian, then social-democratic Liberal William Beveridge who, right at the end of his working life, came up with one of the most moving dreams of associationism I have come across. And it was in direct response to a large-scale working-class association. The friendly societies commissioned him to make a report on their situation after the statist 1948 National Insurance Act had finally marginalised them. At the end of *Voluntary Action: A Report on Methods of Social Advance* (1948) Beveridge wrote:

> restoration may come through one spirit breathing again through many men, as it did in the special field from which this study began. So at last human society may become a friendly society – an Affiliated Order of branches, some large and many small, each with its own life in freedom, each linked to all the rest by common purpose and by bonds to serve that purpose. So the night's insane dream of power over other men, without limit and without mercy, shall fade. So mankind in brotherhood shall bring back the day.[104]

NOTES

1 The Bakunin quote, and much else on this topic, is in A.
d'Agostino, 'Intelligentsia Socialism and the "Workers'
Revolution": the views of J. W. Machajski', *International Review
of Social History*, vol. XIV, 1969, pt I, 54–89. For Machajski and
the literature of the 'new class' more generally, see Carl Levy's
contribution to this volume.

2 'In its most general sense this can be expressed, simply, as a
widespread loss of the future. It is remarkable how quickly this
mood has developed' – R. Williams, *Modern Tragedy*, London,
Verso, 1979, p. 208.

    'The project of Socialism is guaranteed BY NOTHING –
certainly not by "Science", or by "Marxism–Leninism" – but can
find its own guarantees only by reason and through and upon
choice of values. . . . And it is here that the silence of Marx and
most Marxisms is so loud as to be deafening' – E. P. Thompson,
The Poverty of Theory, London, Merlin, 1978, p. 362.

    'The various mechanisms on which Marxists, more or less loosely
basing themselves on Marx's analysis, have relied for the
replacement of capitalism by socialism are not working: neither in
the developed countries, nor in most of the "third world" – itself
a concept whose looseness is now obvious. As for the actual
socialist states, their internal problems and the uncertainties of
their own future are not to be denied. Moreover, even for those of
us who refuse to diminish their extraordinary historic
achievements, they are in their present form difficult to accept as
models of a desirable socialist future. Capitalist society is at present
in global crisis, but few can believe that its probable, or even in
the short term, its possible, outcome in any country will be
socialism. On what then, other than blind will or an act of faith in
historical inevitability, are we to base our hopes? But Marxists
have never been blind voluntarists, nor have they ever based
themselves on historical inevitability or philosophical
generalisation in the abstract. They have always sought to identify
specific conjunctures and situations, which would dig capitalism's
grave' – E. J. Hobsbawm, 'Some Reflections on *The Break-up of
Britain*', *New Left Review*, 105, Sept./Oct. 1977, pp. 15–16.

3 S. Rowbotham, 'The Women's Movement and Organising for
Socialism', in *Beyond the Fragments*, London, Merlin, 1980,
p. 48.

4 *The Reasoner and Herald of Progress*, no. 2, 10 June 1846, pp. 26–
7; 'Co-operation and Socialism', in *Subjects of the Day*, Aug.
1890, p. 96. I owe these references to Peter Gurney, working on
the social history of co-operation at the University of Sussex.

5 I owe this material on Hall to Logie Barrow's unpublished ms. on schemes for trade-union federation 1897–1900. The quotes are from Hall's pamphlet, and from *The Clarion*, February 1896.

6 E. Durkheim, *Socialism* (1896), ed. A. Gouldner, New York, Collier Books, 1962, pp. 61–2; A. V. Dicey, for example, in his 1914 Introduction to *Lectures on the Relations between Law and Public Opinion*, London, Macmillan, 1905, 1962 edn, p. XL, made a similar distinction, based on a similar fear of workers' socialism.

7 I. Bullock, 'Socialists and Democratic Form in Britain, 1880–1914', D.Phil. thesis, University of Sussex, 1981. For example the ILP Treasurer, T. D. Benson (*Labour Leader*, 7 June 1914), in an article on socialism and syndicalism: 'there will be a governing or organising class, corresponding to the brain, but an organising class whose only motive for existence is service to the community – a class which, also, may be hereditary under Socialism, perhaps must be so'.

Or 'Marxian' (George A. N. Samuel) (*Labour Leader*, 14 February 1897) was awaiting the arrival of a 'man strong in the pride of birth or in the conquest of fortune, a man destined to play the great card in the grand style; and the people will follow him to Social Democracy as they have never followed one of their own class'. For 'Marxian' (*Labour Leader*, 1 October 1898), 'socialism was essentially an aristocratic creed . . . just imagine, or study the clod-pated bundles of nerves and appetites that constitute the human produce of the Capitalist system: and then picture the sort of "Democrat" who seeks definite and helpful guidance from such a mob'.

Or H. M. Hyndman, leader of the SDF (*Social Democrat*, February 1901), in an article on 'Democracy': 'If enfranchisement of a mass of deteriorated, uneducated voters would tend to throw back this essential education, then I am not in favour of such enfranchisement, of such "democracy", however convinced I may be of the truth that the whole adult population will take an active and intelligent part in the administration of socialism when Social Democracy itself is constituted. If however anyone could thoroughly convince me (seeing education must inevitably come, in the first instance, from above, that is to say from those who are already themselves educated) that we should make more progress in educating the people under a capable Caesar than we should with a fully enfranchised democracy – then I am for a Caesar for the time being, always provided the capable Caesar presents himself.'

8 See S. Buck-Morss, 'Walter Benjamin – Revolutionary Writer (I)', *New Left Review*, 128, July–August 1981, pp. 52–60.

9 'Conversations with Brecht', in Walter Benjamin, *Understanding Brecht*, London, New Left Books, 1977, pp. 105–21.

10 'The Author as Producer', ibid., p. 103.

11 T. G. Ashplant, 'The CIU and the ILP: Working Class Organisation, Politics and Culture *c.* 1880–1914', D.Phil. thesis, University of Sussex, 1983, ch. 5 'Membership and leadership of the CIU and ILP'.

12 E. J. Hobsbawm, 'The Fabians Reconsidered', *Labouring Men*, London, Weidenfeld, 1964, pp. 250–71.

13 R. H. S. Crossman, *The Backbench Diaries of Richard Crossman*, London, Hamish Hamilton, 1981, pp. 769–70.

14 Beatrice Webb's Diary, entry for 18 April 1940, in Passfield Papers, Vol. 54.

15 *Justice*, 9 March 1901.

16 See CAB 24/98 (1920), pp. 78–9, in the PRO for 'Report from the Ministry of Labour on the Labour Situation' for the week ending 11 February 1920; and CAB 24/98 CP 686 for Directorate of Intelligence, Home Office 'Report on Revolutionary Organisations in the UK', 19 February 1920, p. 322. I owe these references to Paddy Maguire.

17 *New Moral World*, 11 July 1839.

18 M. Hales, *Living Thinkwork: Where Do Labour Processes Come From?*, London, CSE Books, 1980, p. 110.

19 See a forthcoming volume in the Routledge History Workshop Series, S. Yeo (ed.), *New Views of Co-operation*, 1988; plus two chapters I have written in other books: 'State and Anti-State, Reflections on Social Forms and Struggles from 1850', in P. Corrigan (ed.), *Capitalism, State Formation and Marxist Theory*, London, Quartet, 1980; 'Working-Class Association, Private Capital, Welfare and the State in the Late-Nineteenth and Twentieth Centuries', in N. Parry, M. Rustin and C. Satyamurti (eds), *Social Work, Welfare and the State*, London, Edward Arnold, 1979.

20 Reworked in a Communist Party tradition going back at least to Theodore Rothstein's *From Chartism to Labourism*, 1929. J. Saville, 'The Ideology of Labourism', in R. Benewick *et al.*, *Knowledge and Belief in Politics*, London, Allen & Unwin, 1973, pp. 213–26.

21 A. E. Bestor, 'The Evolution of the Socialist Vocabulary', *Journal of the History of Ideas*, IX (3), 1948, 259–302; R. Williams, *Keywords*, London, Fontana, 1983 edn, entry on 'Socialist'.

22 T. W. Mercer, *The Co-operative Movement in Politics*, Manchester, Co-operative Union, 1920. In a series of articles in the *Reasoner*, nos. 150–2, 1849, Holyoake argued for 'association' as the best label for the 'communistic question' and for socialism. Much later

J. A. Schumpeter labelled the socialism of the period 1790–1870 as 'associationist', in his *History of Economic Analysis*, Oxford, OUP, 1954, pp. 452–62. *Associazionismo* is a common, and current, Italian category. The Istituto Socialista di Studi Storici put on a conference in April 1983 on 'Associazionismo e case del popolo in Europa 1900–1939'; see also G. Levi, 'Associazionismo Operaio a Torino e in Piemonte, 1890–1926', in A. Agosti and G. M. Bravo (eds), *Storia del Movimento Operaio del Socialismo e delle Lotte Sociali in Piemonte*, Bari, De Donato, 1979, pp. 481–550; G. Sapelli (ed), *Il Movimento Co-operativo in Italia*, Turin, Einaudi, 1981; M. Degli Innocenti, *Storia del Movimento Cooperativo*, Rome, Riuniti, 1978. In an interesting article, 'The Co-operative Conquest of Industry', *Society for Co-operative Studies Bulletin*, no. 26, February 1976, pp. 32–53, Prof. G. Davidovici slipped into 'socialistes associatonistes' when trying to distinguish co-operative from other politics. For France, see B. Moss, *Origins of the French Labour Movement: The Socialism of Skilled Workers 1830–1914*, Berkeley, University of California Press, 1976; W. H. Sewell, *Work and Revolution in France: The Language of Labour from the Old Regime to 1848*, Cambridge University Press, 1980.

23   With Andry Durr and Paddy Maguire I experienced this when writing 'Notes for Friday Night' for *History Workshop*, 15, 6–8 November 1981, pp. ii–xiv, and when presenting those notes to a large and bewildered audience attending the opening session of the workshop. A huge anthology could be collected on these tensions. Ada Nield Chew went to a Fabian summer school in 1915 and confessed to her 'rather foolish and shrinking objection to close contact with [middle- and upper-class Fabians] on all fours with, and just as silly and snobbish as, the shrinking of many middle and upper class people from working folk', *Cotton Factory Times*, 1 October 1915, quoted in B. Waites, 'The Language and Imagery of Class in Early-Twentieth-Century England', *Literature and History*, no. 4, 1976, p. 41. The point would be to see them as powerful tensions/contradictions in British culture rather than moralising them as 'foolish and shrinking', 'silly and snobbish'. In 1910 John Burns let his feelings out to H. G. Wells, referring to 'the new helotry in the servile state run by the archivists of the London School of Economics'; this 'means a race of paupers in a grovelling community ruled by uniformed prigs' – Burns papers, B. M. Add. MS 46301, p. 121, quoted in J. Harris, *William Beveridge: A Biography*, Oxford University Press, 1977, p. 265, n. 8. Burns was full of feeling of this kind, about 'Bounders on the Bounce', etc., which meant that at times *The Clarion* democrats could quote him with approval in their work

against 'wire-pullers and intriguers'; see P. J. King and R. Blatchford, *Trades Federation*, Clarion pamphlet no. 17, 1897. For recent examples, see P. Whiteley, *The Crisis of the Labour Party*, London, Methuen, 1983.

24 I tried to convey the facts and the feel of this in 'A New Life: The Religion of Socialism in Britain, 1883–1896', *History Workshop Journal*, 4 (Autumn), 1977, pp. 5–56.

25 B. Webb, *My Apprenticeship*, 1926, Cambridge University Press, 1979 edn, p. 151.

26 S. Collini, *Liberalism and Sociology*, Cambridge University Press, 1979, p. 59.

27 B. Webb, op. cit. (note 25), p. 161.

28 B. Potter, *The Co-operative Movement in Great Britain*, London, Sonnenschein, 1891, pp. 235–9; Collini, op. cit. (note 26), p. 65.

29 The quotations are from B. Webb, op. cit. (note 25), chapter VII, 'Why I became a Socialist'. The Mitchell speech in full is in the *Report of the Nineteenth Annual Co-operative Congress*, 1887, pp. 6–7.

30 L. T. Hobhouse, *The Labour Movement*, 2nd edn, London, Unwin, 1898.

31 Collini, op. cit. (note 26), pp. 62–5, explains Fabian political economy and their theory of rent, and puts Hobhouse's *The Labour Movement* and its successive editions in this context; see also A. M. McBriar, *Fabian Socialism and English Politics 1884–1918*, Cambridge University Press, 1962, chapters II–V; and an unpublished paper by C. Levy, 'Fabianism, the Nursery of Organised Socialism: 1884–1900'.

32 *The Producer*, 15 February 1917.

33 Jeremy Seabrook is the writer to have got nearest to the historical and political importance of this question. He is more subtle than his detractors sometimes suggest: 'The passing of the old shoe-making community represents for me something beyond a subjective feeling about the ruin and dispersal of my own extended family. Somehow, that community – closed and impoverished though it was – held within itself a possibility and a promise of an alternative future: nobody wanted to perpetuate those conditions. But that alternative has not been realised; on the contrary, it has been slowly extinguished by the events of the past thirty or forty years. The suppression of the possibility of their change was an act of violence against them and the way they lived and the hope they cherished. Their change was eclipsed and deformed by the change that actually occurred' – *What Went Wrong?*, London, Gollancz, 1978, p. 276; but see also Fiona McFarlane on her mother in J. McCrindle and S. Rowbotham (eds), *Dutiful Daughters*, London, Allen Lane, 1977, p. 223: 'they go through this period when they

see great injustices and they want the injustices put right, and when they see the injustices largely not getting put right but slightly improved then they, I think – they don't like the consequences'.

34 In many works; but see, for example, J. Langley, *Always a Layman*, Brighton, Queenspark Books, 1976; McCrindle and Rowbotham, op. cit. (note 33); Seabrook, op. cit. (note 33); the work of the Federation of Worker Writers and Community Publishers is crucial here.

35 I am thinking of work like L. T. Hobhouse's *Democracy and Reaction*, London, T. Fisher Unwin, 1901–4. The early Gramsci (1914–19) was extremely interested in English liberalism in all its varieties. For the Hammonds, see D. Sutton, 'Radical Liberalism, Fabianism and Social History', in R. Johnson *et al.* (eds), *Making Histories*, London, Hutchinson, 1982. J. A. Hobson became a major critic of Ramsay MacDonald's statism before 1914.

36 G. Stedman Jones, 'Engels and the Genesis of Marxism', *New Left Review*, 106, November/December 1977, is excellent on actual class struggle in relation to epistemological breakthroughs, in this case in the 1840s.

37 P. Corrigan, 'State Formation and Moral Regulation in 19th Century Britain: Sociological Investigations', D.Phil. thesis, University of Durham, 1977, p. 96, is good on this theme of how 'the working class demonstrate future social forms in their *current* organisations of struggle'. He grounds this notion thoroughly in Marx.

38 J. Harris, *William Beveridge: A Biography*, Oxford, Clarendon, 1977, pp. 2, 85–9.

39 For the impact this had on a Congregational minister who was a leading light of Liberalism in Reading, see S. Yeo, *Religion and Voluntary Organisations in Crisis*, London, Croom Helm, 1976, p. 295; for Lord Rosebery and the 'Limps', see H. C. G. Mathew, *The Liberal Imperialists: The Ideas and Politics of a Post-Gladstonian Elite*, Oxford University Press, 1973, p. 146; and Collini, op. cit. (note 26), p. 83.

40 *Labour Leader*, 14 February 1891, 20 August 1898, 1 October 1898.

41 See L. T. Hobhouse, 'The Career of Fabianism', *The Nation*, 30 March 1907.

42 Collini, op. cit. (note 26), p. 32.

43 For instance, P. Redfern, *Journey to Understanding*, London, Allen & Unwin, 1946, pp. 18–19, describing 1893 during a miners' strike (as a shopkeeper's apprentice): 'In the dark of the · evenings, after eight o'clock, I packed myself with the crowd, whilst socialist lecturers simplified everything. Eloquent hands pictured the round cake of the national income. The workers

made it; the capitalists and landlords took it. One slice only, a mere third, they gave back to the workers, just to keep their slaves alive! Thus did Marxian doctrine and Fabian diagrams reach the people. . . . It was not this caricature, with its kernel of bitter half-truth, that Margaret McMillan brought to the market place. She came with a vision of health, joy and beauty in working lives, to be demanded and created by the people themselves.'

44   Its range of usages at the time has been clearly analysed in Collini, op. cit. (note 26), pp. 34–5. Anna Davin gave me two interesting ones. Canon Gregory interrogating Mark Wilks (chair of the London School Board Management Committee) on the Cross Commission in 1887, asked: 'Is it not opening the way to socialism to give them [mothers] these rooms in which to have their babies nursed?' Wilks replied: 'Socialism is a wide term'; see Cross Commission, 3rd Report, Minutes of Evidence, pp. 49, 123, *Parliamentary Papers*, 1887, XXX. And T. J. Macnamara, ex-schoolmaster and Liberal MP, proposed in 1905 school canteens, free transport, baths, etc. in the *Contemporary Review*: 'All this sounds like rank Socialism. I'm afraid it is; but I am not in the least dismayed. Because I know it also to be first-rate Imperialism'; see A. Davin, 'Imperialism and Motherhood', *History Workshop Journal*, 5 (Spring), 1978, p. 17.

45   Like co-operators, e.g. Edward Vansittart Neale, who wrote extensively on socialism in the *Co-operative News*, e.g. 'The Relation of Co-operation to Socialism', 8 March 1879; 'The Demon of Socialism', 4 May 1878; 'What is Socialism?', 14 June 1878. Or like J. M. Ludlow (1821–1911), who in his autobiography, written late in life, wrote: 'In these days, when the term "socialism" is sought to be narrowed in the using to this or that particular system, and the patent meaning of the word, and its history in this country as well as elsewhere, are so overlooked that "Co-operation" and "Socialism" are actually treated as antagonistic, both by men who call themselves Socialists and by men who call themselves Co-operators' – A. D. Murray (ed.), *John Ludlow: The Autobiography of a Christian Socialist*, London, Cass, 1981, p. 188.

46   Socialists like William Morris and Joseph Lane used the label 'communist' with great pride, and as a sign of affiliation to one kind of socialism rather than another. The same conflicts within socialism were expressed in the SDF in terms of 'conscious social democrats' (good) versus 'socialists' (bad); see Reading supplement to *Justice*, 25 April, 1896, p. 1, through to May 1897. Ex-Owenite co-operators like Dr J. Watts and G. J. Holyoake in the 1860s and 1870s also called themselves 'communists'. For the adoption of 'communism' by the Third International, see A. Lindemann, *The Red Years: European Socialism versus Bolshevism 1919–1921*,

Berkeley, University of California Press, 1974. For fascinating traces in the memories of an 'unpolitical' East Ender of earlier uses of 'communism', see R. Samuel, *East End Underworld: Chapters in the Life of Arthur Harding*, London, Routledge & Kegan Paul, 1981, pp. 172–3, 262, 273.

47 The earliest English example of 'collectivism' cited in the *OED* is from *The Saturday Review*, 8 May 1880, and it is quite far from, indeed opposite to, dominant usages as described in my notes here. The piece is on 'The International', and deals with the development of anarchist ideas within it: 'the doctrine of Collectivism forced its way to the front. . . . By Collectivism is meant that everything is done and managed by a society. Railways, mines, forests, and even the soil, are to be worked by associations. . . . What is remarkable in this impracticable conception is that it gets rid of the idea of the State. The associations include everyone, but there is nothing above the associations' – cited in Collini, op. cit. (note 26), p. 33, n. 78. Hilaire Belloc's *The Servile State*, 1912, London and Edinburgh, T. N. Fouks, was careful to distinguish between the collectivism he was attacking (which he called the servile state) and socialism. His work was not a generalised attack upon socialism at all, but a specific critique of a state which he thought was the emerging result of the interaction between capitalism and its socialist critics: 'the Socialist ideal, in conflict with and yet informing the body of Capitalism, produces a third thing very different from the Socialist idea – to wit, a Servile State: . . . This book does not discuss the Socialist State. Indeed it is the very heart of my thesis that we are not, in fact approaching Socialism at all, but a very different state of society: to wit, a society in which the Capitalist class shall be even more powerful and far more secure than it is at present: a society in which the proletarian mass shall not suffer from particular regulations oppressive or beneficient, but shall change their status, lose their present freedom and be subject to compulsory labour' – see Preface to 2nd edn (1913) in the 3rd edn (1927), pp. ix–xi. I owe this material to Ian Bullock's thesis, op. cit. (note 7).

48 Collini, op. cit. (note 26), pp. 66–7.

49 *Justice*, 9 May 1903. *Justice* is a key source for critique of collectivism and statism in this period. It is a vehicle for worry about personality cults in the ILP, and for worry about experts and bureaucrats in socialism; see 15 November 1902 and 8 August 1905.

50 P. Redfern, *Journey*, op. cit. (note 43), p. 102.

51 P. Redfern, 'The Conflict of Capitalism and Democracy' in *CWS Annual*, 1910. This is a full articulation of one version of CWS

ideology in the post-Mitchell era. Redfern also applied 'collectivist' to Mitchell, in his brief biography of him.

52 *The Wheatsheaf*, vol. II, no. 1, (May 1898), p. 162. Neither Ben Jones on the CWS 'materialist'/'federalist' side of the great arguments which divided the movement in the second half of the nineteenth century nor Edward Vansittart Neale on the Christian Socialist 'idealist'/'individualist' side have yet been given enough credit for their (sometimes) deliberate eclecticism, and their critiques of divisive heresies from a whole, united-movement point of view.

53 The collection includes: 'labourism' (John Saville), 'labour socialism' (Stuart Macintyre), 'Working classism' (Timothy Ashplant), 'collective labourism' (Fred Reid); 'socialist collectivism' (Harold Laski) – all, no doubt, meaning quite different things.

54 The quotes are from R. Johnson *et al.*, op. cit. (note 35), p. 300; the context is a critique of 'the autobiographical mode' of the worker–writer movement and of some oral history.

55 In these two sections I am drawing heavily on the work of the Brighton Labour Process Group, which was affiliated to the Conference of Socialist Economists and without which I could not have considered writing these notes. Having first worked on the labour process in Marxism, the group then did original work on 'the three socialisms', with a particular input from Robin Murray. Publications of the group consisted of pieces for *Capital and Class*, of papers for the CSE annual conferences, and of weekly memoranda for discussion; my writing here draws on the latter verbatim.

56 There is a growing body of work on authority relations based on expertise as pivotal within capitalist class systems today, as well as within 'socialist' ones. See John Roemer, *A Theory of Exploitation and Class*, Cambridge, Mass., Harvard University Press, 1982; K. Kumar, *Prophecy and Progress*, Harmondsworth, Pelican, 1978; E. O. Wright, *Class, Crisis and the State*, London, New Left Books, 1978, and *Class Structure and Income Determination*, London, Academic Press, 1979; N. Poulantzas, *Classes in Contemporary Capitalism*, London, New Left Books, 1975, and *State, Power, Socialism*, London, New Left Books, 1978; F. Parkin, *Marxism: A Bourgeois Critique*, London, Tavistock, 1979; T. Nichols, 'The "Socialism" of Management', *Sociological Review*, vol. 23, no. 2, May 1975.

57 See E. M. Wood, 'The Separation of the Economic and the Political in Capitalism', *New Left Review*, no. 127, May/June 1981, pp. 66–95. For the emergence of a cadre of people with a vested interest in their own movement, in the ILP in the early years of the twentieth century, see T. G. Ashplant, 'The CIU and the ILP:

Working-Class Organisation, Politics and Culture, *c.* 1880–1914',
D.Phil. thesis, University of Sussex, 1983, chapter 3.

58 P. Williams, *Hugh Gaitskell: A Political Biography*, London, Cape,
1979, p. 391.

59 See S. Webb, 'Social Movements', in *Cambridge Modern History*,
Vol. XII, Cambridge University Press, 1910.

60 From 1908 there was an international journal of, in effect,
collectivism. It started off as *Annales de la Régie Directe*. By 1925
it was coming out in an English edition too, as *Annals of Collective
Economy*, edited by Edgar Millhaud of the University of Geneva.
In 1947 it became the official organ of the International Centre of
Research and Information on Collective Economy, and in 1964
Annals of Public and Co-operative Economy.

61 K. Hardie, *The ILP: All About It*, London, National Labour
Library, 1908, p. 4. For a sharp attack on statism as a 'nebula',
see P. Anderson, *Arguments within English Marxism*, London,
Verso, 1980, pp. 202–4.

62 For Marx on 'bourgeois socialism' and 'the Social Democracy', see
the *Communist Manifesto*, 1848, and the *Eighteenth Brumaire*,
1851; for Trotsky on statism, see *The Revolution Betrayed* (1937),
New York edn, Merit Publishers, 1965, p. 246.

63 *Labour Leader*, 31 May 1912. I owe this quotation to Ian Bullock's
thesis, op. cit. (note 7).

64 *Annual Conference of Trades Councils*, Report, 1946. I owe this
reference to Michael Bor.

65 See, for instance, H. Jephson, *The Platform: Its Rise and Progress*,
Vols. I and II, London, Macmillan, 1892.

66 I owe this Special Committee Report quote to Ian Bullock's thesis,
op. cit. (note 7). It was published by the Fabian Society in November
1906.

67 These constitute a surprisingly full body of work: *Socialism and
Society* (1905); *Socialism* (1907); *Socialism and Government*, 2
vols. (1909); *The Socialist Movement* (1911); *Syndicalism: A Critical
Examination* (1912); *The Social Unrest: Its Cause* (1913). See also
Bernard Barker (ed.), *Ramsey MacDonald's Political Writings*,
London, Allen Lane, 1972.

68 D. Marquand, *Ramsey MacDonald*, London, Cape, 1977, p. 83.

69 'In so far as scientific Socialism began by uniting the working
classes in a political movement and in centring that movement
round certain abstractions in political and economic theory, it only
followed the method that every other movement has ever followed
or can ever follow. Thus Socialism towards the middle of the
nineteenth century became a political movement. Its growth since
then has been the growth of a political movement, and what
prospects it has at the present moment of succeeding are due to

the fact that it is a political movement' – *The Socialist Movement*,
p. 103. Much of MacDonald's work is a specific attack upon the
social critique of politics which is such an important strand in
nineteenth-century working-class association, and upon the rich
inheritance of inventiveness about democratic forms which is such
an important strand in nineteenth- and twentieth-century
working-class and other radicalism.

70 *Socialism and Government*, 1909, Vol. I, pp. 11–12.
71 S. and B. Webb, *The History of Trade Unionism 1666–1920*,
    London, Longmans, 1920 edn, 'Preface to the Original edition of
    1894', pp. vii–viii.
72 A South Wales miner, b. 1919, quoted in Seabrook, op. cit. (note
    33), p. 59; see also p. 183.
73 Corrigan, op. cit. (note 37), p. 96.
74 Yeo, op. cit. (note 39); see index entries for Rabson, J. (1894–
    1936) and Morse, E. R. T. (1858–1923), covering activity in the
    Reading Athletic Club, the Reading Football Club, the Royal
    Berkshire Hospital and the Co-op, among other associations.
75 S. and B. Webb, op. cit. (note 71), revised edn, 1926, p. 563.
76 Marx, *Capital*, Vol. I, Harmondsworth, Penguin, 1976, p. 171.
77 Dr Wade at the 1832 Co-operative Congress, *Proceedings of the
    3rd Co-operative Congress*, London, April 1832, ed. William
    Carpenter, p. 79.
78 R. Bahro, *The Alternative in Eastern Europe* Eng. trans., London,
    NLB, 1978, pp. 287–8.
79 S. Yeo, 'A New Life: The Religion of Socialism in Britain, 1883–
    1896', *History Workshop Journal*, 4 (Autumn), 1977, pp. 5–56; I
    tried to go a bit beyond my 1977 arguments in 'Towards "Making
    Form of More Moment than Spirit": Further Thoughts on
    Labour, Socialism and the New Life from the Late 1890s to the
    Present', in J. A. Jowitt and R. K. S. Taylor (eds), *Bradford
    1890–1914: The Cradle of the ILP*, Bradford, University of Leeds,
    Centre for Adult Education, 1980, pp. 73–88.
80 F. Boos, Introduction to the reprint of William Morris's Socialist
    Diary, *History Workshop Journal*, 13 (Spring), 1982, p. 2. Boos is
    excellent on these essays. The Diary came from 1887; so did
    'Monopoly', 'Feudal England', 'The Policy of Abstention', 'The
    Society of the Future', 'The Present Outlook in Politics' and 'True
    and False Society'. There is a fascinating example of the contrast
    between Morris's Diary jottings on his 1887 meetings, and the view
    from the consumers in Boos, p. 33 and n. 90. Morris was usually
    despondent, e.g. after a meeting in February 1887 in Mitcham:
    'Except a German from Wimbledon (who was in the chair) and
    two others who looked like artisans of the painter or small builder-
    type, the audience was all made up of labourers and their wives:

they were very quiet and attentive except one man who was courageous from liquor, and interrupted sympathetically: but I doubt if most of them understood anything I said; though some few of them showed that they did by applauding the points. I wonder sometimes if people will remember in times to come to what a depth of degradation the ordinary English workman has been reduced.' In contrast, the Mitcham branch report of the same meeting, in *Commonweal*, reported thus: 'In the evening in our club-room, comrade Morris lectured to a very large audience on "Monopoly", and met with enthusiastic reception. Eden, Harrison, Gregory and others took part in the discussion. We closed as usual with singing. Four new members made.'

81 'True and False Society' (1887), in W. Morris, *The Collected Works*, London, Longmans, 1910–1915, Vol. XXIII, p. 230.

82 'The Policy of Abstention', in M. Morris, *William Morris: Artist, Writer, Socialist* (1936), New York, Russell, 1966, Vol. II, p. 453.

83 Morris to Joseph Lane, 20 March 1887, quoted in Boos, op. cit. (note 80), p. 7.

84 E. D. LeMire, *The Unpublished Lectures of William Morris*, Detroit, State University Press, 1969, p. 216. LeMire has an invaluable Appendix I, a year-by-year 'Calendar of William Morris's Platform Career', enabling a detailed study of a single year, such as 1887.

85 N. Mackenzie (ed.), *The Letters of Sidney and Beatrice Webb, Vol. II, Partnership 1891–1912*, Cambridge University Press, 1978, p. 144.

86 The Morris letter is in *Commonweal*, July 1885.

87 'The Society of the Future', *Commonweal*, 13 April 1885.

88 W. Morris and B. Bax, *Socialism, its Growth and Outcome*, London, Sonnenschein, 1896, p. 282. 'How Shall We Live Then', quoted in P. Meier, *William Morris: The Marxist Dreamer*, Eng. trans., Brighton, Harvester, 1978, Vol. II, p. 315.

89 'The Socialist League, it can be argued, collapsed due to a complex combination of differing political styles, different life experiences, and to a certain but crucial extent opposing class backgrounds. William Morris effectively, but only temporarily, bound the romantic anti-capitalist revolt of the *nouvelle couche sociale* (the new professional class) together with the quite different tradition of London plebeian "club socialism", Morris, whom Frank Kitz once called "nature's nobleman", was a craftsman and a middle-class intellectual and through sheer charisma could weld these forces together' – C. Levy, *History Workshop Journal*, 18 (Autumn), 1984, p. 188.

90 Boos, op. cit. (note 80), p. 10.

91 'The Policy of Abstention'; see M. Morris, op. cit. (note 82).

92   'True and False Society' (1886); see W. Morris, op. cit. (note 81).

93   'Artist and Artisan', *Commonweal*, 10 September 1887. On these themes chapter 8 of Meier, op. cit. (note 88), Vol. II, 'To everyone according to his needs', is excellent.

94   'True and False Society'; see W. Morris, op. cit. (note 81).

95   'The Policy of Abstention'; see M. Morris, op. cit. (note 82).

96   'True and False Society'; see W. Morris, op. cit. (note 81).

97   W. Morris, 'A Dream of John Ball', in M. Morris, op. cit. (note 82), Vol. XVI, pp. 231–2.

98   H. Herbert, 'Red Roads but No Soviets Here', *Guardian*, 31 January 1979, p. 19.

99   See K. Worpole, 'Volunteers for Socialism', *New Society*, 29 January 1981, p. 199.

100 J. Foster, 'Imperialism and the Labour Aristocracy', in J. Skelley (ed.), *The General Strike* (1926), London, Lawrence & Wishart, 1976 edn, p. 52. See also H. Beynon, *Digging Deeper: Issues in the Miners' Strike*, London, Verso, 1985; Barnsley Women Against Pit Closures, *Women Against Pit Closures*, Barnsley, 1984.

101 For more on the Labour Party, see G. Stedman Jones, 'Why Is the Labour Party in a Mess?', in *Languages of Class*, Cambridge University Press, 1983, pp. 239–56. For the new class and new social movements in less parochial settings, see A. Touraine, *The Post-Industrial Society*, London, Wildwood House, 1971; *Mouvements Sociaux d'Aujourd'hui, Acteurs et Analystes*, Paris, Éditions Ouvrières, 1982; A. Gouldner, *The Future of Intellectuals and the Rise of the New Class*, London, Macmillan, 1979.

102 See A. Heath, *Social Mobility*, London, Fontana, 1981, esp. chapter 4.

103 R. Williams, *Politics and Letters*, London, Verso, 1979, p. 255.

104 W. H. Beveridge, *Voluntary Action*, London, Allen & Unwin, 1948, pp. 323–4.

8
Conclusion: Historiography and the New Class
Carl Levy

This volume has demonstrated that in the period before 1914 many ideas strikingly similar to concepts of the 'New Class' were employed, in application both to the growing 'middle layers' of society and specifically to their roles in and around the socialist and labour movements. What use do these concepts have for historians? Can we embrace a 'post-Marxism' which argues that the educated middle classes are not only central to the politics and social structures of today's capitalist and socialist societies but were, in fact, more significant to human societies than the emergence of the industrial working class during the past two hundred years? In my concluding remarks I will analyse critically a series of 'meta-theories' which attempt to do precisely this, and then suggest what aspects of these theories may be useful to historians.

VARIETIES OF 'NEW CLASS'

Modern sociological theories of the 'New Class' centre upon the questions of how far it is possible to identify a 'class' among those in controlling, highly skilled or specialised occupations entered via advanced education in contemporary industrial societies whether socialist or capitalist. Much of this literature is concerned primarily with the social structures of political elites in what Rudolf Bahro has defined as 'actually existing socialism', and specifically the conditions and characteristics of their self-reproduction after revolutionary overturns.[1] Another collection of approaches attempts to apply this concept of a 'New Class' to late capitalist societies. Here it is argued that the educated middle classes, lacking large-scale property, have established and enlarged their social position through political means, mostly by drawing upon and extending their affinities with the state's role in social management or by creating a socially dominant 'world-view' based upon the meritocratic principles of their professional or academic life-styles. Concerning the 'new class' under capitalism, there are three fields of inquiry:

(1) those concentrating on the emergence of corporate technostructures, technocrats and the new technical working class;[2]

(2) those revealing connections between the rise of services and the state sector relative to private industry and the occupational and social consequences of post-industrialism;[3]

(3) and, finally, those adopting a more openly Marxist approach, identifying new middle strata of controllers within the very heart of the capitalist production process and broader systems of social reproduction. These comprise the 'class boundary' separating rulers from subordinate producers in late capitalism, and are a group whose 'contradictory class location' may shift them towards a progressive alliance with the manual working class or conversely in a conservative direction as the servants or mandarins of capitalist and politico-military elites.[4]

Alvin Gouldner and Ivan Szelényi have been two of the most rigorous sociological proponents of a 'New Class' on the left. Moreover, both have attempted to trace the origins of the 'New Class' through history.[5] Alvin Gouldner's corpus of work is more all-encompassing, and he has dealt more consistently with a 'New Class' within Western capitalism. However, since the term 'New Class' was popularised in the context of the debate about how one should classify 'actually existing socialism', I should like to make a few brief comments about Eastern 'New Class' theories.

THE EASTERN NEW CLASS

By now it is commonplace to separate the Eastern intelligentsia from national groups of Western intellectuals. Thus many writers differentiate the two by tracing diverse occupational and cultural patterns open to each group.[6] The argument goes like this: Western feudalism gradually disintegrated through the subversive influence of isolated but vibrant urban cultures; the clerisy passed through an intermediate stage of patronage from enlightened despots and landed aristocrats, but finally modern intellectuals become dependent upon a modern economy which guaranteed them productive and socially integrative work. In the East however, civil society was, to quote Antonio Gramsci, 'gelatinous'; lacking independent and countervailing sources of power and income, the Eastern intelligentsia remained isolated both from the state and from the lower orders.[7]

The second part of the argument draws the political moral. Here it is shown how a part of this Eastern intelligentsia secured its social and psychological moorings during the late nineteenth and early twentieth centuries by discovering a transformative/teleological agent in the small, compact but rapidly increasing urban proletariat, after an earlier generation had sought similar salvation via the peasantry.

The young working class became a form of human dynamite, a tool capable of demolishing the edifice of the Asiatic state. After 1917 the politically successful elements of the intelligentsia laid the foundations for a 'New Class'. The decimation of revolutionary workers during civil war and famine, and the Stalinist purges of errant colleagues and rebellious peasants, allowed this party intelligentsia to create its own self-perpetuating political *apparat* which guaranteed its existence as a distinct class in Soviet society.[8]

Such a family portrait of the 'New Class' has found its advocates across the ideological spectrum. They all exhibit a rather cavalier attitude towards the effects of historical conjunctures and even accidents on political outcomes. These accounts fail to explain how to distinguish an incipient pre-1917 Bolshevik 'New Class' from a similar social group of intellectuals within the Mensheviks and Social Revolutionaries, and how they arrived at such different, indeed mutually hostile, strategies.

Furthermore, the historiography of the Russian revolutions (1905 and 1917) and their outcomes had remained until very recently either political biography, prosopography or institutional history, and we lacked detailed accounts of the social life and customs of the industrial proletariat. Even the peasantry could do with more social historical or sociological treatments on a par with Theodor Shanin's pioneering monographs. It may well be that standard accounts of the immense influence of the revolutionary educated middle classes within the Russian context will have to be re-evaluated once recent case studies are synthesised into a living portrait of the intelligentsia's putative agents.[9]

Then, of course, there is the sticky problem of post-1917 history. When indeed does a full-blown 'New Class' gain power, and what social groups and historical processes are involved in its formative stages? For instance, it is not at all clear whether the Soviet 'New Class' emerged from a fusion of War Communism bureaucrats and 'Nepmen', or during Stalin's forced collectivisation and industrialisation of the 1930s. Or, quite possibly, is this 'New Class' a product of the post-1945 era – a result of convergence with a Western pattern of rapid growth in both the tertiary sector and higher education?[10]

In Szelényi's most recent work the 'New Class' is identified with university graduates.[11] Milovan Djilas, the Yugoslav populariser of the term, had imagined a quite different animal.[12] For him the 'New Class' was a product of the bureaucratic machine. Its members consisted of former peasants and workers (or at least young Stalinists from humble social backgrounds) transformed into white-collar *apparatchiks* during the 1930s in order to replace the purged generations of technicians and Bolshevik intellectuals.

The Hungarian's 'New Class' is the generation of post-war university graduates who are currently challenging the power and prerogatives of the older Stalinist bureaucracy.

Clearly, here is a concept chasing after its own rapidly changing reference group. Power may be exercised through political groupings without these becoming classes. But it seems particularly difficult for Marxists to realise this embarrassing fact.

THE WESTERN NEW CLASS

Gouldner's central concerns are different. Following a large group of social theorists and historians, he suggests that the new educated middle classes of the late nineteenth and early twentieth centuries in Western Europe were first and foremost modernisers, social controllers and self-interested agents of professionalisation and credentialism. He also attempts to argue that some components of this/these diverse social group(s) employed socialist and reformist movements to reorganise civil society along more congenial lines, suitable for the triumph of their 'world-view'.[13]

Gouldner produced evidence that concepts similar to those of a 'New Class' had been employed before 1914. One could extrapolate from the 'Gouldnerian model' and construct a general case for an 'intelligentsia socialism', socialism as state collectivism, as reforms initiated or stage-managed by a well-educated elite. Socialism was not, such a formulation would show, first and foremost about an egalitarian reordering of society and the achievement of grass-roots democratic political and industrial control, but what dull sociology books describe as modernisation.

Take a famous example much examined in this book and else-where: British Fabianism. It did appear to combine an appeal for 'social service' with schemes which substituted for traditional elites and capitalist entrepreneurs a stratum of managers and experts. Furthermore, the Fabian road to modernity could, it seemed, be implemented under the guises of apparently alien and hostile brands of socialism. Thus (as Royden Harrison writes in this volume and Theodor Shanin has demonstrated in the course of a description of the encounter between 'scientific socialism' and untidy 'less progressive' 'vernacular radicalisms') socialism as a positivist science of development (Marxist or otherwise) could be used in very different national contexts.[14] It aimed firstly, to create effective collectivist forms of capital accumulation in mature industrial capitalist states, and secondly to bring into being 'healthy' productivist bourgeoisies and their disciplined 'proletarian negators' in adolescent second-comers. Who, in fact, can deny that heavy doses of these remedies are present in the literature of pre-1914 Italian and French positivist or German and Russian Marxist socialisms.[15]

My 'Gouldnerian model' would not stop here, however. Allied to its role as a positivist science of rational development, socialism as a religion, as a form of *solidarisme* or social service, provided a much-needed spiritual resonance to generalise the appeal of the scientistic message. The Webbs, as Royden Harrison has shown here, were always attracted to this religion of socialism and thought they had finally found it in the Soviet Union of the 1930s. But it should also be recalled that Bolshevik 'god-builders' and 'god-searchers' before 1914 had embodied similar tendencies.[16]

But socialism was more than just a positivist religion of development for those intellectuals who joined movements and parties in the late nineteenth and early twentieth centuries. In Italy, for example, the rapid proletarianisation of sharecroppers and freeholders in the decades following unification stirred the consciences of *Risorgimento* patriots. And the gap between the flowery rhetoric of the Italian national movement and the appalling conditions they found in the countryside shocked many young professionals. It was not very different from the mental agonies suffered by their English contemporaries on discovering 'Outcast London'.[17]

Yes, socialism could be a form of paternalistic or maternalistic social service, but it also was repentance, a way to cleanse oneself of sins, as Beatrice Webb noted in her diary, the collective sins of those who lived on the labours of others.[18] In the Po Valley the selfless intellectual or professional was greatly admired, Socialist rural district doctors were loved by the local peasantry. Socialist general practitioners in industrial Britain; lawyers who defended strikers and demonstrators in German courts; or Swedish hygenists and social workers who uncovered the effects of poverty in city or countryside were motivated, at least partially, by guilt and love, and long remembered by the weak and inarticulate. We should not reduce all their efforts to fears of the *lumpenproletariat*, to social control, even if there is abundant evidence that these motives were not absent.[19]

Socialism for this emergent group of criminologists, sociologists, practitioners of industrial or occupational medicine or urban planners meant a new life style, it meant modernity: 'free marriages', garden city suburbs, utilitarian clothing and new occupations. In this regard the manifesto of the Milanese *Lega Socialista*, (1890) a local variation on Fabianism, possesses universal resonance.

The nearly complete dissolution of the patriarchical family, the relaxation in custom, if not in law, of marital and paternal power, the relaxation of matrimonial custom, the rapid increase in marital separations, the institution of divorce, the free unions contracted by conviction and not through recklessness; the access of women to almost all work and social activities; the consequent transferral of almost all life outside the domestic walls; the education and instruction of children entrusted to the State, the Communes, localised and concentrated in nurseries, schools and colleges, far from interference or even vigilance of parents; the same, no matter how imperfect, but always vaster organisation of public welfare which tends . . . to coordinate and modernise itself outside of every religious influence, the spread of free thought in opposition to dogma and religious practices; are all attempted and accomplished . . . preparing the structure of the new socialist society.[20]

The manifesto and its contemporary equivalents throughout Europe reflected the corporate, one might be tempted to say, class consciousness of this new stratum of intellectuals, drawing their sustenance from a desacralisation of traditions and the rapid expansion of a modern professional meritocracy. But if their encounters with working-class organisations might appear to bear similarities to 'crypto-leninism' as these positivist or Marxist 'scientific socialists' imported 'modern socialism' into working-class organisations, they were, in fact, too much free-floating intellectuals to imagine or join a political party in which workers and professional brain-workers would have to obey an inflexible iron discipline.

THE PUBLIC SPHERE IN THE LATE NINETEENTH CENTURY

The project, I believe, should be less ambitious. It should be respectful of historical periods and it ought to be open-ended. As we have seen in this volume, there is considerable evidence that the educated middle classes were of very great importance during the formative stages and heyday of the Second International. In what ways did the membership and activities of the educated middle classes actively influence programmes, organisational structures and procedures, and the very political language of socialism itself? Perhaps the first place to look is at those bourgeois 'renegades', the university graduates, professionals and literati, whom Marx and others predicted and hoped would join the socialist movement.

How, then, did middle-class socialists experience their new

political home? A discernible set of behaviour, verbal procedures and rules of the game had already been digested by these 'bourgeois renegades' before they deserted their class. Where did they learn the tricks of their trade? I would suggest that Pierre Bourdieu's and Jürgen Habermas's similar investigations of new discursive practices arising from an 'intellectual field' or 'public sphere' supply some possible answers.

Habermas's 'public sphere' is that autonomous space developed by the professional classes in the nineteenth century.[21] It emerges with the arrival of the market economy, the constitutional state and the weakening of aristocratic patronage of intellectuals. In a similar vein Bourdieu demonstrates how notions of artistic autonomy arose from an 'intellectual field'.[22] Through the creation of literary and artistic markets intellectuals were freed from the whims of single patrons. It was within these fields of force that liberal, nationalist and socialist ideologies evolved.

Educated middle-class socialists' political apprenticeships were experienced within this 'print capitalism'. The newspapers, magazines and books of the 'public sphere' or 'intellectual field' were an essential training ground.[23] Thus there are still little-studied connections between free-lance, popular or 'labour' journalism, avant-garde literary movements, and socialism in the 1880s and 1890s. One can almost identify quarters in Milan, Paris, London and Berlin where this manifested itself.[24]

We need studies which illuminate the material culture of this educated middle class: social histories of socialism's brains trusts.

Naturally the language and assumptions of the nineteenth-century educated middle-class socialist pioneer were particularly prominent in that first wave of socialist leaders (*circa* 1860–90) who came largely from literary or university backgrounds. Robert Michels and his more recent admirers became very excited about a working-class authoritarianism and hero worship linked to these 'regal professionals'.[25]

The Lassalles, Ferris and Hyndmans are almost too well known to bear repetition. Michels, for one, made a serious mistake by lifting phenomena linked to specific historical conjunctives onto a timeless plane. To cite the German example, the development of working-class self-education and the availability of party finances tempered the worship of 'regal' free professionals. The rhetorician gave way to the 'machine man' perhaps best exemplified by Frederich Ebert.[26]

DIVISIONS OF LABOUR IN SOCIALISM: *1890–1914*

On the other hand, did emergent self-educated trade-union or party officials like Ebert have their own social space? Some years ago two socialist scholars associated with Habermas, Oskar Negt and Alexander Klüge, suggested a 'proletarian sphere' where workers express publicly in their own fashion their experiences and needs.[27] But the question which must be put is whether the political division of labour within the socialist movement and outside would have allowed this possibility ever to occur.

If, as Oskar Negt and Alexander Klüge (summarised by Hans Medick) argue that, the 'proletarian public' is 'characterised by its "direct", sensual and collective mode of experience' in contradiction to the 'mediated, intellectual, mode of the bourgeois', and it is 'a public grounded in the process of production' as opposed to the bourgeois separation of private and public,[28] then as socialist trade unionists or working-class party activists become white-collar professionals they tend to imitate the 'bourgeois renegades'. These specialists, Bakunin rightly noted, were not workers but *ex-*workers.[29]

To what extent, therefore, did socialist organisations become mirror images of the emergent capitalist and state white-collar organisations around them? Did they come to embody the same concern for professionalism and credentials? The more acute bourgeois critics of socialism, such as Max Weber, judged all socialist programmes on their ability to accept a 'realistic' rather than a 'utopian' definition of both the political and the economic division of labour. Did socialist organisations before 1914 not only accept Weber's advice but produce activists and leaders who deepened this very process? It depends.

While socialist parties may have been capable of awarding members from working- or middle-class backgrounds a species of white-collar respectability, their numbers, their social mix and their ultimate destination were dependent upon particular national conditions. But this does not preclude social histories of the division of labour within socialist parties before 1914, based upon the assumption that these were public arenas whose various forms of knowledge and expertise encountered each other. Thus the self-educated manual worker, the 'middle-class renegade', the 'machine man' and the lower-middle-class 'nothing' need their historians. Particularly important, as case studies, are periods when debates over education and culture were directly linked to concerns about party structures, party bureaucracy and the social composition of party membership.

I can suggest two periods:

(1) The 1890s when locally based 'workerism', founded on self-taught culture (e.g. the French Allemanistes, the *Partito Operaio Italiano*, the early Russian Economists, the North of England – and Scottish – labour clubs and 'unions' or German educational clubs and localistic SPD party structures) confronted the formally trained 'metropolitan scientific socialists'.[30]

(2) The so-called Syndicalist Revolt (*c.* 1910–14), when forms of self-education (e.g. the Ferrer Schools, the Plebs Leagues, the *Bourses de Travail* and *Camere del Lavoro* educational experiments, etc.) combined with worker anti-officialist (i.e. anti-professional labour leaders) and anti-state socialist intelligentsias in 'rebel movements'. The fortune of the English notion of a new 'servile state' – a marriage of the interventionist state (just flexing its muscles), big capital and professional socialist/labour leaders – would be very interesting to trace. My own, albeit preliminary, investigations suggest that its imagery travelled quite rapidly around Europe.[31]

In neither of these two historical examples should it be assumed that revolts against 'intelligentsia' or 'official' socialism were merely led by 'autonomous working-class producers'. Indeed, in the 1880s and 1890s the German *Jungen* (largely literati) and the Morrisite Socialists (similarly), or the Guild Socialists of the Syndicalist Revolt (literati and academics) lived in close and at times tense proximity with self-taught rebels. Neither should it be assumed that most workers were disenchanted with reformist trade unionism or electoralism. I am referring to a small, buoyant group whose effects upon broader working-class life fluctuated quite dramatically.[32]

Appropriation of culture and knowledge within socialist movements meant negotiation. For if there existed a line of cleavage running through socialist parties' educational policies, and these very organisations as forms of education and cultural formation in themselves, pitting scientifically or classically educated middle-class socialists against worker autodidacts and lower middle-class enthusiasts, it seems to me to be too neatly defined. It is not merely a struggle between clearly defined usurpatory actions from below and another opposing closure strategy from above. Indeed, the self-educated did not shun the classical heritage. On the contrary they respected it, along with their own scientific culture based upon that fascinating plebeian materialism which Carlo Ginsburg and Christopher Hill have traced back to early modern Europe and Rée, Eric Hobsbawm and Logie Barrow have extended into our own century, embodied in the scientific revolution's unsung partners, the artisans.[33]

Appropriation of culture and knowledge also depended on control of one's free-time. But, as I suggested earlier in my introduction, it was the unintended effects of free time which fuelled the political division of labour. In this respect one of the 'New Class' theorists, Rudolf Bahro, may help us understand this process.

Using his own experiences in the DDR, but extending them to the capitalist West, he developed a theory of the division of labour which, as Yeo discussed in his contribution, owes as much to Weber as it does to Marx and the utopian tradition.[34] He describes how modern bureaucratic societies are arranged through these inequalities which arise between individuals who control, to varying degrees, their personal time. Thus 'economies of time', interestingly present in Marx's *Grundrisse*, would demonstrate how those closer to the bureaucratic pyramid's apex, rather than mundane time-bound operators at its base, appropriate greater quantities of power.[35] Bahro had his mind concentrated by examples other than Frederich Ebert, Karl Kautsky or Ramsay MacDonald. Nevertheless, as a metaphor his suggestions stimulate my imagination more than Robert Michels's iron law ever has.

CONCLUSION

Studies of the educated middle classes and socialism have most been restricted either to aspects of wider institutional histories or to histories of ideas. We have been deluged by accounts in which ideas feed on other ideas. What I have suggested in my Introduction can be taken as a possible multi-causal model which grounds these ideas in structural realities. But it should be borne in mind that its applicability would fade for the period after 1914. The high tide of mass manual communist or social democratic parties, the emergence of the disenfranchised, was due to an altered relationship between state, economy and the lower classes caused by world wars, revolutions and resistance. The histories of radical professional groups and the violent political oscillations of the lower middle class between 1920 and 1945 deserve their own discrete set of guidelines. Finally, the rapid growth of higher education after 1945 and graduate participation in new social movements and workers' parties throw up other problems.

Perhaps the relationship between socialist propositions and the working class was always problematic, but I do believe that at mid-century (and until the early 1970s) in many Western European countries there was a noticeable convergence. Today, without policies which can win professionals' and white-collar workers' endorsement, socialism is in danger of becoming a political irrelevance. But the impelling need for a redefinition of socialism's agenda should not cause us to forget its long-standing goal of modifying our dismal political and economic divisions of labour through policies inspired by democratic and *collectivist* values. We might even sustain that dream of William Morris, that reconciliation of the mental and manual, that generation of human friendship and love, that good and peaceful Utopia, which the English artist and artisan shared with his less 'certified' comrades.

NOTES

1 R. Bahro, *The Alternative in Eastern Europe*, London, New Left Books, 1978. Good summaries of Eastern 'New Class' theories can be found in E. Kamenka and M. Krygier (eds), *Bureaucracy: The Career of a Concept*, London, Edward Arnold, 1979, chapter 4; A. Westoby, 'Conceptions of communist states', in D. Held (ed.), *States and Societies*, Oxford, Martin Robertson, 1983. A. Westoby, Introduction to Bruno Rizzi, *The Bureaucratisation of the World*, London, Tavistock, 1985 (originally published in French, Paris, 1939), pp. 1–33. Other important texts are M. Djilas, *The*

New Class: An Analysis of the Communist System, New York, Praeger, 1957; I. Konrad and G. Szelényi, *The Intellectuals on the Road to Class Power*, Brighton, Harvester, 1980.

2 For corporate technostructures and technocrats, see A. A. Berle and G. C. Means, *The Modern Corporation and Private Property*, New York, Macmillan, 1933; J. Burnham, *The Managerial Revolution*, New York, John Day Co., 1941; Rizzi, op. cit. (note 1); J. K. Galbraith, *The New Industrial State*, New York, Houghton Mifflin, 1967. For the new technical working class, see A. Gorz, *Strategy for Labor*, Boston, Beacon Press, 1967; S. Mallet, *Essays on the New Working Class*, St Louis, Telos Press, 1975; J. R. Low-Beer, *Protest and Participation: The New Working Class and Italy*, Cambridge University Press, 1978. See also the telling criticisms by Duncan Gallie, *In Search of the New Working Class*, Cambridge University Press, 1978.

3 D. Bell, *The Post-Industrial Society*, London, Heinemann, 1974; A. Gouldner, *Intellectuals and the Rise of the New Class*, London, Macmillan, 1979; R. Collins, *The Credential Society: An Historical Sociology of Education and Stratification*, New York, Academic Press, 1979; J. Roemer, *A General Theory of Exploitation and Class*, Cambridge, Mass., Harvard University Press, 1982.

4 N. Poulantzas, *Classes in Contemporary Capitalism*, London, New Left Books, 1975; G. Carchedi, *On the Economic Identification of Social Classes*, London, Routledge & Kegan Paul, 1977; N. Poulantzas, *State, Power, Socialism*, London, New Left Books, 1978; E. O. Wright, *Class, Crisis and the State*, London, New Left Books, 1978; E. O. Wright, *Class Structure and Income Determination*, London, Academic Press, 1979; E. O. Wright, 'Intellectuals and the class structure of capitalist society', in P. Walker (ed.), *Between Labour and Capital*, Brighton, Harvester, 1979, pp. 181–211; B. and J. Ehrenreich, 'The professional-managerial class', in P. Walker, ibid., pp. 5–45; G. Carchedi, *Problems in Class Analysis: Production, Knowledge and the Function of Capital*, London, Routledge & Kegan Paul, 1983.

For a hilarious criticism of 'class boundary hunters', see F. Parkin, *Marxism and Class Theory: A Bourgeois Critique*, London, Tavistock, 1979, pp. 11–28. See also the criticisms by John Goldthorpe, 'On the service class, its formation and future', in A. Giddens and G. Mackenzie (eds), *Social Class and the Division of Labour*, Cambridge University Press, 1982, pp. 162–81.

An approach employing notions of a 'power elite' (derived respectively from Weber and the anarchists) can be found in C. W. Mills, *White Collar*, New York, Oxford University Press, 1956;

N. Chomsky, *American Power and the New Mandarins*, New York, Pantheon, 1969.

5 Most recent publications are I. Szelényi, 'The intelligentsia and the class structure of state socialist societies', *American Journal of Sociology*, vol. 88, supplement, 1982, pp. 5287–326; B. Martin and I. Szelényi, 'Beyond Cultural Capital: Toward a Theory of Symbolic Domination', in R. Eyerman, L. Svensson and T. Söderqvist (eds), *Intellectuals, Universities, and the State in Modern Western Societies*, Berkeley, University of California Press, 1987; Gouldner, op. cit. (note 3). The major proponent of symbolic or cultural capital is Pierre Bourdieu. However, he has retained a curious attachment to the concept of these cultural credentials being physically inherited by an old-fashioned petit bourgeoisie; see P. Bourdieu and J. C. Passeron, *Reproduction in Education, Society, Culture*, London, Sage, 1977; P. Bourdieu and J. C. Passeron, *The Heirs*, University of Chicago Press, 1979; P. Bourdieu, *The Distinction*, London, Routledge & Kegan Paul, 1984. Martin's and Szelényi's piece is an ambitious attempt to synthesise Frank Parkin's neo-Weberian notion of 'social closure' with conceptions of cultural, symbolic and human capital.

6 R. Pipes (ed.), *The Russian Intelligentsia*, New York, Columbia University Press, 1961; A. Gella (ed.), *The Intelligentsia and the Intellectuals*, London, Sage, 1976; Konrad and Szelényi, op. cit. (note 1).

7 A. Gramsci, *Quaderni del carcere*, ed. V. Gerratana, Turin, Einaudi, Vol. II, p. 866.

8 For the Populist period, 1860–80, see, F. Venturi, *Roots of Revolution: A History of the Populist and Socialist Movements in Nineteenth-Century Russia*, New York, Grosset & Dunlap, 1966; A. Gleason, *Young Russia*, University of Chicago Press, 1980. For later periods, see below.

9 T. Shanin, *The Awkward Class: Political Sociology of the Peasantry in a Developing Society: Russia 1910–1925*, New York, Oxford University Press, 1972; T. Shanin (ed.), *Late Marx and the Russian Road*, London, Routledge & Kegan Paul, 1984; T. Shanin, *The Roots of Otherness: Russia's Turn of the Century*, London, Macmillan, 1985; A. Rabinowitch, *The Bolsheviks Come to Power*, New York, W. W. Norton, 1976; C. J. Sirianni, *Workers' Control and Socialist Democracy: The Soviet Experience*, London, Verso, 1982; V. Bonnell, *Roots of Revolution*, Berkeley, University of California Press, 1983; S. A. Smith, *Red Petrograd: Revolution in the Factories, 1917–1918*, Cambridge University Press, 1983.

10 For good historical accounts of the Soviet Union's elites, see K. E. Bailes, *Technology and Society under Lenin and Stalin*, Princeton University Press, 1978; N. Lampert, *The Technical Intelligentsia*

and the Soviet State, London, Macmillan, 1979; S. F. Cohen,
Rethinking the Soviet Experience: Politics and History since 1917,
Oxford University Press, 1985; M. Lewin, *The Making of the
Soviet System: Essays in the Social History of Inter-War Russia*,
London, Methuen, 1985.

Good sociologies of modern Soviet social structure are D. Lane,
The Socialist Industrial State, George Allen & Unwin, 1976; D.
Lane, *The End of Social Inequality?*, London, Allen & Unwin,
1982 edn; G. Littlejohn, *A Sociology of the Soviet Union*, London,
Macmillan, 1984.

For a good critical summary of convergence theories, see K.
Kumar, *Prophecy and Progress*, Harmondsworth, Penguin, 1978,
pp. 164–240.

11 Szelényi, 1982, op. cit. (note 5).

12 Djilas, op. cit. (note 1). For the 'New Class' debate within the
Fourth International, see Westoby's Introduction to Rizzi, op. cit.
(note 1).

13 Gouldner, 1979, op. cit. (note 3); Gouldner, *Against
Fragmentation*, New York, Oxford University Press, 1985. A
summary of theories of modernisation as social control can be
found in Z. Bauman, *Memories of Class: The Prehistory and
After-Life of Class*, London, Routledge & Kegan Paul, 1982. See
also N. Elias, *The Civilising Process*, Oxford, Blackwell, 1978/82,
Vols. 1 and 2; J. Frykman and O. Löftgen, *Den Kulterverade
Manniskan*, Lund, Liberförlag, 1979; P. N. Stearns, 'The middle
class: toward a precise definition', *Comparative Studies in Society
and History*, vol. 21, no. 3, 1979, pp. 376–96; P. N. Stearns,
'The effort at continuity in working-class culture', *Journal of
Modern History*, vol. 52, no. 4, 1980, pp. 626–55.

To a certain extent Foucault's work concerning the social
constitution of penology and modern sexuality should be included
here. However, it is not clear if a class should be held to represent
this modernisation process. An account of his work can be found in
A. Sheridan, *Michel Foucault: The Will to Truth*, London,
Tavistock, 1980; J. Weeks, 'Foucault for historians', *History
Workshop Journal*, no. 14 (Autumn), 1982, pp. 106–19; and the
critical comments of S. Cohen, *Visions of Social Control*, Cambridge,
Polity Press, 1985. Harvey Mitchell and Peter Stearns are advocates
of socialism as functionalist modernisation see, H. Mitchell and
P. N. Stearns, *The European Labor Movement, the Working
Classes and the Origins of Social Democracy 1890–1914*, Ithaca,
Illinois, F. E. Peacock Publishers, 1971: p. 151, 'in the long run
the politicization of the labor movement helped turn it away from
revolution; in this sense even middle-class radicals may have helped
tame the working class. It is relevant to note the role of the labour

movement in inculcating among the workers other essentially middle-class values: temperance and sobriety; regularity of work and savings; even better treatment of women and children in the family. From a variety of vantage points the role of the middle-class elements in socialism cannot be ignored.' p. 152: 'Socialism did help spread to workers many values already developed in middle-class culture albeit in different form. It stressed progress, the importance of politics, even the acceptability of industrial (though not capitalist) society, a society open to technological change and steadily increasing production and prosperity. Along with its message of class consciousness it may ultimately have helped integrate workers within modern industrial life.' p. 207: 'In fact the separate Socialist society helped integrate workers into the industrial world in a variety of ways. It discouraged and provided alternatives to heavy drinking. It encouraged literacy and acquaintance not just with Socialist work but with traditional culture as well. For many it provided organizational experience and even upward mobility in the Socialist administration itself. Socialism drew many of the lonely. It gave them an ideology which they could sincerely maintain but it also made it difficult for them to preserve their sense of isolation.'

14 Shanin, 1984, op. cit. (note 9), pp. 243–79; R. Jacoby, *Dialectic of Defeat*, Cambridge University Press, 1981.

15 A superb review of pre-1914 Marxism can be found in E. J. Hobsbawm *et al.*, *Storia del marxismo*, Turin, Einaudi, 1978 and 1979, Vols. 1 and 2.

16 J. Schurrer, 'Bogdanov e Lenin: bolscevismo al bivio' in Hobsbawm *et al.*, 1979, op. cit. (note 15), Vol. 2, pp. 495–546; C. Read, *Religion, Revolution and the Russian Intelligentsia 1900–1912*, London, Macmillan, 1979; D. C. Williams, 'Collective immortality: syndicalist origins of proletarian culture, 1905–1910', *Slavic Review*, vol. 39, no. 3, 1980, pp. 389–422.

17 G. Stedman Jones, *Languages of Class*, Cambridge University Press, 1983, pp. 20–2.

18 B. Webb, *My Apprenticeship*, London, Longmans, Green & Co., 1926, p. 126.

19 For Swedish professionals see, K. Jonsson, 'Towards the administered Welfare State', Umea University, 1984, Ms.

20 I. M. Ottolenghi, 'Filippo Turati, *La Critica Sociale e la formazione della borghesia industriale*, Italia: Dalle origini all'eta giolittiana', *Ricerche storiche*, January–June, p. 356. For crowd psychology and the socialists see: R. L. Geiger, 'Democracy and the crowd: the social history of an idea in France and Italy, 1890–1944', *Societas*, 8, 1, 1977, pp. 47–71; R. A. Nye, *The Anti-Democratic Sources of Elite Theory: Pareto, Mosca, Michels*, London, Sage, 1977. S.

Barrows, *Distorting Morrors*, New Haven, Yale University Press, 1981; R. D. Nye, *Crime, Madness and Politics in Modern France*, Princeton University Press, 1984; S. Mosovici, *The Age of the Crowd*, Cambridge University Press, 1985; D. Pick, 'The Faces of Anarchy: Lombroso and the Politics of Criminal Science in Post-Unification Italy', *History Workshop Journal*, no. 21, 1986, pp. 60–86.

21   J. Habermas, *Strukturwandel de Offentlickheit: Untersuchungen zur einer Kategorie der burgenlichen Gesellschaften*, Neuweid, Luchterhand, 1962; D. Held, *Introduction to Critical Theory*, Berkeley, University of California Press, 1980, pp. 260–7.

22   P. Bourdieu, 'Intellectual field and creative project', in M. F. D. Young (ed.), *Knowledge and Control*, London, Collier-Macmillan, 1971, pp. 161–88. For Habermas/Bourdieu, see P. Schlesinger, 'In search of the intellectuals: some comments on recent theory', *Media, Culture and Society*, vol. 4, 1982, pp. 206–7.

23   The term 'print capitalism' is derived from L. Febvre and H. J. Martin, *The Coming of the Book: The Impact of Printing 1450–1800*, London, New Left Books, 1976. For the 'creation' of national traditions and nationalism by the educated middle classes, see B. Anderson, *Imagined Communities*, London, Verso, 1983; E. J. Hobsbawm and T. Ranger (eds), *The Invention of Tradition*, Cambridge University Press, 1983.

24   E. J. Hobsbawm, 'La cultura europa e il marxismo', in Hobsbawm *et al.*, 1979, op. cit. (note 15), Vol. 2, pp. 62–106; M. Reberioux, 1967, 'Critique litteraire et socialisme au tounart du siècle', *Mouvement Social*, vol. 59, 1967, pp. 3–28. E. Herbert, *The Artist and Social Reform*, New Haven, Conn., Yale University Press, 1961; D. D. Egbert, *Social Radicalism and the Arts*, New York, Knopf, 1970; G. Fülberth, *Proletarsche Partei und bürgliche Literaten*, Neuwied, Luchterhand, 1972; H. Scherer, *Burgerlich oppositionelle literaten und sozial democratie Arbeiterbewegung nach 1890*, Stuttgart, Metzler Studienaugabe, 1974; G. H. Rohr, 'The revolt of the Jungen', Ph.D. thesis, University of Rochester, 1975; P. Weinard, 'Revoluzzen und Revisionisten, Die Jungen in der Soziademocratie vor der Jahrhundertwende', *Politische Vierteljahresschrift*, vol. 17, 1976, pp. 208–41; V. Lidtke, 'Naturalism and socialism in Germany', *American Historical Review*, vol. 79, 1974, pp. 14–37; R. Fedi, 'Socialismo e litteratura', in various authors, *Prampolini e il socialismo riformista*, Rome, Mondoperaio/Edizioni Avanti!, 1979, pp. 127–61; G. Bertone, 'Parlare ai borghesi: De Amicis, il Primo Maggio e la propaganda socialista', *Movimento Operaio e Socialista*, vol. 3, nos. 2/3, 1980, pp. 155–73; G. Turi, 'Socialismo e cultura', *Movimento*

Operaio e Socialista, vol. 3, nos. 2/3, 1980, NS, pp. 143–53; I. Britain, *Fabianism and Culture*, Cambridge University Press, 1983.

The Austro-Marxist milieu is of extreme interest, especially Max Adler's attempts to win over the apolitical intellectuals of Vienna's 'intellectual field' to socialism. See Leonardi Paggi's Introduction to *Il socialismo e gli intellettuali*, Bari, De Donato, 1974. For the background, see C. Schorske, *Fin-de-Siècle Vienna*, London, Weidenfeld & Nicolson, 1980; L. Olausson, 'Socialism and intellectuals in fin-de-siècle Vienna. Max Adler on socialism and intellectuals. A case study', MS, University of Gothenburg, 1984. Vienna could be profitably contrasted to the noticeable politicisation of Paris's 'intellectual field' in the 1890s; see C. Charle, 'Champ litterataire e champ du pouvoir: les écrivans et l'Affaire Dreyfus', *Annales*, vol. 32, no. 2, 1977, pp. 240–64.

25 An early but still useful study is E. Bernstein, *Ferdinand Lassalle: As a Social Reformer*, New York, Scribner's, 1893; S. Na'aman, *Lassalle*, Hannover, Verlag für Literatur und Zeitgeschehen, 1970. On Ferri and other 'regal professionals', see A. Riosa, 'Il PSI tra democrazia e socialismo', in Fondazione Brodolini, *Storia del Partito Socialista Italiano*, Venice, Marsilio, pp. 94–5.

26 C. E. Schorske, *German Social Democracy 1865–1917*, Cambridge, Mass., Harvard University Press, 1983 edn (1st edn 1955), pp. 116–45; D. K. Buse, 'Fredrich Ebert and German socialism 1871–1919', Ph.D. thesis, University of Oregon, 1972.

27 O. Negt and A. Klüge, *Öffentlichkeit und Ertahrung: Zur Organisationanalyse von bürgerlichen und proleterischer öffentlchkeit*, Frankfurt, Suhrkamp, 1972.

28 H. Medick, 'Plebian culture in the transition to capitalism', in R. Samuel and G. Stedman Jones (eds), *Culture, Ideology and Politics*, London, Routledge & Kegan Paul, 1982, p. 87.

29 See Bakunin's *Statism and Anarchy* (1873), cited in G. P. Maximoff (ed.), *The Political Philosophy of Bakunin: Scientific Anarchism*, London, Collier-Macmillan, 1964, p. 288.

30 On the Allemanistes, see S. Reynolds, 'Allemane, the Allemanists and *Le Parti Ouvrier*: the problems of a socialist newspaper 1888–1900', *European Studies Quarterly*, vol. 15, no. 1, 1985, pp. 43–70; M. Winnock, 'La scission de Châtellerault et la naissance du parti allemaniste, 1890–1891', *Mouvement Social*, no. 71, 1971, pp. 33–62; B. Moss, *Origins of the French Labor Movement*, Berkeley, University of California Press, 1976. On the Partito Operaio, see C. Levy, 'Origins of the Italian Socialist Party's intelligentsia: 1870–1840', MS, Open University, 1983; C. Levy, 'Italian socialism and the professors' socialism and the educated elite in the 1890s', MS, Open University, 1983. For the Russian case, see A. Westoby, 'Social democracy and the Russian

intelligentsia: the birth of mass influence', MS, Open University, 1983; A. Westoby, 'Social democracy and the Russian intelligentsia: the campaign for a party, 1898–1903', MS, Open University. For the German case, see Fülberth, op. cit. (note 24); Scherer, op. cit. (note 24); Rohr, op. cit. (note 24); Weinard, op. cit. (note 24).

31 C. Levy, 'Malatesta in exile', *Annali della Fondazione Luigi Einaudi*, vol. XV, 1981, pp. 270–80.

32 B. Holton, *British Syndicalism*, London, Pluto, 1976. For some good examples of 'servile state' cum rank-and-file approaches, see K. H. Roth, *Die 'Andere' Arbeiterbewegung*, Munich, Werkshutz U.A., 1974; E. Lucas, *Zwei Formen von Radikalismus und den deutsche Arbeiterbewegung*, Frankfurt, Roter Stern, 1976; S. Yeo, 'Working-class association, private capital, welfare and the state in the late nineteenth and twentieth centuries', in N. Parry, M. Rustin and C. Satyamurti (eds), *Social Work, Welfare and the State*, London, Edward Arnold, 1979; A. Pepe, *Lotta di classe e crisi industriale in Italia*, Milan, Feltrinelli, 1978.

For opposing viewpoints, see M. Reberioux, 'Les tendances hostiles a l'état dans le SFIO', *Mouvement Social*, no. 65, 1968, pp. 21–37; K. Schönhoven, *Expansion und Konzentration: Studien zur Entwicklung der Freien Gewerkschaften im Wilhelminischen Deutschland 1890 bis 1914*, Stuttgart, Klett-Cotta, 1980; J. Zeitlin, 'Trade unions and job control: a Critique of "rank and filism"', MS, 1982; V. Gore, 'Rank-and-file dissent', in C. J. Wrigley (ed.), *A History of British Industrial Relations*, Brighton, Harvester, 1982, pp. 47–73; P. Thane, 'The working class and state "welfare" in Britain 1880–1914', *Historical Journal*, vol. 27, no. 4, 1984, pp. 877–900.

For the relationship between the educated and rank-and-file revolts, see: for the *Jungen*, Rohr, op. cit. (note 24); Morrosite socialists, E. P. Thompson, *William Morris*, London, Merlin Press, 1977 edn; and Yeo's remarks in this volume. For the 'syndicalist revolt', see A. W. Wright, *G. D. H. Cole and Guild Socialism*, Oxford, Clarendon Press, 1979; S. Pierson, *British Socialism: The Journey from Fantasy to Politics*, Cambridge, Mass., Harvard University Press, 1979.

33 See Hill's life work; C. Ginsburg, *The Cheese and the Worms*, London, Routledge & Kegan Paul, 1978; P. Burke, *Popular Culture in Early Modern Europe*, London, Temple Smith, 1978; J. Rée, *Proletarian Philosophers*, Oxford, Clarendon Press, 1984; E. J. Hobsbawm, *Worlds of Labour*, London, Weidenfeld & Nicolson, 1984, chapter 14, L. Barrow, 'Determinism and environmentalism in socialist thought', in Samuel and Stedman Jones, op. cit. (note 28), pp. 194–214; L. Barrow, *Independent Spirits. Spiritualism*

and English Plebeians 1850–1910, London, Routledge & Kegan Paul, 1986. Vernon Lidtke demonstrates that German workers appropriated those elements in bourgeois culture they felt relevant to their needs. If Marxist intellectuals praised classical humanist culture, many workers were attracted to naturalism. His book is an important study of the process of working-class appropriation of culture and the relationship between Marxist intellectuals and the rank-and-file of the SPD and the Free Trade Unions. See V. L. Lidtke, *The Alternative Culture: Socialist Labor in Imperial Germany*, New York, Oxford University Press, 1985.

34 Bahro, op. cit. (note 1), pp. 163–82: Yeo discusses this point in his contribution.

35 'Economy of time, to this all economy ultimately reduces itself' – Marx, *Grundrisse*, Harmondsworth, Penguin, 1973, p. 173. See also the interesting essay by Adam Westoby, 'Mental work, education and the division of labor', in Eyerman, Svensson and Söderqvist, op. cit. (note 5).

Index

reformism, 118–19, 124–8; unity
of, 65
Labour Party: and co-operative
movement, 232–3; and
community action, 256; in
government, 70–3, 79, 82–3;
middle class in, 68; and statism,
242
Labour Representation Committee,
13, 135, 183
'labourism', 6, 13, 139, 175, 192,
226–7, 239n.
labourism, collective, 239n.
Labriola, Arturo, 109, 110–11, 113,
115n.
Lacquer, Thomas, 167
Lagardelle, Hubert, 109, 111–12,
116, 122–3
laissez-faire policies, 49, 127
Landauer, Gustav, and 'New Class',
17
Lane, Joseph, 236n.
Laski, Harold, 79, 239n.
Lassalle, Ferdinand, 15, 278
Leach, William, 142
Leatham, James, 146n.
Leeds, Independent Labour Party in,
140
Leicester, Independent Labour Party
in, 141
Lenin, V. I., 14, 17, 59–60, 68–9,
226, 235; on intellectuals, 121–2,
129; on reformism, 117–18, 121–2,
124, 127–9; on socialist education,
22–3
Levy, Carl, 135–210, 271–90
Lewes, G. H., 215
Liberal Party, Britain: and
association, 234–8; and
collectivism, 4, 174, 232, 235–6;
and ILP, 139–40, 145, 151, 163;
Webb and, 45–6, 62–3, 67
Liberals: New, 235; Radical, 136,
140, 144, 147, 163, 182, 184
Lidtke, Vernon, 15n., 281n.
Liebknecht, 120n.
Lister, John, 176n.
Littlewood, Francis, 142, 176n.,
178n.
Lloyd George, David, 63, 66–7

London School of Economics and
Political Science, 60–1, 62, 63, 80,
81, 162, 232
London Technical Education Board,
60, 81
London University, reshaping of,
60–1
Lough, Thomas, 161
Ludlow, J. M., 236n.
Lukacs, Georg, 91
Lunarchasky, 22
Luxemburg, Rosa, 10, 14, 125–6
Lynd, Helen, 236

Macclesfield, Independent Labour
Party in, 179
MacDonald, Ramsey: and
Independent Labour Party, 150–1,
159–63, 172, 177–8, 182, 183–4;
and Liberal Party, 182; and 'New
Class', 21, 82, 190, 281; as Prime
Minister, 71–2; statism, 235n.,
236, 246–7
McFarlane, Fiona, 233n.
Machajski, J. W., 17, 109, 113–14,
220
Macintyre, Stuart, 239n.
McKibbin, Ross, 184
McMillan, Margaret, 157–8, 168,
182, 192, 236n.
McMillan, Rachel, 157
Macnamara, T. J., 236n.
Macpherson, Fenton, 140n.
Maguire, Tom, 135, 146, 156
Maguire, Paddy, 228n.
Mainwaring, Sam, 171
Maisky, Ivan, 73–4
Majority Socialist Party, Germany,
101–2
Manchester, Independent Labour
Party in, 140–1, 186
Manchester Guardian, 141
Mann, Tom, 54, 146, 151, 164–7,
169, 171–3, 178–9, 181, 232
Marquand, David, 161, 247
Marshall, Alfred, 230
Martyn, Carolyn, 156–7
Marx, Eleanor, 54, 153, 164n.
Marx, Karl: on man, 40; on middle
class, 277; and political division of